变化中的中国

Reading Into a New China

Integrated Skills for Advanced Chinese

Volume 2

Duanduan Li • Irene Liu

CHENG & TSUI

BOSTON

18 17 16 15 14 13   2 3 4 5 6 7 8 9 10

Published by
Cheng & Tsui Company, Inc.
25 West Street
Boston, MA 02111-1213 USA
Fax (617) 426-3669
www.cheng-tsui.com
"Bringing Asia to the World"™

ISBN: 978-088727-693-4

Acknowledgments and copyrights can be found at the back of the book on p. 355, which constitutes an extension of the copyright page.

Library of Congress Cataloging-in-Publication Data
Liu, Ruinian.
[New text for a modern China]
Reading into a new China : integrated skills for advanced Chinese = [Bian hua zhong de Zhongguo] /Irene Liu, Duanduan Li.
          p. cm.
Originally published: A new text for a modern China, 1998.
Parallel title in Chinese characters.
Includes index.
Chinese and English.
ISBN 978-0-88727-627-9 (v.1 pbk.) -- ISBN 978-0-88727-693-4 (v.2 pbk.)
1. Chinese language--Textbooks for foreign speakers--English. I. Li, Duanduan. II. Title. III. Title: Bian hua zhong de Zhongguo.

PL1129.E5L585 2009
495.1'82421--dc22

2009075154

Printed in the United States of America

变化中的中国
Reading Into a New China
Integrated Skills for Advanced Chinese
Volume 2

READING INTO A NEW CHINA
INTEGRATED SKILLS FOR ADVANCED CHINESE

变化中的中国

目 录（下册）

语法介绍	练习与活动	阅读短文
■ Ellipsis ■ "可"的用法 ■ 既然	语音 词汇与句型 语法 综合 阅读 口语 写作	■ 超越时空的爱恋 ■ 女儿为妈妈找伴侣 ■ 外婆的"老伴儿"
■ 中文表被动的方式（一）	语音 词汇与句型 语法 综合 阅读 口语 写作	■ 您愿意做个全职太太吗？ ■ 妻子下岗又上岗 ■ 女人为什么要工作？
■ 中文表被动的方式（二） ■ Discourse Function of the Passive in Chinese	语音 词汇与句型 语法 综合 阅读 口语 写作	■ 现代中国的"小皇帝" ■ 开学第一天 ■ "80后"这一代

Audio Downloads

Users of this textbook have access to free, downloadable audio files that correspond to *Reading Into a New China.* To download the audio files, you simply need to register your product key at our website:

1. Visit the Cheng & Tsui download center at **www.cheng-tsui.com/downloads** and follow the instructions for creating a user account.

2. Register your product key.

3. Download the audio files.

5. For technical support, please contact support@cheng-tsui.com or call 1-800-554-1963.

If you have purchased a used copy of this book, or one without a valid product key, you may purchase a new key on our website (www.cheng-tsui.com) or by contacting our customer service department at 1-800-554-1963.

Your Product Key: U2UM-EDUT

PREFACE

It has been a decade since the publication of the advanced reading textbook *A New Text for a Modern China*. Since then, many things related to the book have changed. First, the social and economic situation in China has undergone a tremendous transformation. Second, in recent years, research in the field of second language reading pedagogy has produced a rich pool of findings on how people process texts when reading. This knowledge has enabled teachers to develop approaches to teach reading more effectively. Third, the linguistic theory of Chinese discourse grammar is now more developed. A functional, discourse-based grammar, according to many experts, is more suitable than a less contextualized sentence-based grammar to explain how the Chinese language works. All this new information has continuously reshaped our teaching philosophy over the years. We felt it was time to revise and re-envision *A New Text for a Modern China*, transforming it into a timely, updated textbook that takes into account all of these developments, reflecting new conditions and contemporary issues in the "New China."

Before revising this textbook, we went about a series of tasks to ensure that the new edition would meet the needs of students and teachers. We first carefully re-examined *A New Text for a Modern China* in order to understand the areas that needed changes. Next, we reflected on our own teaching experiences and studied the most current research findings in reading pedagogy and discourse grammar. We also asked our students who were using that textbook for comments and suggestions. Based on that review process and the information that emerged, we developed a group of guiding principles that we have used to write the new textbook, now titled ***Reading into a New China: Integrated Skills for Advanced Chinese***《变化中的中国》. Apart from the many improvements in content, this book also features a completely new design, tailored for maximum ease of use for students and teachers. The textbook is now divided into two volumes, with each volume including practice exercises as well as instructional material.

■ The Target Learners

Reading into a New China: Integrated Skills for Advanced Chinese is designed mainly for students of Chinese as a foreign language at a high intermediate or beginning advanced level of proficiency, as designated by ACTFL standards (or third-year Chinese language courses at most North American universities and colleges). Heritage students at the intermediate level can also take advantage of the many new features of this textbook to advance their language and especially literacy skills.

■ Our Guiding Philosophy: Skill Integration with a Special Focus on Reading

Reading into a New China: Integrated Skills for Advanced Chinese aims to develop both fluency and accuracy in Chinese through a topic-based syllabus. The topics are of high interest to students and provide maximum opportunities for thinking and discussion, promoting the development of both linguistic and communication skills. While we have adopted an integrated approach to teach all language skills coherently, it is on reading and building reading skills that we place our special focus.

The reason for this focus is that in beginning and intermediate levels of Chinese study, oral communication skills are usually stressed in order to build a strong foundation in spoken Chinese. However, at the advanced level, it is not enough to be proficient only in oral communication skills. Students must also have well-developed written communication skills to meet the challenges of potential employment and increased engagement in Chinese-speaking communities. Third-year students, with their sound foundation of first- and second-year Chinese, are at the ideal stage to begin to learn formal written Chinese.

One of the unique features of this reading textbook is that the reading is supported by other skills. Students are encouraged and facilitated to further advance their oral proficiency while developing reading and writing skills. Third-year students should learn to expand their speaking repertoire from topics of everyday routines and interests to more intellectually and linguistically challenging topics, such as social issues and current events. The combination of writing exercises and discussion questions in this book provides ample opportunities for students to go beyond the reading text and put all their integrated skills to work.

■ Some Pedagogical Considerations on the Use of English in Instructions

In language teaching, we take the position that an effective language classroom should be one where active student participation in Chinese is the norm. It should not be a place where the instructor lectures and students passively listen. The instructor's role in the class is to create an environment in which students can actively discuss the content of the lessons; to reinforce and build upon previous learning; and to clarify specific difficult or confusing points in the lessons. This ideal situation cannot happen unless the students are well prepared before class. In order to help students prepare effectively, we have written all explanations about grammar, reading skills, and general instructions in both Chinese and English for easy comprehension. Chinese sentences used as examples are provided with English translations. However, simple instructions (especially repeated ones) will only be given in Chinese to increase the target language input and reduce over-reliance on English for learners.

■ About the Lessons

One of the keys to teaching a language effectively is to present high-interest, provocative material that will engage the readers. The readings of this book have been carefully chosen to include a variety of viewpoints on current issues of population, education, family, gender, environment, business, and technology in the rapidly changing China. Vocabulary and concepts related to these issues are recycled throughout the text, building up a basic core of knowledge.

The transition from dealing with spoken-style materials to written-style materials can be a demanding but gratifying process for learners. Well-chosen materials at an appropriately challenging level can maintain learners' interest and inspire them to continue to develop their language and literacy skills, as well as their knowledge of Chinese culture and current social issues and events. Texts that are well beyond the students' linguistic competence might cause anxiety and frustration. For this reason, we have chosen to use mostly modified materials written specifically to suit the literacy level and linguistic needs of third-year students, rather than purely "authentic" materials taken directly from magazines or newspapers, which might be too difficult for learners at this level.

The genres of writing presented and developed in this book are of three kinds: narrative, expository and news features. These lessons can help students build up their knowledge and skills concerning general literary styles normally used in Chinese works of literature, official documents, essays, and news, and thus are a good source for understanding twenty-first-century Chinese society. This serves as good preparation for learners' future reading of unmodified authentic written materials in real life.

■ Features

1. Pre-reading Activities

Each chapter starts with a brief overview in English to introduce the thematic content of the lesson. Visual stimuli (photos or illustrations) related to the theme, followed by discussion questions, are also provided. The intention is to help activating students' prior knowledge and prepare them mentally for the main text. In addition, the overview also provides information about the text organization and genre of the main reading. The information in this section can benefit students in three major ways:

- by enhancing students' opportunities to make sense of the information they will encounter in the text;

- by increasing students' interest and confidence in the topic and thus motivating them to read the text; and

- by establishing realistic reading expectations about the lesson and the skills required to read the material effectively.

2. Vocabulary

The vocabulary learning in each lesson is divided into two parts. The first part is a new feature called "Vocabulary Building Skills." Designed for self-study, this part presents ten to fifteen new words composed of characters known to the students. Students are asked to guess the meaning of the compound words based on the meaning of the known characters. This activity encourages students to make intelligent guesses and helps build students' knowledge of Chinese morphology in order to increase their speed and effectiveness in vocabulary acquisition. Another advantage of this practice is to let students get used to seeing new words without anxiety. Students in the habit of reading from word to word tend to stop at every unfamiliar word to look up the meaning in a dictionary. If the pauses are long and frequent, comprehension will suffer because the train of thought is interrupted. The ability to make intelligent guesses from context can help students take the risk of tolerating some ambiguity or uncertainty while reading, and thus improve their reading fluency.

The second part is the new vocabulary of the lesson. In addition to the common practice of providing parts of speech and English meanings of words in the vocabulary list, each entry also includes the Vocabulary Level[1] of *HSK* (*Hanyu Shuiping Kaoshi* 汉语水平考试) to indicate the frequency (or difficulty) level of the words we are learning. The words listed in the official *Outlines for Chinese Proficiency Words and Characters in HSK* are categorized into four levels:

- Level A (甲), the basic level, includes 1033 words which can satisfy the minimum language requirements for staying and traveling independently in China.

- Level B (乙), the intermediate level, includes 2018 words. Mastery of Level A and Level B (3051 words and phrases altogether) will enable the learner to understand 85% of the words used in newspapers and popular magazines.

- Level C (丙), the advanced level, includes 2202 words and phrases. Level A, B, and C cover 90% of the words in general use.

- Level D (丁), the higher advanced level, includes 3569 words and phrases to enable learners to understand 95% of the words in articles of general topics.

This information lets students know the level of the words they are learning and also directly benefits those students who are preparing to take the HSK test.

---

[1]There are a few words in each lesson that are not included in the HSK list, so no level can be indicated. They are:

1. set phrases (e.g., 成语)

2. newly emerged words (e.g., 上网)

3. proper names

4. some specific terms (e.g. 本科、大专)

5. some compounds (e.g., 餐饮, although HSK has 餐 and 饮 separately)

3. Approaches to Teaching Reading

The most common method of teaching reading in Chinese at present typically involves decoding, "bottom-up" information processing through word-by-word translation of the text for comprehension. This is not efficient and often leads to slow, inaccurate reading. Our position is that both top-down (activating readers' background and expectations for comprehension) and bottom-up (decoding words, phrases, sentences for comprehension) processes are important to tackle the complexity of reading. Thus, in *Reading into a New China*, we emphasize both strategies by asking students to use their prior knowledge to understand the main idea of the text, and relate it to their own worldview and opinion. At the same time, they should also pay close attention to detailed information and deeper meaning by decoding important vocabulary, phrases and sentences. Skill-focused activities that highlight the thinking process of proficient Chinese readers are carefully designed. For example:

> 1. *First Reading: Skimming for the Main Idea*
>
>   This activity requires students to read the whole text without stopping and then select the main idea of the text from three provided statements. This is the goal of the first read-through of each chapter.
>
> 2. *Second Reading: Looking for Details*
>
>   This activity requires students to look for specific information in each text. Typically, students respond to true/false and multiple-choice questions, link specific solutions to problems, and locate technical terms and definitions.

Other specific skills of the reading process are articulated for the students in each lesson. They include the skills of *guessing meaning from context, understanding written structures, identifying text organization, making inferences, distinguishing facts from speculation*, and many others. The objective is to gradually build up students' abilities to read Chinese independently in the future.

4. Word Usage and Sentence Patterns

This section uses contexts provided by the text to focus students' attention on the usage/function of 10–15 target items of vocabulary and sentence patterns. These target items have been selected for their usefulness in communication, especially in formal and written styles. Extra examples are provided to illustrate varied usages and functions in different contexts beyond the text.

5. Grammar

To reach the goal of developing integrated language skills, *Reading into a New China* gives systematic attention to grammar for both fluency and accuracy in Chinese. Each chapter not only introduces new grammar features or rules (e.g., word formation rules, idiomatic expressions, topic chains, rhetorical devices, formal and informal styles, etc.), but also reviews and summarizes previously learned fragmentary grammatical items in a more systematic and functional way (e.g., categorizing functions of connectives for cohesion and coherence in reading and writing in discourse-level communication). Grammar is explained in clear and plain language, from a pedagogical perspective, without using unnecessary technical terms or jargon.

6. Contextualized and Communicative Exercises for Integrated Language Skills

Reading into a New China provides students with ample exercises for learning and practicing the integrated skills of reading, speaking, and writing, in addition to vocabulary and grammar. We have significantly increased the number and variety of exercises in the textbook, eliminating the need for a separate workbook. These contextualized exercises offer students opportunities to carry out communicative tasks that require exchanging information and negotiating meaning. For example, vocabulary exercises are always provided at an extended discourse level so that students can use the newly acquired language for comprehension and communication. Grammar exercises provide both controlled practice and communicative activities. Reading skills covered in the text are practiced in interesting and relevant supplementary reading tasks to reinforce the training. In the speaking activity, students are given a chance to make connections between the readings and their own lives and opinions, to recycle newly learned vocabulary and structures, to develop their oral communication skills, to approach the readings more critically, and to share their opinions with their classmates. The final exercise is always writing, which provides another chance for vocabulary recycling, writing skill practice, and closure for each chapter.

7. Audio Recordings

Audio recordings include new words and main text of every chapter. Each copy of this book includes a passcode on page viii that enables the user to download free MP3 audio recordings from **http://www.cheng-tsui.com/downloads**. These recordings can be played on a computer or portable MP3 player, or burned onto a CD. We hope that these supplementary audio recordings will be especially useful for auditory learners and students seeking extra practice in fluent and natural pronunciation. The downloadable audio recordings are also available for separate purchase from **www.cheng-tsui.com**.

■ Organization

This textbook (Volume Two) contains ten lessons, with each lesson including the following sections.

Section	Objective(s)
1. Overview	To provide background (cultural, social, historical) information and text-feature knowledge
2. Photo or Illustration	To provide visual clues about the lesson and stimulate discussion
3. Pre-reading Questions	To activate students' background knowledge about the theme
4. Main Text	To present high-interest topics that can develop students' reading skills and stimulate discussion
5. Vocabulary Building Skills	To develop students' vocabulary-building skills so as to increase speed and effectiveness in vocabulary acquisition
6. Vocabulary	To broaden students' knowledge and use of vocabulary words, idioms and phrases
7. Reading Skills	To introduce various important skills used in the reading process
8. Word Usage and Sentence Patterns	To present and explain model language use of new words and sentence patterns
9. Grammar	To introduce new structures and grammar items To summarize previously learned structures and grammar items To illustrate how previously learned structures and grammar items can be used in more complex ways
10. Exercises	To provide contextualized exercises for integrated language skills development: ■ pronunciation ■ words and sentence patterns ■ grammar ■ comprehensive exercises ■ reading ■ speaking ■ writing

We hope this new textbook can help our students develop language proficiency that can live up to the name of "advanced Chinese." We are also aware of the fact that, despite our best efforts, it will have its shortcomings. We welcome your ideas and hope that teachers and students who use it will provide us with any feedback or suggestions for improvement by contacting the publisher at editor@cheng-tsui.com.

The Authors
March, 2009

ACKNOWLEDGMENTS

Writing this book has been a wonderful experience. During this period of time we have received great deal of help, encouragement and support from our dear friends and colleagues, for which we are grateful. We wish to acknowledge their contributions to this book project and express our appreciation and gratitude to them.

First of all, we would like to thank John Meskill and Patricia Duff who offered us their professional advice, scholarly feedback on second language learning, particularly for Chinese language learning, and expert help in English editing throughout the writing process. This book would not have been possible without their sustained support and encouragement.

In addition, we would like to thank the following colleagues and students at the University of British Columbia who contributed in various ways to the creation of this book, from technical help to content editing, proofreading and audio recording. They are: Pan Luo, Jingchan Liu, Rachel Wang, Hui Yu, Xinxin Wu, Xihua Guan, and Wanhui Qing. We also acknowledge, with thanks, practical and financial support received from the University of British Columbia Centre for Research in Chinese Language and Literacy Education and from the Social Sciences and Humanities Research Council of Canada that enabled us to remunerate these assistants.

The preparation and completion of this book were greatly facilitated by the editors and staff at Cheng and Tsui Company, whose assistance and professional work on the manuscript was superb. We are particularly grateful to Jill Cheng, for her great confidence and support in this project, and our excellent editor, Laurel Damashek, for her sharp mind, keen eye and guiding hand in helping bring this project to closure.

Finally, we thank the Chinese language learners in the United States, Canada and elsewhere who have provided so much inspiration to us over the years and who have been the impetus for this new textbook. We hope you will enjoy it!

缩略语表
Abbreviations

adj.	adjective
adv.	adverb
attr.	attribute
conj.	conjunction
interj.	interjection
m.	measure word
n.	noun
num.	numeral
ono.	onomatopoeia
part.	particle
prep.	preposition
pron.	pronoun
p.n.	proper noun
i.e.	idiomatic expression
v.	verb
v.o.	verb-object
v.p.	verb phrase

黄昏之恋

课文提要

In China, 11 percent of the total population consists of elderly people, among whom 35 percent are widowed. These people who have lost their spouses might wish to find a new love and create a new family. But the prospect of remarriage can be plagued with issues such as personal property disputes, children's objections or even social prejudice.

According to the traditional moral values that guided Chinese society for thousands of years, a person was expected to be faithful and loyal to his or her spouse for life, although in a male-dominant society this moral code was not equally applied to men and women. In practice, a widower could remarry with much less stigma, while a widow's remarriage was viewed as "shameful."

In recent years, romance and remarriage among elders have gradually become accepted in Chinese society, although people are still influenced by the traditional ideas. The story in this lesson is about the love and remarriage of two elderly people and the reactions of their family members.

阅读前讨论：

1. "黄昏恋"是什么意思？根据这个题目，猜猜这篇课文会讲什么？
2. 谈谈上面这张照片。
3. 老年人最需要的是什么？优越的生活条件还是亲人的关心？
4. 你认不认识因黄昏恋而幸福的老人？讲一讲他们的故事。
5. 你知道哪些跟"老人"有关的词汇？

自学生词

Match each new word in the left column with its English translation in the right column by guessing the word's meaning from the characters that it is composed of. (The first one is done for you).

	生词	繁体	序号	英文
(3)	当年	當	1.	split in two
( )	听话	聽話	2.	old man, old father
( )	谁知	誰	3.	that year, in those years
( )	来得快	來	4.	heed advice; be obedient
( )	开心	開	5.	unexpectedly, who knows…
( )	一分为二	為	6.	quick in responding
( )	老爷子	爺	7.	in this way
( )	这样一来	這樣來	8.	can get along well with
( )	合得来	來	9.	needless to say
( )	不用说	說	10.	look at each other
( )	对看	對	11.	feel happy, rejoice

生词

简体	繁体	拼音	词性	英文	HSK 等级
1. 黄昏		huánghūn	*n.*	dusk, twilight	丙
2. 不禁		bùjīn	*adv.*	cannot help (doing sth.)	丙
3. 叹	嘆	tàn	*v.*	sigh	丁

简体	繁体	拼音	词性	英文	HSK 等级
4. 指挥	揮	zhǐhuī	*v.*	command, direct, conduct	乙
5. 团	團	tuán	*n.*	regiment (in army)	乙
6. 愣		lèng	*adj.*	dumbfounded, stupefied	丙
7. 连忙	連	liánmáng	*adv.*	hastily, hurriedly	乙
8. 端		duān	*v.*	hold sth. level	丙
9. 热腾腾	熱騰	rèténgténg	*adj.*	steaming hot, piping hot	
10. 羹		gēng	*n.*	a thick soup, custard	
11. 媳妇	婦	xífu	*n.*	daughter-in-law	丙
12. 惦记	記	diànjì	*v.*	keep thinking of, miss	丙
13. 疑惑		yíhuò	*v.*	be doubtful, uncertain, perplexed	丁
14. 琢磨		zuómo	*v.*	ponder, think over	丁
15. 闹	鬧	nào	*v.*	make a noise; give vent	乙
16. 顺路	順	shùnlù	*adv.*	on the way	丙
17. 怪		guài	*v.*	blame	丙
18. 呜	嗚	wū	*ono.*	sound of crying, wind, siren	丁
19. 宝贝	寶貝	bǎobèi	*n.*	treasure; endearment (children)	丁
20. 搂	摟	lǒu	*v.*	hold in one's arms, hug	丙
21. 别扭	彆	bièniu	*adj.*	awkward, uncomfortable	丁
22. 表态	態	biǎotài	*v.o.*	make one's position known	乙
23. 看		kān	*v.*	look after, take care of	丙
24. 家务	務	jiāwù	*n.*	household duties	丁
25. 省心		shěngxīn	*v.o.*	save worry, avoid worry	
26. 太平		tàipíng	*adj.*	peaceful	丁
27. 瞧		qiáo	*v.*	look, see, watch (colloquial)	乙
28. 挑		tiāo	*v.*	choose, select	乙
29. 赞成	贊	zànchéng	*v.*	approve, endorse, agree with	乙

课文

■ 第一读：掌握课文大意

快速阅读课文，看下面三个选择中哪一个最能说明本课主要意思：

1. 中国三代人家庭生活的故事
2. 爷爷和孩子的故事
3. 一对老年人恋爱的故事

黄昏之恋

"聪聪，走吧，爷爷送你上幼儿园。"

"不去，爷爷，我不去。幼儿园老师要我表演，我不要表演，我不去嘛！"

爷爷一听，心想糟糕了，上星期六就约好了，星期一把聪聪送进幼儿园，他就到她那里去。谁知道今天聪聪特别不听话，说什么也不肯去幼儿园。他不禁叹了口气，唉，想当年，自己能指挥一个团，现在却连一个五岁的孙子都指挥不了。

于是他只好带着聪聪一起到她那里去。她住在北海公园附近，虽然只有一间小小的屋子，但是屋内收拾得干净整齐，屋前还种着各种好看的花草。

他推门进去，让聪聪叫"奶奶"。

"奶奶！"聪聪甜甜地叫了一声。

她一愣，没想到他把聪聪带来了。"哎，"她连忙把聪聪拉过来，拍拍他的头，让他坐下，然后端出一碗热腾腾的鸡蛋羹来。这碗鸡蛋羹原来是为他做的，既然聪聪来了，就一分为二，让他和聪聪各吃半碗吧。

他吃了一口鸡蛋羹，叹了口气："哎，星期天最不好过，儿子媳妇都在家，不好意思出来，可心里又惦记着你。"

"等哪天把事跟他们说明了，咱们去登记一下，就好了。"她说。

小聪聪疑惑地看看爷爷，又看看"奶奶"，琢磨着他们说的"登记"是什么意思。他只知道，爷爷奶奶一"登记"，他就有鸡蛋羹吃，所以，他希望他们天天都去"登记"，这样他一定能天天吃到鸡蛋羹。

因为遇到一个好奶奶，聪聪一定要玩到吃完晚饭才走。晚饭后，爷孙两个终于回家了。聪聪边走边唱，可高兴了。

谁知家里已经闹翻了天。

原来，幼儿园老师看见聪聪一天没来，心里有点担心，下班后顺路赶到聪聪家，想看看聪聪是不是病了。这样一来，可就急坏了聪聪的妈妈："都怪你！都怪你！自己不送孩子，一定要那么早去上班，现在可好，老爷子送孙子去幼儿园，连自己都送丢了！呜……"

"妈妈、爸爸，"聪聪猛然推开门，飞跑进来。妈妈一看见宝贝儿子就立刻上去搂住他，又高兴又着急地问："宝贝儿，你可回来了！上哪儿去啦？快告诉妈妈。"

"到奶奶家去了，"聪聪高兴地说，"奶奶可好了！给我做鸡蛋羹吃，带我去公园玩儿，还说要给爷爷和我做新衣服呢。"

小两口先对看了一下，然后一起看着老爷子，心想：哪儿来的这位"奶奶"？怎么从来没听说过啊？可嘴里又不好明明白白地问。

"是这样的，"老爷子不自然地看了看他们，说："我给聪聪找了个奶奶，我们俩很合得来。你们小两口商量商量吧，要是没意见，我就把她接过来一起住；要是有意见，我就搬到她那里去住。"

儿子一听就觉得别扭。老爷子这把年纪，还搞起自由恋爱来了，这可让作儿子的怎么表态呢？于是他看了看妻子。

倒是儿媳妇来得快，她心想，老爷子可不能走，走了谁看聪聪？来个奶奶也不错，一定比爷爷还能干，这样家务、孩子就都省心了。而且老爷子开心、身体好，家里也太平啊。于是她就很快表了态："爸，瞧您说的，当初我们结婚，您操了那么多心；现在您要办喜事，我们哪能反对呢？我一百个同意！您就挑个好日子吧。""是啊，我们完全赞成！"儿子也立刻接着说。不用说，小聪聪也把两只小手举得高高的。

■ 第二读：细节和理解

1. **按照这篇文章的意思，下面的说法对不对？(T/F)**

   (　　) 1. 聪聪家有五口人：爷爷、奶奶、爸爸、妈妈和他。

   (　　) 2. 聪聪很喜欢上幼儿园。

   (　　) 3. 聪聪的爷爷每天都去看奶奶。

   (　　) 4. 奶奶给爷爷做了一件新衣服。

   (　　) 5. 聪聪的妈妈很高兴，因为爷爷找到了一位合适的伴侣。

   (　　) 6. 聪聪的妈妈做事很快。

   (　　) 7. 聪聪的爸爸很赞成爷爷再婚。

   (　　) 8. 爷爷和奶奶正在热恋中，他们很快就要结婚了。

2. **根据课文内容回答下列问题：**

   1. 为什么爷爷当年能指挥一个团，现在却连一个五岁的孙子也指挥不了？

   2. 为什么爷爷星期天最不好过？

   3. 聪聪的爸爸妈妈听说了爷爷的婚事后各有什么反应？他们的反应说明了什么？

   4. 聪聪的爸爸本来不赞成爷爷再婚，可是为什么后来改变了态度？

   5. 聪聪家里谁的权力最大？从什么地方可以看出来？

   6. 你觉得爷爷奶奶结婚后住在哪儿会比较幸福？为什么？

■ 阅读技巧：理解和运用语气词

Understanding the "Mood Words" — Learning Sentence Final Particles (SFPs)

The text of this lesson is a narrative. In a narrative, speech is often quoted in dialogues among characters in the story. One special feature of Chinese dialogue is its frequent and numerous sentence-final particles (in Chinese: 语气词, literally "mood words"), a linguistic feature that may be new to English speakers.

These "mood words" do not have semantic content per se, but rich contextual meanings are generated when they are used in discourse, providing information about the speaker's intentions, perspectives, attitudes, or impressions. SFPs are usually pronounced in the neutral tone, and they are literally the last element in a sentence. Their usage and meaning are usually determined by different discourse factors related to the intentions of the speaker and the speaker's relationship to the person being addressed. For example, the following sentences all include the same clause 纽约的冬天很冷, but with the different SFPs, they have different meanings:

我在纽约住过，纽约的冬天真冷啊！(expressing strong feeling)

你在纽约住过吗，纽约的冬天很冷吧？(asking for confirmation)

我要带厚衣服吗，纽约的冬天很冷吗？(asking for information)

你一定要带件大衣，纽约的冬天很冷呢？(reinforcing an assertion)

The most common (and well-studied) of these particles are listed in the following table, along with a non-exhaustive summary of their possible "functions"(i.e., added emotive, modal, pragmatic or discourse contributions to the utterance).

Particle	Functions	Examples
啊 showing strong feelings	exclamation (usually with 多, 多么，真)	它们多么快乐、自由啊！ 多好的地方啊！
	confirmation, certainty	你这话说得对啊！ 他做这种事也是因为没有办法啊！
	urging, warning	快走啊！一定要小心啊！
	interrogative marker	你去不去啊？她是哪国人啊？
吧 mitigating the force of speech	softening the tone of a request or suggestion	我们一起去看看他吧。
	soliciting agreement or confirmation	你不会反对吧？
	agreement or resignation (often with 就)	好吧，那我就去吧。

Particle	Functions	Examples
吗 questioning	yes/no question marker	你赞成黄昏恋吗？
呢	interrogative marker	我们应该赞成还是反对呢？
	one-word question	我的书呢？ 我们都去。你呢？
	assertion reinforcement (usually with 还)	我这个同学中文很好，他还会唐诗呢！ 我认识她，我还是她同班同学呢。
嘛	obviousness	她当然认识这个字，她是老师嘛。
	insistence	我就是不想去他们公司嘛。
	expectation, persuasion	不要哭嘛，有话慢慢说嘛。

The particle 啊 can be pronounced in different ways, depending on the sound of the previous syllable. These different variants are sometimes written in different characters, such as 呀 (i+a), 哇 (u+a), 哪 (n+a), and 啦 (了+a). The following table lists the most common contexts for the variants of 啊. You don't have to remember all the "rules." Just by linking the sounds naturally, you will pronounce them well.

Context	Variant	Examples
a, e, i, o, ü + 啊	→ ya (呀)	就等你回家啊 (ya)！ 好漂亮的大衣啊 (ya)！
u, ao, ou + 啊	→ wa (哇)	您在哪儿住啊 (wa)？ 他汉语说得真好啊 (wa)！
-n + 啊	→ na (哪)	这件事儿可不简单啊 (na)！ 孩子们笑得真欢啊 (na)！
了 (le) + 啊	→ la (啦)	宝贝儿，上哪儿去啦？ 毕业啦！再也不用考试啦！

Reading Skill Practice:

1. **The writer of this narrative didn't describe the characters in detail. Rather, the personalities of the characters in the story are revealed through their "voices." Read the following sentences (with sentence final particles) in the voices of the different characters from this text, and decide from the context which "mood" they express.**

   爷爷

   1. 聪聪，走吧，爷爷送你上幼儿园。
      a. softening the tone of a request or suggestion
      b. soliciting agreement or confirmation
      c. agreement or resignation

   2. 你们小俩口商量商量吧。
      a. softening the tone of a request or suggestion
      b. soliciting agreement or confirmation
      c. agreement or resignation

   聪聪

   1. 我不要表演，我不去嘛!
      a. obviousness
      b. insistence
      c. expectation, persuasion

   2. 还说要给爷爷和我做新衣服呢!
      a. interrogative marker
      b. one-word question
      c. assertion reinforcement

   奶奶

   1. 既然聪聪来了，就让他们各吃半碗吧。
      a. softening the tone of a request or suggestion
      b. soliciting agreement or confirmation
      c. agreement or resignation

儿子

1. 哪儿来的这位"奶奶"呀 (nai+a)？

    a. exclamation

    b. confirmation, certainty

    c. urging, warning

    d. interrogative marker

2. 让我这作儿子的怎么表态呢？

    a. interrogative marker

    b. one-word question

    c. assertion reinforcement

3. 是啊，我们完全赞成！

    a. exclamation

    b. confirmation, certainty

    c. urging, warning

    d. interrogative marker

儿媳妇

1. 老爷子可不能走，走了谁看聪聪啊？

    a. exclamation

    b. confirmation, certainty

    c. urging, warning

    d. interrogative marker (rhetorical question)

2. 而且老爷子开心、身体好，家里也太平啊。

    a. exclamation

    b. confirmation, certainty

    c. urging, warning

    d. interrogative marker (rhetorical question)

3. 现在您要办喜事，我们哪能反对呢？
   a. interrogative marker (rhetorical question)
   b. one-word question
   c. assertion reinforcement

4. 您就挑个好日子吧。
   a. softening the tone of a request or suggestion
   b. soliciting agreement or confirmation
   c. agreement or resignation

词汇与句型

1. 当年 • that year, in those years, in those days

1. 想当年几乎没有人会首选"公司、企业"。
   In those years, almost nobody would choose "company or corporation."

2. 当年她还是个孩子，现在却已成为一个乐团指挥了。
   She was just a kid in those years. But now she has become the conductor of an orchestra.

3. 刘先生现在走路都走不动了，没人知道他当年曾经是著名的长跑运动员。
   Mr. Liu can hardly walk now. Nobody knows that he used to be a well-known long-distance runner in those days.

2. V 得了/V 不了 • be able to do/unable to do
In this phrase, 了 (liǎo) is used with 得 or 不 after a verb to indicate "possibility" or "capability."

1. 想当年，自己能指挥一个团，现在却连一个五岁的孙子都指挥不了。
   Thinking back, he could command a regiment in those years. But now he can't even command a five-year-old grandson.

2. 你来得了还是来不了？
   Will you be able to come or not?

3. 这件事他跑不了。
   He can't get away with it.

3. 合得来/合不来 • get along well with/can't get along with

1. 我跟说话痛快的人比较合得来。
   Relatively speaking, I get along with those who are straightforward in speech.

2. 你和你的同屋合不合得来（合得来合不来）？
   Can you get along well with your roommate?

3. 我们虽然是姐妹，可是从小就合不来。
   Although we are sisters, we haven't been able to get along with each other since childhood.

4. 怪 • blame, strange, very (colloquial)

1. 都怪我，我不应该发脾气。
   I'm to blame. I shouldn't have lost my temper.

2. 这盘菜的味道有点怪，是不是坏了？
   The dish tastes a bit strange. Has it gone bad?

3. 天气怪热的，我不想穿那件外套了。
   It's quite hot. I don't want to put on that jacket.

5. 不禁 • cannot help (starting) doing...

1. 昨天晚上，我一个人走在树林里，不禁害怕起来。
   Last night, as I walked in the woods alone, I couldn't help feeling scared.

2. 听到被重点大学录取的消息，她非常激动，不禁流下泪来。
   Upon hearing the news that she had been admitted into a key university, she was so excited that she couldn't help her tears running down.

3. 看着小女儿可爱的样子，妈妈不禁微笑起来。
   Watching the lovely expression of her little daughter, the mother couldn't help smiling.

Note: While 不禁 and 不由得 are both adverbs indicating "cannot help (doing), cannot refrain (from doing)" and sometimes they are interchangeable, 不禁 has a more formal tone than 不由得。

6. 一分为二 • (one) split in two

1. 第二次世界大战后，德国被一分为二。
   After the Second World War, Germany was divided in two.

2. 他们都想吃那个苹果，妈妈只好把它一分为二，一人一半。
   Both kids wanted the apple. Mother had to split it in two and gave half to each.

3. 事情总是一分为二的，不要只看消极的方面。
   Everything has two sides. Do not just look at the negative side.

7. 闹翻天 • create a great disturbance, turn a place upside down

1. 昨天妹妹请同学们到我家开生日会，他们简直闹翻了天。
   Yesterday my younger sister invited her classmates to our house for a birthday party. They simply turned our house upside down.

2. 老师刚出去不久，小学生们就在教室里闹翻了天。
   Shortly after the teacher went out, the pupils created a great disturbance in the classroom.

3. 我听到邻居家闹翻天了，发生了什么事？
   I heard a commotion from our neighbor. What happened?

8. 猛然 • suddenly, abruptly, drastically

1. 风猛然把门关上，吓了我一跳。
   The wind forcefully slammed the door, which startled me.

2. 我猛然想起今天下午有英文考试。
   I suddenly recalled that there is an English test this afternoon.

3. 汽车猛然停下来。
   The car jerked to a halt.

9. 瞧您说的 • it's not like what you said... (look what you said...)

This is a rather colloquial expression to show mild "disagreement" or "protest" in order to express politeness or modesty. It is usually used in response to a compliment or someone else's self-deprecating expression. Similar expressions are: "看您说的，" "瞧/看您说到哪儿去了."

1. 瞧您说的，我哪能忘了您呢？
   It's not like what you said. How could I forget you?

2. 看您说的，我可没那么聪明。
   I'm not as smart as you said.

3. 瞧您说到哪儿去了，我当然支持您的决定了。
   It's not like what you said. Of course I will support your decision.

10. 说什么也不 V • won't do… no matter what, absolutely against…

1. 小王深深地爱着这位农村姑娘，可是他的父母说什么也不同意他们结婚。
   Xiao Wang loves the country girl very much. But his parents absolutely disapprove of this marriage.

2. 妈妈想哄孩子睡觉，可是他说什么也不睡。
   The mother wants to put her child to bed, but he refuses to sleep no matter what.

3. 她帮助我复习中文，我想付她一些钱，可是她说什么也不要。
   She helped me review my Chinese. I wanted to pay her, but she refused to take payment no matter what.

11. 谁知 • unexpectedly, it turns out…, who knew…

1. 妈妈以为聪聪丢了，谁知他自己走回家去了。
   Congcong's mother thought he was lost. It turns out he walked home by himself.

2. 奶奶等爷爷过来吃午饭，谁知他把聪聪也带来了。
   The grandma waited for the grandpa to come for lunch. Who would expect him to bring Congcong along with him?

3. 聪聪爸爸以为聪聪妈妈会反对爷爷再婚，谁知她却非常赞成。
   Congcong's father thought his wife would object to Grandpa's remarriage, but was completely surprised to hear her enthusiastic endorsement.

12. 这样一来 • in this way, so, therefore

1. 聪聪希望爷爷奶奶赶快去"登记"，这样一来，他就能天天吃鸡蛋羹了。
   Congcong hopes that his grandpa and the grandma will go to "register" soon, so he will get to eat steamed egg custard every day.

2. 他们把工作重新安排了一下，这样一来，就不必聘新人了。

They rearranged the work so they didn't have to hire anyone new.

3. 听说三个公司跟这件事故有关，这样一来，问题就更复杂了。

It is said that three companies are involved in this accident. In this way, the issue becomes more complicated.

13. 倒是 • but, rather, otherwise, actually *, contrast*

倒是, used as an adverb, indicates contrast or something contrary to common sense, fact, general opinion or expectations. It can appear either before or after the subject of the clause. Its meaning is highly versatile, depending on the context of the discourse.

1. 倒是儿媳妇来得快。

(In contrast to the son's hesitant response) The daughter-in-law was rather quick-minded.

2. 天气预报说今天下雨，结果今天倒是个大晴天。

The weather forecast said it would rain today, but it turned out to be a sunny day.

3. 人人都说他性情很怪，我倒是跟他很合得来。

Everyone says he is kind of eccentric, but I actually get along pretty well with him.

4. 这个工作累了点，其他方面倒是挺让人满意。

This job is a little too tiring, but otherwise it is quite satisfactory.

语法

1. 省略 • Ellipsis

Ellipsis involves the omission of an item: a case of leaving something unsaid which is nevertheless understood. Ellipsis occurs more frequently in Chinese than in English, because of the *topic-prominent* features and very flexible syntactic rules of the Chinese language. In clearly contextualized utterances, some language features (e.g., conjunctions, noun phrases and pronouns) can become redundant; therefore, they are often omitted.

Clarity is the key governing when ellipsis can occur in discourse and when it cannot. Ellipsis occurs more often in oral discourse because in spoken conversation, there are many other cues such as intonation, body language, or visual aids that can assist in achieving clarity. In written discourse, the understanding of omitted elements depends mainly on the context (and sometimes on the reader's background knowledge).

Ellipsis is an important discourse device that makes both oral and written discourse more coherent and less redundant. Being able to detect ellipsis in discourse (both oral and written) and recover the implied information in an unstated slot is a very important part of learning the Chinese language. The following are the most common situations for ellipsis:

1.1. In oral discourse (particularly in dialogue), any noun phrases or pronouns may be omitted as long as they are conceptually clear to listeners. For example:

- "聪聪，走吧，爷爷送你上幼儿园。"

- "（我）不去（幼儿园），爷爷，我不去嘛。"

1.2. In written discourse, pronouns in the subject position are more likely to be omitted than those in the object position, when they refer to the same topics of the discourse. (See "topic-chain" in Lesson 5).

爷爷一听，心想糟糕了，上星期六（他们）就约好了，星期一（他）把聪聪送进幼儿园，他就到她那里去。谁知道今天聪聪特别不听话，（他）说什么也不肯去幼儿园。他不禁叹了口气，想当年，自己能指挥一个团，现在（他）却连一个五岁的孙子都指挥不了。

1.3. In complex sentences, ellipsis can be applied to the cue words or connectives that link the clauses within a sentence, *if* the relationship between the clauses is clear from context (see Lesson 9 for the table of connectives).

聪聪因为遇到一个好奶奶（所以）一定要玩到吃完晚饭才走。

星期天最不好过，（因为）儿子媳妇都在家，（所以）不好意思出来，可是（我）心里又惦记着你。

原来，幼儿园老师看见聪聪一天没来，（所以）（她）心里有点担心，（于是）下班后她顺路赶到聪聪家，想看看聪聪是不是病了。

2. "可" 的用法

2.1. (conj.) but, yet, however（= 可是）

1. 星期天最不好过，儿子媳妇都在家，不好意思出来，可心里又惦记着你。

2. 哪儿来的这位 "奶奶"？……可嘴里又不好明明白白地问。

2.2. (adv.) really, indeed, must

As an adverb, 可 is used (in colloquial-style discourse) before a verb or an adjective to express emphasis. The sentences often end with particles such as 了、啊、呢、啦, etc.

The following examples from this lesson illustrate the different facets of its emphatic function:

1. 现在可好了，老爷子送孙子去幼儿园，连自己都送丢了！
   Now that's terrific (ironic tone)! The old grandpa even got himself lost by walking his grandson to kindergarten!

2. 这样一来，可就急坏了聪聪的妈妈。
   This situation really devastated Congcong's mother.

3. 这可让作儿子的怎么表态呢？
   How could I, indeed, as his son, tell him what I really think?

4. 结婚可是一生的大事，你可不能随随便便的。
   (Warning) Marriage is a big thing in one's life. You cannot take it too lightly.

5. 我可不想结婚，做一个单身的自由人不是更好吗？
   Indeed, I don't want to get married. Isn't it better to be a free single person?

3. 既然…… • since (now that, under these circumstances)

既然 is a conjunction that introduces a clause indicating an already existing condition or situation. The second clause (usually with 就, 也, or 还) introduces suggestions, inferences, and deductions based on the existing condition. 既然 can appear either before or after the subject, but 就 (or 也，还) can only be placed before the verb phrase.

既然聪聪来了，就一分为二，让他和聪聪各吃半碗吧。
Since Congcong is here, then (let me) divide the egg custard so he and Congcong can each have half of it.

你既然来了，就别走了，在这儿吃晚饭吧。
Since (it is the case that) you are already here, don't leave. Have dinner with us.

这其实完全是他的事情。既然他不去，那我为什么要去？（= 我也不去。）
This is actually his business. Since he is not going, why would I bother to go?

Compare "既然…就…" and "因为…所以…"

Both 既然…就… and 因为…所以… indicate a cause/effect relationship. The basic difference is that 既然…就… expresses a more subjective opinion of the speaker or writer. It is worth noting that the English word "since" may have different Chinese equivalents due to its multiple functions. For example:

自从他走了（以后），我们就再也没有得听到过他的消息了。
Since he left, we have never heard from him. (time)

既然他已经走了，我们就找别的会计师吧。
Since he's gone, let's look for another accountant. (premise for suggestion)

因为他走了，（所以）我们公司不得不再找一位会计师。
Since he's gone, our company has to find another accountant. (reason for situation)

练习

1. 语音

Write pinyin for the following underlined Chinese characters. Pay special attention to their different pronunciations in different contexts:

着急（　）	指挥不了（　）	看孩子（　）	特别（　）
带着（　）	太晚了（　）	对看（　）	别扭（　）
挑战（　）	各种各样（　）	当年（　）	不禁（　）
挑选（　）	种树（　）	当作（　）	禁止（　）

2. 词汇与句型

2.1. 词语搭配 Match the following words by considering their appropriate collocations.

Group One (Verb + Object)			**Group Two** (Adj. + Noun)		
1. 办	_____	屋子	1. 热腾腾的	_____	答案
2. 指挥	_____	门	2. 甜甜的	_____	孩子
3. 推	_____	乐队	3. 疑惑的	_____	感觉
4. 登记	_____	手	4. 听话的	_____	饭菜
5. 收拾	_____	喜事	5. 明明白白的	_____	眼光
6. 举	_____	结婚	6. 别扭的	_____	声音

2.2. 用括号内的词语完成对话：

1. A: 我的同屋性格太怪了。跟她住在一个房间里，真难受。

   B: _____（既然）

2. A: 你们老师今天上课的时候为什么那么生气？

   B: _____（是这样的）

3. A: 这家饭馆的四川菜怎么样？

   B: 不太好，_____（倒是）

4. A: 你们假期去中国玩儿得怎么样？

   B: 别提了，本来我们打算去很多地方，_____（谁知）

2.3. 选择填空

A. 选择合适的语气词（吗、啊、呢、吧、嘛）填空：

1. 虽然你们之间曾经有过不愉快的事儿，可他现在病了，你还是去看看他 _____！

2. 这么晚了，恐怕他不会来了 _____？

3. 你怎么能这样对待生你养你的父母 _____？

4. 你知道到底有多少人会参加我们的晚会 _____？

5. 一个人出去旅行，你可要多加小心 _____！

6. 真快 _____！四年的大学生活马上就要结束了！

7. 听说你们星期天要去爬山，我可以跟你们一起去 _____？

8. 你这个人哪，总是这么糊里糊涂的，让我说什么好 _____？

9. 你的要求也不算太高，她应该会答应 _____？

10. 你不是说你不想来 _____？怎么又来了 _____？

11. 有话好好说，不要太激动 _____！

12. 独生子女就是这样，他们是小皇帝 _____！

B. **Fill the blanks with the most suitable *sentence final particles* based on your understanding of the *mood* of the speakers in the following dialogue: Each sentence final particle may be used more than once.**

A: 王阿姨，您好！

B: 小林 _____！好久不见，今天什么风把你给吹来了？

A: 今天进城，我妈让我顺路到您家看看。向您问好 _____！

B: 谢谢！你妈还好 _____？她回乡下有半年了 _____？我们常惦记着她 _____。

A: 她很好。听说大龙哥下个月要结婚了，是 _____？

B: 是 _____！我们正要寄请帖请你们全家来喝喜酒 _____。

A: 我妈让我问问您，那天有什么需要我们帮忙的 _____？

B: 瞧你说的！怎么敢要你们来干活 _____？到时候只要你们来捧场就行了！

A: 那不用说，您是妈的老朋友 _____，我们当然会来给您道喜 _____！

B: 我有什么喜 _____！只要他们小夫妻合得来，我这个做妈的就省心了。

2.4. 选词填空 Choose the most appropriate words to fill in the blanks of the passage:

a. 幸福	b. 合得来	c. 自然	d. 对看	e. 疑惑	f. 住
g. 同意	h. 奶奶	i. 然后	j. 登记	k. 反对	

当小王听说他的 ＿＿＿＿ 搬出了他父母的家，不禁 ＿＿＿＿ 了。他 ＿＿＿＿ 地看着他父母，问道："她去哪儿了？"他父母 ＿＿＿＿ 了一下，＿＿＿＿ 他父亲很不 ＿＿＿＿ 地说："她在老年人俱乐部 (jùlèbù, *club*) 认识了一位老先生，两个人很 ＿＿＿＿，就去 ＿＿＿＿ 结婚了。我们也不好 ＿＿＿＿。只好 ＿＿＿＿ 了。"

3. 语法

3.1. Ellipsis

The following sentences are taken from the text in this lesson. Fill in the nouns, pronouns and connectives that are omitted in the original text, based on the contextual meaning. Each space is for only one word.

1. "（　　）都怪你！（　　）都怪你！（　　）自己不送孩子，（　　）一定要那么早去上班，现在可好，老爷子送孙子去幼儿园，（　　）连自己都送丢了！呜……"

2. 她一愣，（　　）没想到他把聪聪带来了。"哎，"她连忙把聪聪拉过来，（　　）拍拍他的头，（　　）让他坐下，然后（　　）端出一碗热腾腾的鸡蛋羹来。

3. ■"哎呀！宝贝儿，你可回来了！（　　）上哪儿去了，快告诉妈妈。"
   ■"（　　）到奶奶家去了，"聪聪高兴地说，"奶奶可好了！（　　）给我做鸡蛋羹吃，（　　）带我去公园玩儿，（　　）还说要给爷爷做新衣服呢。"

4. 倒是儿媳妇来得快，（　　）心想，老爷子可不能走，（　　）走了谁看聪聪啊？来个奶奶也不错，（　　）一定比爷爷还能干，这样家务、孩子就都省心了。而且（　　）老爷子开心、身体好，家里也太平啊。于是（　　）就很快表了态。

3.2. Ellipsis

Rewrite the following sentences by joining the pairs of clauses according to their logical relationships, using appropriate connectives from the following list.

因为、所以、如果、即使、无论、不然、由于、虽然、可是

1. 他的思想原来很保守。现在越来越开放了。

   _____

2. 他认为废品回收是一种环保行业，毕业以后开办了一家废品回收公司。

   _____

3. 政府在房地产上的收入较少，很难维修旧房和兴建新房

   _____

4. 中学生毕业后，想继续读大学，就要参加全国统一的大学入学考试。

   _____

5. 芳芳！快起床，上课要迟到了。

   _____

6. 政府分配你做什么，你就做什么。

   _____

7. 你们店做的饭菜太没特色，再不改进，我们就换别的店了。

   _____

8. 结婚后，不幸福也不敢或不能离婚。

   _____

9. 老年人恋爱就会受到子女和周围人的反对。

   _____

3.3. 汉译英（请注意"可"在句子中的不同意思）

1. 想当年，自己能指挥一个团，可现在却连一个五岁的孙子都指挥不了。

_____

2. 她心想，老爷子可不能走，走了谁看聪聪？

_____

3. 奶奶可好了！给我做鸡蛋羹吃，还带我去公园玩儿。

_____

4. 聪聪边走边唱，可高兴了。

_____

5. 宝贝儿，你可回来啦！

_____

3.4. 英译汉（请注意 since 在句子中的不同意思）

1. Since you know he is not able to come, why don't you make some other arrangement?

_____

2. Since my early childhood, I have always liked music.

_____

3. Since he wants to go to the #1 university in China, he has been working very hard for the past two years.

_____

4. The two lovers have been working in different cities since they graduated from university.

_____

5. Since he is sick, he didn't come to class.

   _____

6. Since he got sick two weeks ago, he hasn't been to class.

   _____

7. Since you are sick, then why don't you ask your teacher for sick leave?

   _____

8. Since you eat at that restaurant every day, their food must be really good.

   _____

9. Since he doesn't have much money, he seldom eats at restaurants.

   _____

10. Since she didn't like Italian food, we had Japanese food instead.

   _____

11. Since she doesn't like Italian food, let's go to a Japanese restaurant.

   _____

12. Since you are so interested in business, you should have studied business management in college, not English literature.

   _____

4. 综合练习

4.1. 用所给词语将下列句子译成中文：

1. He suddenly pushed the door open and ran out, shouting: "Fire! Fire!" (猛然)

_____

2. Seeing these poor people who couldn't even afford food, he couldn't help signing. (不禁……起来)

_____

3. Xiao Wang was admitted into Beijing University. His father was very happy after hearing the news. (可 + Adj + 了)

_____

4. My sister and her roommate get along with each other very well. (合得来)

_____

5. Even though he was opposed to his father getting married again, he didn't show it. He only said to his father, "Since you love her so much, Dad, marry her." (表态，既然……就……。)

_____

4.2. 短文填空：

超越 (transcend) 时空的爱恋

a. 热恋	b. 惦记	c. 例如	d. 传统	e. 与	f. 疑惑	g. 赞成	h. 合得来
i. 关注	j. 年轻	k. 报道	l. 不管	m. 更	n. 开心	o. 呢	p. 门当户对

　　长久以来，中国人的爱情婚姻一直讲究 _____。在古代，那就是老百姓找老百姓，做官的找做官的。后来，又变成了农民找农民，工人找工人，干部找干部…… 除了"门当户对"以外，传统的爱情世界里还有很多别的"规则"。_____，男的应该比女的学历高、工作好、收入多；女的则应该长相漂亮，而且比男的年龄小、身材矮、性情好，等等。自从中国实行改革开放之后，人们的这些 _____ 观念慢慢改变，并对一些"非主流 (non-mainstream)"的恋情有了越来越多的尊重和接受。

2004 年 12 月，一家报纸 _____ ：现年 82 岁的第一位华人诺贝尔 (Nobel) 奖获得者杨振宁教授，将 _____ 广东外语外贸大学一位 28 岁的硕士生结婚。这条新闻引起了全社会 _____。有人震惊 (shocked)，有人 _____，但更多的人表示理解和祝福。

当记者问杨振宁有没有感觉到压力时，杨振宁回答："我们当然都能感觉到压力。有人可能想，她那么 _____，跟我结婚是不是为了我的名利？可能还有更多的人想，是不是我骗了一个年轻的女孩子？事实上 _____，我们两个人确实是真情相爱，在一起很 _____。不管现在别人怎么讲，将来大家一定会 _____ 我们的结合是一个美丽的浪漫故事。"

爱可以超越年龄，也可以超越国界。路小月毕业于北京大学法语系，一次聚会时，她认识了在北京工作的法国人 Claude。他们在一起总能找到互相感兴趣的话题，分别时总是互相 _____ 着对方，于是他们很快就进入了 _____ 之中。

"我和 Claude 都属于那种性格开朗 (sanguine, cheerful) 和独立的人。所以特别 _____。我觉得两个不同国家的人相恋，文化上的差异肯定是有的，但重要的是看两个人怎样对待这种差异。比如，我会告诉他我父母对我们的关系的担心，而他也愿意从一个中国女孩的角度来考虑我们的未来。_____ 我们之间的差异有多大，至少现在我们都认为彼此是最理想的恋人。"

"超越时空的爱情"只与相爱的两个人有关，不需要向其他人作任何解释，_____ 不需要符合任何外在的"准则 (norm, rule)"。

按照上面这篇文章的意思，下面的说法对不对？ (T/F)

_____ 1. 这篇文章的主要意思是恋爱婚姻必须讲究门当户对。

_____ 2. 传统的中国爱情观是女的应该比男的收入少，可是长相无所谓。

_____ 3. 中国人的爱情观从改革开放后开始改变。

_____ 4. 人们对杨振宁婚姻表示震惊的原因是双方年龄差距太大。

_____ 5. 杨振宁觉得和那么年轻的女孩结婚并没有什么压力。

_____ 6. 小月和 Claude 虽然国籍不同，但是文化上没有什么差异。

_____ 7. 小月的父母担心她恋爱关系的原因是 Claude 不是中国人。

_____ 8. "超越时空的爱情"的意思是爱情应该不受年龄和地区的限制。

回答下面问题

1. 这篇文章的主要意思是什么？

2. 中国的传统爱情观是怎么样的？

3. "非主流"恋情是什么意思？

4. 杨振宁的婚姻为什么会受到很多压力？

5. "超越时空的爱情"指的是什么？

5. 阅读练习

阅读短文（一）
女儿为妈妈找伴侣

他，六十六岁。她，五十七岁。他们虽然离得很远，却成了一对好伴侣。

男的叫王路中，以前是一个企业单位的经理，现在已经退休了。二十年前他和妻子离了婚，一个人带着四个孩子生活。现在孩子们都长大了、结婚了，家里只剩下他一个人，才觉得日子过得太<u>冷清</u> (*cold and cheerless*)了，该找个老伴了。

一天，他给《老人天地》杂志寄出了一则征婚启事。几天以后，就收到了十几封应征者的来信。应征者们的经济条件和学历都不错，但其中一封广州姑娘的来信特别引起了他的注意。信上写着：

"母亲只有我一个女儿，虽然我想尽了办法让母亲生活好，可是母亲总觉得孤独，她缺少一个生活中的伴侣…… 我认为老人晚年应该生活得更幸福，他们也要追求爱情。请您不要笑我，女儿为母亲找伴侣，在这个新时代已经不是什么新闻了……"信里还有一张母亲的照片。看着这封信，看着照片，王路中心动了，于是他拿起笔，给姑娘回了一封很长的信。

原来，姑娘的母亲是一个很有文化的人，年轻时也长得很美。结婚后，生了一儿一女，生活很幸福。没想到，儿子突然得病死了，丈夫又有了别的女人，和她离了婚，她的生活一下子全变了。虽然女儿关心她、爱她，但是在她的生活里缺少了一种不能替代 (replace) 的感情 — 夫妻情。

她从来不好意思跟女儿讲，可是女儿最了解母亲。为了母亲的晚年生活，她开始注意报上登的各种征婚启事。当她从《老人天地》杂志上看到王路中的信息后，觉得他可能是个合适的人选 (candidate)。她没有告诉母亲，就给王路中写了那封信。现在，回信收到了，她把信拿给母亲看。母亲看着信封，觉得很奇怪，但当她知道了一切经过后，被女儿的爱深深地感动了。

半年以后，两颗孤独的心紧紧地连在了一起，两位老人开始了共同的新生活。

1. 根据短文内容，选择最佳答案回答问题

　1. 两位老人是怎样认识的？
　　a. 通过"电话红娘"服务
　　b. 通过报纸征婚启事
　　c. 通过杂志征婚启事
　　d. 通过电视征婚

　2. 关于两位老人的情况，下面哪项**不正确**？
　　a. 她五十七岁；他六十六岁。
　　b. 她生了两个孩子；他有四个孩子。
　　c. 她以前又漂亮又有文化；他以前是一家企业的经理。
　　d. 他在《老人天地》登了征婚启事；她看到了那个征婚启事。

3. 两位老人有什么共同之处？
    a. 他们都和儿女住在一起。
    b. 他们的儿女都很关心他们。
    c. 他们都觉得一个人生活很孤独。
    d. 他们的老伴都去世了。

4. 根据短文内容，下面哪句话是正确的？
    a. 母亲希望女儿能帮自己找个老伴。
    b. 一年以后，两位老人结婚了，开始了共同的新生活。
    c. 两位老人的儿女都很支持他们结婚。
    d. 女儿成了母亲的红娘。

5. 以下哪项最好地说明了短文的主题？
    a. 新时代的人对老年人追求爱情的态度越来越开放。
    b. 女儿的爱感动了两位老人的心。
    c.《老人天地》把很多孤独的老人的心连在一起。
    d. 为了让母亲过上幸福的晚年，女儿为母亲找到了合适的伴侣。

2. 按照上面这篇文章的意思，下面的说法对不对？ (T/F)

_____ 1. 王路中因为要带四个孩子，白天晚上都很忙，所以日子不好过。

_____ 2. 王路中觉得生活太孤独，就在报上登了一个征婚广告。

_____ 3. 王路中觉得应征者中那位广州姑娘的条件对他最合适，最吸引他。

_____ 4. 女儿为妈妈找伴侣，这种事在九十年代已经不算很奇怪了。

_____ 5. 王路中一看姑娘的妈妈的照片就喜欢上她了。

_____ 6. 妈妈原来的丈夫不爱她了。

_____ 7. 母亲跟女儿之间的感情和妻子跟丈夫之间的感情不一样。

_____ 8. 女儿为妈妈找伴侣，是为了让妈妈晚年生活更幸福。

_____ 9. 女儿没有告诉妈妈就替妈妈应征，使妈妈觉得很奇怪，很生气。

_____ 10. 半年以后，两位老人就结婚了。

阅读短文（二）
外婆的"老伴儿"

外婆 80 岁了，退休前曾是小学校长。坐在她身上的小狗是我五年前送给她的生日礼物。现在外婆叫它"老黄"，就像当年称呼我的外公。

外婆这辈子共有 4 个儿女、我这个外孙女和 3 个孙子。从我们很小时候起，我们就记得外婆从来都是这世界上最忙的人，没见过她有休息的时候。可是自从她退休以后，生活就变得单调起来。尤其是外公去世以后，她更是感到孤独。每到周末或是寒暑假，外婆就盼望着我们去看她。可是后来家中最小的孩子都上了大学，各忙各的，有时外婆一个月也盼不到我们一个人回去。她渐渐毛病 (illness) 多起来 – 身体越来越弱，精神也越来越不好。

小狗做了外婆的"老伴儿"后，外婆除了料理自己生活以外，每天要惦记着给它按时喂食，早中晚还要带它外出<u>散步</u> (walk) 3 次。小狗跟外婆也很亲，从早到晚都跟着她，还能帮她找东西，开关房门。外婆的身体越来越好，人也变得越来越有精神。过去外婆很少出门，上街也没人跟她打招呼。现在很多人见了她和可爱的小狗都不由得停下来摸摸小狗的头，跟外婆说上几句话。外婆也整天笑容满面，主动和不同的人聊天，交了很多新朋友。

可爱的小狗成为了外婆生活中的一个忠实伴侣，它让外婆每天的生活更加充实。它让外婆与外面的世界有了更多的交流，让她的晚年生活更加幸福多彩。最重要的是，它让外婆真切地感受到生活的意义。因为外婆知道世界上又多了一个<u>依恋</u> (attached to) 自己的小生命。

根据短文内容，选择最佳答案回答问题

1. 为什么作者说小狗是外婆的"老伴儿"？
   a. 小狗的名字叫"老黄"，和当年外公的名字一样
   b. 外婆觉得小狗就像老伴儿一样重要
   c. 小狗让外婆想起了死去的外公
   d. 小狗是外婆生活中的忠实伴侣

2. 关于外婆身体越来越不好的原因，以下哪项<u>不符合</u>原文？

　　a. 外婆年纪大了，所以身体不好

　　b. 外婆退休以后生活太单调

　　c. 外公去世以后，外婆感到孤单

　　d. 外婆的子女和孙子孙女没有时间去探望她

3. 外婆养了小狗以后，生活有哪些变化？

　　a. 子女经常去看望小狗和外婆

　　b. 外婆经常带小狗出门看老朋友

　　c. 外婆的身体越来越好，人也越来越精神

　　d. 外婆必须料理自己的生活

4. 以下哪项最好地说明了这篇短文的主题？

　　a. 老年人的生活要充实，最好的办法就是养宠物

　　b. 小狗增加了外婆和外面世界的交流，使她更好地珍惜生活

　　c. 现在的晚辈因为工作太忙，常常忽略了老年人

　　d. 单身老年人的生活很单调

5. 口语练习：

5.1. 小组练习（2-3 人）

Based on the "tones" or "moods" of their speech and the whole story, select from the provided list the expressions that best describe the characters from "黄昏恋." (Note: Not every word can be used, but some words can be used more than once. You can also add your own words.)

热心	活泼	可爱	听话	能干	客气	善良	厉害
传统	开放	聪明	骄傲	细心	有礼貌	有爱心	胆小
天真 (naïve)		有心计 (calculating)			头脑简单 (simple-minded)		
自私 (selfish)		保守 (conservative)			通情达理 (reasonable)		
有耐心 (patient)		体贴人 (considerate)			宠坏的 (spoiled)		

爷爷 _____

奶奶 _____

聪聪 _____

儿子 _____

媳妇 _____

5.2. 小组之间比较结果

Compare your answers for the preceding exercise with another group. If there are different opinions, try to support your selection with facts and clues from the text.

5.3. 讨论

1. 黄昏恋对老人有什么好处？也可能会有什么问题？

2. 谁会反对黄昏恋？

3. 爱情婚姻应不应该受年龄与国度的限制？

4. 年龄相差太大的婚姻会有什么问题？

5. 国籍或种族不同者的婚姻会有什么问题？

6. 什么是主流婚姻和非主流婚姻？

7. 你对非主流婚姻有什么看法？

8. 宠物是不是老人理想的"伴侣"？为什么？

6. 写作练习（500-600 字）

作文题：一个<u>不寻常</u> (bùxúncháng, *unusual*) 的爱情故事

Write a narrative about an unusual love story. Try to use dialogues (and sentence final particles) to express different feelings and moods of the characters in your story.

Use at least 10 of the following new vocabulary and sentence patterns:

当年	谁知	开心	不禁	指挥	连忙	惦记	疑惑	琢磨
怪别扭	表态	省心	太平	赞成	这样一来	合得来	不用说	来得快
一分为二		说什么也不……		这样一来				

女性走回厨房：是进步还是倒退？

课文提要

This lesson is an expository essay concerning an issue related to the changing social status of women in China. Chinese women have come a long way in the fight to gain equal rights with men. Before the 20th century, Chinese women had always been at the bottom of society. They were deprived of the right to receive education and were economically dependent. The first glimmer of hope for women to break the bonds of traditional roles cropped up in the Hundred Days Reform movement in 1898, which aimed at making sweeping social and institutional changes. The movement ignited a wave to ban foot binding and establish schools for women. After that came the 1911 revolution, which kindled a feminist movement that focused on equal rights for men and women. Although neither of these two movements was successful in making fundamental changes for Chinese women, they raised women's consciousness for the more serious women's liberation movement in the 1940s and 1950s. In terms of government policies and law, Chinese women now enjoy equal rights with men in politics, education, economic opportunities and social life. Many are as successful as men in their professional positions. However, in recent years some successful professional women have quit their high-paying jobs and returned home to become full-time housewives. This trend makes people wonder if "returning to the kitchen" means progress or regression in women's long struggle for emancipation.

阅读前讨论：

1. 根据课文题目，猜猜这篇课文的内容会是什么。
2. 举例说明什么叫"进步"，什么叫"倒退"。
3. 在你们国家，女性在社会上的地位及作用近 50 年来有什么改变？
4. 你知道哪些跟"女性"和"女性解放"有关的词汇？

自学生词

Match each new word in the left column with its English translation in the right column by guessing the word's meaning from the characters that it is composed of.

	生词	繁体	序号	英文
( )	养家	養	1.	self, oneself, ego
( )	看望		2.	regain, get back
( )	外出		3.	wash clothes, do laundry
( )	自我		4.	young couple
( )	洗衣		5.	housewife
( )	意愿	願	6.	raise a family
( )	小两口	兩	7.	wish, desire
( )	家庭主妇	婦	8.	go out (esp. on business)
( )	找回		9.	call on, pay a visit

生词

简体	繁体	拼音	词性	英文	HSK 等级
1. 倒退		dàotuì	*v.*	go backwards, regress	丁
2. 历来	歷來	lìlái	*adv.*	always, all through the ages	丁
3. 人格		réngé	*n.*	moral integrity, human dignity	丁
4. 全职	職	quánzhí	*n.*	full-time position	丙
5. 出于	於	chūyú	*v.p.*	out of, stem from, be due to	

简体	繁体	拼音	词性	英文	HSK 等级
6. 精力		jīnglì	*n.*	energy, vigor	乙
7. 主		zhǔ	*v.*	lead, manage, take charge of	丁
8. 赚	賺	zhuàn	*v.*	make money, make a profit	丙
9. 解放		jiěfàng	*v.*	liberate	乙
10. 运动	運動	yùndòng	*n.*	movement	甲
11. 享有		xiǎngyǒu	*v.*	enjoy (rights, privileges, etc.)	丁
12. 责任	責	zérèn	*n.*	responsibility	乙
13. 肩头	頭	jiāntóu	*n.*	shoulder	乙
14. 卸		xiè	*v.*	unload, remove	丙
15. 保姆		bǎomǔ	*n.*	nanny, housekeeper	丁
16. 反而		fǎn'ér	*adv.*	on the contrary, instead	丙
17. 压力	壓	yālì	*n.*	pressure; burden	丙
18. 重		chóng	*adv.*	again; once more	乙
19. 人事		rénshì	*n.*	personnel matters	丁
20. 部		bù	*n.*	unit, ministry, department	丙
21. 强	強	qiǎng	*v.*	force, make an effort, strive	丙
22. 晚餐		wǎncān	*n.*	dinner; supper	丁
23. 清理		qīnglǐ	*v.*	clean up, clear up, tidy up	丁
24. 公公		gōnggong	*n.*	husband's father, father-in-law	丁
25. 婆婆		pópo	*n.*	husband's mother, mother-in-law	丁
26. 放松	鬆	fàngsōng	*v.*	relax	丙
27. 繁忙		fánmáng	*adj.*	busy, bustling	丁
28. 挽救		wǎnjiù	*v.*	save, rescue	丙
29. 暂时	暫時	zànshí	*attr.*	temporary	乙
30. 辞职	辭職	cízhí	*v.o.*	resign, quit one's job	丁
31. 休闲	閑	xiūxián	*n.*	leisure	丙
32. 甜蜜		tiánmì	*adj.*	sweet, happy, comfortable	丙
33. 添		tiān	*v.*	add, have a baby	乙

简体	繁体	拼音	词性	英文	HSK 等级
34. 宝宝	寶	bǎobǎo	*n.*	baby, "little treasure"	丙
35. 理由		lǐyóu	*n.*	reason	乙
36. 支出		zhīchū	*n.*	expenses, expenditure	丁
37. 究竟		jiūjìng	*adv.*	actually, exactly, after all	乙
38. 度		dù	*m.*	occasion, time	
39. 返回		fǎnhuí	*v.*	return, come back, go back	丁

成语和惯用语

成语/惯用语	繁体	单字解释	意思
生儿育女 shēng ér yù nǚ	兒	生儿：give birth to a son 育女：give birth to a daughter 生儿育女 = 生养孩子	bear children 例：生儿育女负担太重，所以很多年轻夫妇选择不要孩子。
井井有条 jǐng jǐng yǒu tiáo	條	井：neat, orderly 条：order 有条 = 有条理	be in perfect order 例：自从新的人事部经理来了以后，一切都安排得井井有条。
争执不休 zhēng zhí bù xiū	執	争：argue 执：persist in 休：stop, cease 不休 = 不停	argue opinionatedly and endlessly 例：夫妻之间应该互相谅解，不要为了一点小事就争执不休。

■ 第一读：掌握课文大意

Read the text without stopping and choose from the following options the one that best captures the main idea of the text:

    a. 全职太太现象出现的原因和社会影响。

    b. 全职太太现象是社会进步的表现。

    c. 全职太太现象是社会倒退的表现。

女性走回厨房：是进步还是倒退？

女性从家庭走向社会，历来被看作她们在人格上独立自主、在经济和社会地位上提高的表现。但有意思的是，近年来，不少能干而独立的中国职业女性却又走回家庭，走进厨房，做起"全职太太"来了。这种现象的出现，主要有两个原因：

一是出于时间和精力上的考虑。过去，传统的家庭模式是"男主外，女主内"。男人外出工作，赚钱养家；女人生儿育女，管理家务。可是，在妇女解放运动后走出家庭的妇女们，没多久就发现，如今虽然享有了工作自由，实现了自我价值，但家务的责任并没有从肩头卸下去。这样一来，职业女性一方面要在外工作，另一方面又要照顾全家人的生活，成了"自带工资的保姆"，反而更累了。近年来，职场竞争日益激烈，职业女性的压力也越来越大。于是，有些女性开始考虑重返传统家庭模式。

今年二十七岁的小王，原来是一家公司人事部经理，结婚两年，住在新建的花园公寓，只是离公司太远，每天上下班要花两小时，到家后已经精疲力尽，但仍然要强打着精神准备晚餐。星期六、星期天总算不用上班了，但还得买菜、洗衣、清理公寓，去公公婆婆和自己父母家看望老人。小王一星期七天都让家事排满了，没有一天可以放松。再加上公司人事复杂、业务繁忙，因此精神上压力很大，心情也不好，为了一点小事就和丈夫争执不休。夫妻俩都开始觉得这样的生活没什么意思。为了挽救只有两年的婚姻，小王决定暂时辞职，回家作"全职太太"。现在，小王的生活不像以前那么紧张，精神愉快得多，家里收拾得井井有条，夫妻俩也有时间休息和休闲。钱虽然比以前紧了点，但找回了恋爱时的甜蜜，小两口还打算在不久的将来再添个小宝宝呢。

另一个原因是经济方面的考虑。刚过了三十一岁生日的小刘，自从生了个胖儿子，就不再工作了。她的理由是："现在请个保姆太贵了，又得给她工资，又得给她吃饭，我一个人的工资都不够，而且好保姆也不容易找，不如自己带孩子，对孩子的成长更好。"她打算等孩子上学后，再重返工作。而这段时间里，正好可以学点新知识，为"第二度事业"做些准备。

如今的"全职太太"跟以前的"家庭妇女"有很大的不同。现在的"全职太太"一般都有高等学历，工作能力强，大多在孩子出生后才辞掉工作，她们的丈夫收入较高，能独立负担家庭支出。这种现象究竟是进步，还是倒退呢？有人认为，女性从家庭走进社会是一种进步，而重新回到厨房则是一种倒退。但是也有人认为，应该尊重女性自己的意愿，她们有走出家庭的自由，也有返回厨房的自由，这才是真正的妇女解放。

■ 第二读：细节和理解

1. 按照上面这篇文章的意思，下面的说法对不对？(T/F)

_____ 1. 妇女参加工作，说明她们的社会地位提高了。

_____ 2. 全职太太又要工作又要做家务，觉得很累。

_____ 3. 小王以前在工厂工作的时候特别忙。

_____ 4. 小王觉得自己做全职太太挺不错的。

_____ 5. 现在在中国请一个保姆花的钱可能比一个女工的工资还多。

_____ 6. 小刘觉得自己照顾孩子比请保姆照顾好。

_____ 7. 小刘很喜欢她的胖儿子，打算一辈子在家里做专职家庭妇女。

_____ 8. 现在的全职家庭妇女一般比以前的家庭妇女文化水平高。

_____ 9. 有人觉得妇女应该有选择重新走回厨房的权利。

_____ 10. 真正的妇女解放是让妇女都从家里走出来，走进社会。

2. 根据课文回答下列问题：

1. 妇女从家庭走向社会，意味着什么？

2. 现在妇女又走回家庭，原因是什么？

3. 现在的"全职太太"跟以前的"家庭妇女"有什么不同？

4. 如今妇女又走回厨房，你认为是社会的进步还是倒退？

5. 你觉得这位作者的意见是支持还是反对妇女做全职太太？你从什么地方可以看得出来作者的态度？

■ 阅读技巧：文章结构的分析 • Analyzing How a Text is Organized

The conventional way to read an essay is to start reading from the beginning to the end, sentence by sentence, one sentence after another. However, this is not always an effective way to read because comprehension is not linear but multilayered. A better way is to first find out what the overall idea of the article is. To do so, first, quickly read through the entire article to see how the passage is organized. Is it organized by a deductive or inductive method?[1] When you read through the article, also keep in mind the rhetorical strategies the author uses to arrange the information. Do you see devices such as cause and effect, temporal sequence, contrast and comparison, hypothesis and supporting ideas, etc.? Use your findings to process your reading. They will help you find the major focus of the topic, sort out important messages, and distinguish necessary from unnecessary or redundant information. The following brief outline will help you process your own reading.

1. The basic ideas of an expository essay: Generally speaking, it consists of three parts: a) 论点 lùndiǎn "the central argument or the topic of interest," b) 论据 lùnjù "grounds of the argument," and c) 论证 lùnzhèng "process of developing the argument."

2. The process of reading an expository essay:
   a. 找论点 (zhǎo lùndiǎn): What is the major point or position of the author's argument? The easier way to find it is to read the first and the last paragraph. It can usually be found in either paragraph. Sometimes the title also outlines the argument of the essay.
   b. 理解论据 (lǐjiě lùnjù): On what grounds does the author justify the argument? Generally speaking, the argument can be based on facts or reasoning.

---

[1]See Lesson 10 in Volume 1 for more information.

c. 分析论证 (fēnxì lùnzhèng): How does the author develop his or her argument? Is it based on the deductive method, the inductive method or the contrastive method? What devices does the author use to prove and support his or her argument? Like 找论点，论证 can be found by first skimming the first paragraph, the first sentence of each middle paragraph and the entire last paragraph.

阅读技巧练习

Use the reading instructions explained above to write a simple, brief summary of this lesson's essay in less than ten sentences. Employ these strategies: identify and select main information, get rid of repetitive or trivial information, delete redundant information and examples, and relate important supporting information. Finally, edit the paragraphs you have written.

_____

_____

_____

_____

词汇与句型

1. 主 • lead, manage, be in charge of

1. 传统的家庭模式是"男主外，女主内"。
   In the traditional family model, the man is in charge of external matters while the woman is in charge of domestic matters.

2. 你来主厨，我来给你当二厨。
   You manage the cooking, and I'll be your sous-chef.

3. 谁是这部新电影的主演？
   Who is the leading actress of this new movie?

2. 度 • time, occasion

1. 姐姐打算重返校园，读一个硕士，为她的"第二度事业"充充电。
   My elder sister is coming back to school for a master's program in order to recharge herself for her "second career."

2. 由于金融危机，房价将再度下降。
   Due to the financial crisis, housing prices will go down again.

3. 他下个月将代表我们学校参加本省一年一度的汉语演讲比赛。
   Next month he is going to represent our school in our province's annual Mandarin speech contest.

3. 重…… • re..., again, once more

1. 近年来，职场竞争日益激烈，职业女性的压力也越来越大。于是，有些女性开始考虑重返传统家庭模式。
   In recent years, competition in the job market has become increasingly intense, and career women are under more and more pressures. Therefore, some of them have started to consider returning to the traditional family mode.

2. 工作几年后，小王决定重返校园。
   After several years of work, Xiao Wang decided to return to school.

3. 如果他的回忆录被证明是真的，历史将会重写。
   If his memoir proves to be true, then history will be rewritten.

4. 强 V（强 = 勉强）• force oneself to, make an effort to, strive to

1. 小王到家后已经精疲力尽，但仍然要强打着精神为家人准备晚餐。
   Xiao Wang was exhausted when she got home, but still had to force herself to perk up and make dinner for the family.

2. 我强忍着膝盖的疼痛，最终爬到了山顶。
   Forcing myself to endure the pain in my knees, I eventually made it to the top of the mountain.

3. 她虽然心里紧张得要命，可还是强作镇定，把演讲做完了。
   Though she was extremely nervous inside, she forced herself to appear composed and finished her speech.

5. 出于 • out of, stem from, with the intention of

1. 一是出于时间和精力上的考虑。
   Number one (reason) is our concerns about time and money.

2. 大家都认为，她嫁给那位年老的富商是出于虚荣心。
   People all suspected it was out of vanity that she married that old rich businessman.

3. 虽然他说的话可能有些伤人，但他也是出于好意。
   Though what he said may hurt you, he said it with good intentions.

6. 享有 • enjoy (rights, privileges, etc.)

1. 如今妇女虽然享有了工作自由，实现了自我价值，但家务的责任并没有从肩头卸下去。
   Today, while women enjoy the freedom to work, which realizes their self-worth, the burden of housework has still not been taken off their shoulders.

2. 在这个国家，有钱人享有种种特权，而普通百姓却连基本的生活都没有保障。
   In this country, the rich enjoy various privileges, while the ordinary people can't be assured of having even the basics of life.

3. 所有儿童都应该享有同样的受教育的权利。
   All children should enjoy the same right to education.

7. 究竟 • actually, exactly, on earth;

究竟 is an emphatic adverb usually used in questions, pressing for an exact answer.

1. 越来越多的职业女性又走回家庭，走进厨房，这**究竟**是进步，还是倒退呢？
   More and more career women returned to their home kitchens. Is this actually progress or regression?

2. 你**究竟**跑到哪里去了？我们找你找了一天。
   Where on earth have you been? We have been looking for you the whole day.

3. **究竟**是谁寄给我这张生日卡片，至今我也不知道。
   Who actually sent me the birthday card is still a mystery to me.

究竟 vs. 到底

究竟 and 到底 are similar in their emphatic sense of pressing for exact answers, so sometimes they are interchangeable (as in Examples 1–3 above). The differences between them are:

▶ 究竟 is more formal than 到底。

▶ 究竟 can be used as a noun, indicating an outcome or exactly what happened, but 到底 is not a noun.

   （例：如果你不肯告诉我，我就去他那儿问个**究竟**。
   If you're not willing to tell me, I'll go to him to find out what exactly happened.）

▶ 到底 can be used after a verb, indicating "to the end" (e.g., 坚持到底 persist to the end)，but 究竟 cannot be used in this way.

8. 反而 • on the contrary, instead

反而 is an adverb of transition that connects two clauses. It is used in the second clause to express that in light of the first clause, what happened is contrary to one's expectation or against common sense. The first clause usually includes 不但不/没 or 不仅不/没. This indicates that not only did what was expected not happen, but actually the unexpected opposite happened.

1. 我本来是想帮忙的，结果（不但没帮成）**反而**把事情弄糟了。
   I intended to help, but instead I messed things up.

2. 电脑不仅没有夺去人们的饭碗，**反而**创造了许多就业的机会。
   Instead of displacing people, the computer has created many jobs for them.

3. 已经六月了，天气怎么**反而**冷起来了？
   It is already June, so how come it's getting colder?

9. 不如……

1. (verb) be unequal to; not as good as; inferior to

1. 我的中文不如他的好。
   My Chinese is not as good as his.

2. 他没有自信心，总是觉得自己不如别人。
   He is not confident, always feeling that he is inferior to others.

2. (adv.) it would be better to…; would rather…; had better…

1. 请保姆太贵了，而且好保姆也不容易找，不如自己带孩子，对孩子的成长更好。
   It is too expensive to hire a nanny; plus, it is hard to find a good one. I'd rather raise my child on my own, which is better for the child's development too.

2. 反正你现在也没事，不如来我家喝杯茶。
   You don't have anything to do at the moment anyway. Why don't you come over to my place and have some tea?

3. 这门课很重要，咱们不如提前出发，免得上课迟到。
   This course is very important. We'd better leave early so that we won't be late for class.

10. Adj 的是 • what's adj. is (that)

1. 有意思的是，近年来，不少职业女性又走回家庭，走进厨房，做起 "专职家庭主妇" 来了。
   What's interesting is that in recent years, many career women returned to their home kitchens to be full-time housewives again.

2. 幸运的是，她得到了系里的奖学金，这样她就可以不必为昂贵的学费发愁了。
   What's fortunate is that she was chosen to be the winner of the departmental entrance scholarship. Therefore, she was able to afford the expensive tuition fees.

3. 他失去了工作，更糟的是，因为没工作他女朋友也和他分手了。
   He lost his job, and what's worse is that his girlfriend broke up with him because of it.

11. 一是…… （二是……三是……）● First of all... (second... third...)

This construction is usually used to list evidence, facts or explanations in order to support an argument.

1. 过去，家长为孩子选对象有两个最重要的条件：一是要两家门当户对，二是要对象人品好。

   In the past, parents selected spouses for their children based on two most important conditions: The first is the match in the social and economic status of the two families; the second is the character of the candidate.

2. 老赵一直不敢公开他的 "黄昏恋"，一是怕儿女反对，二是怕邻居笑话。三是担心那位老太太会改变主意。

   Lao Zhao has been keeping a secret of his "twilight romance." First of all, he was concerned about his children's possible objection; second, he didn't want to be ridiculed by his neighbors; and third, he was afraid that the old lady might change her mind.

3. 我问你这个问题，一是出于好奇，二是因为我觉得你可以借这个机会向大家说明一下。

   The reasons why I am asking you this question are: First, I am curious; second, I think you may use this opportunity to clarify in front of everyone.

12. 一方面……，另一方面…… ● on the one hand..., on the other hand

This structure conveys the idea that a person is speaking about two different facts or two opposite ways of thinking about a situation. It may be translated as "on the one hand...but on the other hand..." The predicate following 另一方面 often includes adverbs such as 又, 也, 却 or 还.

1. 他一方面很想帮助那位老人，另一方面又怕因此增添太多负担。

   On the one hand, he wanted to help the old man; on the other hand, he was afraid of taking on too much of a burden.

2. 她一方面想做一个独立的职业妇女，另一方面又渴望有时间多跟孩子在一起。

   On the one hand, she wants to be an independent professional woman; but on the other hand, she longs to spend more time with her children.

3. 对于在公共场合禁烟的问题政府一直没有决策。一方面抽烟者说他们应该享有抽烟的权力，而另一方面不抽烟的人也说他们有权不吸二手烟。

   The government hasn't been able to decide how to handle the non-smoking policy in public areas. On the one hand, smokers claim they should have the right to smoke if they want to; but on the other hand, non-smokers say they should have the right not to breathe second-hand smoke.

13. 而…… • but... (or and...)

As we discussed before, the conjunction 而 can connect two contrasting or two complementing elements (words, phrases or clauses), so it can be interpreted as either "but" or "and." It is often used with the adverbs 则 or 却.

1. 有人认为，女性从家庭走进社会是一种进步，而重新回到厨房则是一种倒退。
   Some people think that women's transition from the home to society is social progress, but the fact that they are returning to the home again is a regression.

2. 接受别人的夸奖在西方文化里是很自然的反应，而在东方文化里则被认为是不虚心的表现。
   It is a natural response to accept others' compliments in Western culture, whereas it is considered to be a reflection of immodesty in Eastern culture.

3. 皮肤是身体的镜子，而身体则是心灵的镜子。
   You skin is the reflection of your body, and your body is the reflection of your heart.

4. 过错是暂时的遗憾，而错过则是永远的遗憾。
   Making a mistake is a regret for the time being; but missing a chance is a regret forever.

语法

1. 中文表被动的方式（一）• Expressing passivity in Chinese (1)

Some people say that Chinese is a language without voice categories such as active voice and passive voice, since a passive sense in Chinese is usually expressed implicitly rather than explicitly. But Chinese does have its own way to indicate that *the subject is the affected entity of the action*.

　　Generally speaking, Chinese passive structure may be roughly classified into two categories: sentences with and sentences without the passive markers (i.e., the "marked" and "unmarked" passives).

The "marked" passives

1. 被

被 is the most common passive marker in Chinese. 被 is used in a rather straightforward construction: **A 被 (B) V + other element**. This describes how a particular object (A) is dealt with or disposed of by the action (V) performed by the agent (B). The following examples illustrate the usage of 被:

A	(adv.)	被	(B)	Verb + other elements
1. 女性从家庭走向社会		被	人们	看作是她们地位提高的表现。
2. 他爸爸	文革中	被		关进了监狱。
3. 这些考生	常常	被		称为"寄托一族"。
4. 我们这些孩子		被	升学率	压得喘不过气来。
5. 我家门前的大树	没	被	风	吹倒。
6. （原来）她	也	被	客户	责备了。
7. 聪聪		被	妈妈	抱在怀里。

Remember:

1. The verbs in 被 sentences, as in 把 sentences, are usually followed by some other elements to indicate the result of the action.

2. The agent (B) can be omitted if it is clear from the context or irrelevant to the meaning of the sentence, as in Examples 2 and 3.

2. 让 and 叫

In spoken Chinese or colloquial writing, 被 is often replaced by 让 and 叫, but *they must take an agent*. In these cases, 给 may also be used before the verb.

A	(adv.)	让/叫	(B)	Verb + Other elements
8. 小王一星期七天	都	让	家事	排满了。
9. 心爱的 iPod 和小说	也	让	妈妈	（给）锁起来了。
10. 我们的秘密		叫	她	说出去了。
11. 这些玩具	都	叫	聪聪	（给）弄坏了。

It is worth noting that the original meaning of 被 is "suffering," so the Chinese passive structures marked by 被 (as well as 让 and 叫) typically express things that are unpleasant or undesirable to the receiver of the action (e.g., 被压得喘不过气来，被责备，让……锁起来了，叫……弄坏了). Although there is a modern tendency towards non-adverse use of these passive sentences, (e.g. "被称为"寄托一族"、"被妈妈抱在怀里"), the fundamental use of this construction is still expressing adversity.

3. 受, 遭, 挨 and 得到

In addition to 被、叫、让 , passives in Chinese can also be marked by the verbs 受 *(receive, suffer)*, 遭 *(zāo, encounter, suffer)*, 挨 *(ái, endure, suffer)*, 得到 *(receive, gain)*, etc. Note that most of these verbs (except 得到) include the meaning of "suffering" as well.

12. 中国教育在文革期间受到很大的损害。

13. 老年人恋爱也会受到子女和周围人的反对。

14. 中国人的恋爱、婚姻在封建社会里一直受到许多限制。

15. 这本小说一出版就受到了年轻人的欢迎。

16. 这男孩不听话挨了爸爸的打。

17. 他的意见刚提出来就遭到了大家的反对。

18. 他的意见刚提出来就得到了大家的支持。

4. 由

The passive structure marked by 由 puts the focus on the agent of the verb, stressing *who* is responsible for (or in charge of) the action. It doesn't have the negative connotation of 被 , it must take an agent, and its verb doesn't need to be followed by other elements.

19. 在公房制度下， 老百姓的住房都由政府兴建。

20. 毕业后的工作也由国家分配。

21. 他们的婚姻要由父母决定。

练习

1. 语音

Write pinyin for the following underlined Chinese characters. Pay special attention to their different pronunciations in different contexts.

倒退 ( )	一天 ( )	不多 ( )	为了 ( )
推倒 ( )	一个 ( )	不累 ( )	认为 ( )
精疲力尽 ( )	重返 ( )	能力强 ( )	能干 ( )
尽管 ( )	尊重 ( )	强迫 ( )	干净 ( )

2. 词汇与句型

2.1. 词语搭配

Match the following words by considering their appropriate collocations.

Group One (Verb + Object)			**Group Two** (Adj. + Noun)		
1. 出于	_____	自我价值	1. 复杂的	_____	业务活动
2. 提高	_____	肩头责任	2. 繁忙的	_____	职场竞争
3. 享有	_____	个人意愿	3. 愉快的	_____	工作安排
4. 实现	_____	社会地位	4. 独立的	_____	人事关系
5. 尊重	_____	经济上的考虑	5. 井井有条的	_____	精神
6. 强打着	_____	特殊权利	6. 日益激烈的	_____	事业
7. 卸下	_____	精神	7. 第二度	_____	人格

2.2. 词汇扩展练习 (Vocabulary expanding exercise)

The following are words and phrases generated from "主","重", and "出于". Choose the most appropriate words to fill in the blanks of the sentences.

主:	主编	主办	主管	主讲	主修	主演	主治

1. 这种中药 ＿＿＿＿＿ 什么病，你知道吗？

2. 听说刘教授在 ＿＿＿＿＿ 一本大字典。

3. 她在公司 ＿＿＿＿＿ 人事部门的工作。

4. 这部电影由著名影星 Jackie Chan ＿＿＿＿＿。

5. 2008 年的世界奥运会由中国 ＿＿＿＿＿。

6. 他上大学时 ＿＿＿＿＿ 的是数学，没想到现在却成了一位有名的电影演员。

7. 下星期的学术报告将由诺贝尔 (Nobel) 奖获得者李教授 ＿＿＿＿＿。

重:	重返	重建	重修	重写

1. 地震发生后，人们纷纷捐 (donate) 款帮助震区人民 ＿＿＿＿＿ 家园。

2. 工作三年之后，他又 ＿＿＿＿＿ 校园读研究生。

3. 两次考试他都没通过，老师说他需要下学期 ＿＿＿＿＿ 这门课。

4. 如果他的回忆录是真实的，那一段历史可能会被 ＿＿＿＿＿。

出于:	出于同情	出于好奇	出于无意	出于礼貌	出于自愿

1. 我们到这儿来帮忙完全是 ＿＿＿＿＿＿，没有谁强迫我们。

2. ＿＿＿＿＿＿，她给了那个可怜的孩子几块钱。

3. 小三是 ＿＿＿＿＿＿ 才犯了错，你们不要骂他，要他下次注意就行了。

4. 他并没有教过我们。我们只是 ＿＿＿＿＿＿ 才称他为老师。

5. 小孩喜欢问问题是 ＿＿＿＿＿＿。我们应该满足他们的求知欲望。

2.3. 选词填空

a. 不如	b. 反而	c. 没多久	d. 出于	e. 历来
f. 第二度	g. 有意思的是	h. 挽救	i. 究竟	j. 休闲
k. 放松	l. 紧	m. 井井有条	n. 强打着精神	

1. 无论把什么工作交给她，她总能安排得 ＿＿＿＿＿＿。

2. 我们公司的工作环境很轻松，上班时甚至也可以穿 ＿＿＿＿＿＿ 服。

3. 我最近手头有点 ＿＿＿＿＿＿，能借我点钱吗？

4. 爷爷是一家之长，咱们家大小决定都听他的，＿＿＿＿＿＿ 如此。

5. 尽管医生尽了最大努力，仍没能 ＿＿＿＿＿＿ 他的生命。

6. 以前，＿＿＿＿＿＿ 对批评的恐惧 (fear)，政府对新闻媒体控制得很 ＿＿＿＿＿＿。
＿＿＿＿＿＿，近几年来，政府 ＿＿＿＿＿＿ 了对媒体的控制，结果对政府的
批评 ＿＿＿＿＿＿ 少多了。

7. 结婚 ＿＿＿＿＿＿，姐姐就成了全职太太。现在，孩子上学了，她打算 ＿＿＿＿＿＿
校园读一个硕士，为她的"＿＿＿＿＿＿ 事业"充电 (recharge)。

8. 小王想买房，可有人说现在房价太贵，买房 ＿＿＿＿＿＿ 租房。他不知道 ＿＿＿＿＿＿
应该怎么办。

2.4. 用指定的词汇或句型完成下列对话：

1. A: 你暑假打算做什么？

B: 还没决定呢! ＿＿＿＿＿＿＿＿＿＿＿＿＿＿＿＿＿＿。（一方面……另一方面……）

2. A: 昨天医生给你开的药吃了吗？

   B: 吃了。可是 _____。（不但没……反而……）

3. A: 她为什么辞职了？

   B: _____。（一是……二是……）

4. A: 你觉得住在城市好还是住在乡村好？

   B: _____。（不如……因为）

5. A: 当职业女性比作全职太太难吗？

   B: 不见得。当职业女性需要有工作能力和社交能力，

   _____。（而……则）

3. 语法练习

3.1. 王丽今天很不走运。请把发生在她身上的这些不幸的事情用<u>被动句</u>表达出来：

1. 一早起来，孩子打破了她最喜欢的花瓶。

   _____

2. 然后她发现丈夫弄坏了她的电脑。

   _____

3. 在公共汽车上，小偷偷走了她的钱包。

   _____

4. 上班时，因为精力不集中，公司老板骂了她一顿。

   _____

5. 回家路上，一个骑自行车的年轻人撞了她。

   _____

6. 一到家她就看到，邻居家的孩子又打破了她家的窗户。

   _____

3.2. 英译汉（不能都用"被字句"）

1. He was praised by his teacher.

2. For a long period to come, most of China's elderly people will continue to be <u>provided for</u>（赡养 shànyǎng）by their families.

3. After the earthquake, the victims were offered a lot of aid by people all over the country.

4. His songs are well received by American young people.

5. Most of the commodities in the US market are manufactured by Chinese factories.

6. Some of the <u>historical relics</u>（文物）were destroyed during the war.

7. Next week's meeting will be led by Mr. Liu.

8. He was scolded by his mother yesterday for playing computer games.

3.3. 上面哪些句子不能用"被"字句翻译？为什么？

4. 综合练习

4.1. 选词填空

a. 职业	b. 出于	c. 精力	d. 赚钱	e. 解放	f. 责任
g. 分别	h. 反而	i. 压力	j. 重返	k. 繁忙	l. 暂时
m. 理由	n. 等于				

您愿意做个全职太太吗？

最近，某市场研究公司就"做全职太太"这一主题开展了一次民意调查，调查对象主要是 18 至 35 岁的年轻女性，参加调查的有 1100 人。调查结果表明，有 82% 的年轻女性表示，在一定条件下会考虑做全职太太。

当问到"您最可能会出于什么原因做全职太太"时，首选 _____ 一是"丈夫事业成功"，二是"更有利于照顾子女"，选择率 _____ 为 45% 和 34%。选择"丈夫提出的要求"的占了 8%，选择"家务太 _____，没有时间和 _____ 工作"的占了 7%，还有 4% 的年轻女性考虑会在"找不到合适的工作"的时候选择做全职太太。调查发现，只有 2% 的女性完全是因为自己喜欢而愿意选择做全职太太的，更多的女性则是 _____ 对婚姻和家庭中某些实际情况的考虑。

在调查中，认为"全职太太也是一份工作，而且需要更大 _____ 心才能做好"的女性占了 68%。可见现代女性已基本从思想上 _____，"全职太太"已不 _____ 传统意义上的"家庭主妇"。调查还发现， 年龄和学历上的差异明显影响着女性对"全职太太"的肯定看法。有意思的是，年纪越轻，学历越高的女性，这种观念 _____ 越强。此外，认为"做全职太太是女性权益提高的表现， 因为她们不必再为养家 _____ 而外出 _____"的女性有 24%，这类女性以 28 岁以上的为主，她们已有自己的家庭，而且经济条件较好。

这个调查也反映出，绝大多数的女性不会把"全职太太"作为自己的长久 _____，而更愿意看作是 _____ 的特殊工作。当问到"如果您是全职太太，最大的担心是什么"时，有 43% 的女性表示是"失去和社会联系，跟不上社会"，32% 女性认为" _____ 职场困难大，不好找工作"，还有 16% 的女性则担心"在家庭中地位下降"，9% 的女性怕"生活太单调没有意思"。

4.2. 按照上面这篇文章的意思，下面的说法对不对？(T/F)

_____ 1. 调查显示，82% 的年轻女性喜欢并且愿意做全职太太。

_____ 2. 许多女性为了方便照顾子女而放弃工作。

_____ 3. 大多数女性并不愿意主动选择成为全职太太。

_____ 4. 学历高的女性认为全职太太等于传统意义上的家庭主妇。

_____ 5. 绝大多数的女性都希望全职太太不是终生的职业。

_____ 6. 将近一半的女性担心做全职太太会令她们在家庭中的地位下降。

_____ 7. 做过全职太太的妇女回到社会找工作会比较困难。

_____ 8. 这篇文章主要是说明为什么女性应该回到家庭做全职太太。

4.3. 英译汉

1. Not only did he not own up to his own mistakes, but he actually blamed other people for things that were his responsibility.

_____

2. At the time of parting, I forced back my tears and said goodbye to father.

_____

3. You are such a competent housewife! You always make your home tidy and clean in perfect order.

_____

4. On the one hand, I'd like more money, but on the other hand, I'm not prepared to work the extra hours in order to get it.

_____

5. What's worrisome is that many teachers had to change professions due to poor salary and low social status, which resulted in the even more serious teacher shortage in elementary and middle schools. (令人……的是)

_____

6. To solve housing and employment problems for the people has always been a focus for the government. Although the government has changed their housing policies while developing a number of affordable residence buildings in recent years, the increasing housing needs of the people still have not been met. (历来，但……并没有……)

_____

_____

_____

5. 阅读练习

阅读短文（一）妻子下岗又上岗[2]

妻子的工厂关门了。妻子和她的同事们，离开工作了 20 年的工厂，成了下岗女工。妻子刚下岗，我还真舒服了一阵，下班回家，热腾腾的饭菜就已经摆在桌子上了。可是没过几天，我发现妻子总是不开心，不管我说多少好话，她总是说："我可不能整天在家呆着，女人 40 岁，孩子大了，正是工作的好时候，不管什么单位，只要要我，哪怕工作累点我都愿意。"于是她东奔西跑，终于找到了一个小工厂，又上岗了。

妻子重新上岗后，第一天就上夜班。虽然她为我和女儿准备好了晚饭才走，可是一到家，我还是觉得好像家里少了点什么。女儿也总是问："爸爸，妈妈不上夜班行吗？如果你不在，妈妈又上夜班，我怎么办？"

妻子重新就业，给我们这个小家庭带来了新的挑战。以前，家里早餐吃什么，我从来不用管，每天早上我到公园去跑步，回来吃完早饭就上班。现在不行了，得早早起床，为自己和女儿做早饭，忙得团团转。以前，下班后，我可以在办公室和同事们聊聊天，不用考虑什么时候回家。现在不行了，想到妻子要上夜班，哪怕同事们说我"怕老婆"，也得抓紧时间往家里跑，不放心女儿一个人在家。以前，妻子工厂里的工作很轻松，回到家还能把家务全做了。现在，妻子下班一到家，就倒在沙发上睡着了。看她累成那个样子，我也很心痛，就主动多干家务，不但做饭、洗碗、收拾房间，连衣服我也全洗了。我好几次跟她说："别干了，再找个好点儿的单位吧！"她却说："那怎么行？"

一个月过去了，妻子拿着刚发的工资回到家，高兴地说："怎么样，老公 (hubby)，比以前多一倍呢！"妻子下岗又上岗，重新找回了自己，我这个当丈夫的也得到不少意想不到的锻炼。

---

[2]下岗 (xiàgǎng): being laid off, a euphemism for "unemployed"

5.1. 根据短文内容，选择最佳答案回答问题：

1. 妻子下岗以后，
    a. 感觉很轻松 (*relaxed*)。
    b. 感觉很不高兴。
    c. 舒服了一阵子。
    d. 忙得团团转。

2. 妻子为什么要重新上岗？
    a. 因为女儿上大学需要很多钱。
    b. 因为她以前的工厂重新开门了。
    c. 因为另一家工厂的工资很高。
    d. 因为她不愿意在家里呆着。

3. 妻子重新上岗后，为家人带来什么挑战？
    a. 我早上要照顾女儿吃早餐，不能去公园跑步了。
    b. 我下班后要赶快回家，不能在办公室聊天了。
    c. 因为妻子太累，我要帮忙做家务。
    d. 以上都是。

4. 作者对妻子重新上岗的态度？
    a. 很生气，因为觉得家里少了点什么。
    b. 很高兴，因为妻子的工资比以前多了一倍。
    c. 很心痛，因为妻子工作得太累了。
    d. 很不满 (*unsatisfied*)，因为要多做很多家务。

5. 妻子对重新上岗的态度？
    a. 很高兴，因为重新找回了自己。
    b. 很难过，因为不能照顾女儿。
    c. 很生气，因为同事们说我"怕老婆"。
    d. 很不满，因为工作太累，工资又少。

6. 以下哪项最好地说明了这篇短文的主题？
    a. 我和女儿都不希望妻子上夜班。
    b. 下岗女工往往感到自己没价值。
    c. 经过锻炼，我做家务的能力提高了。
    d. 下岗和重新上岗为家庭结构带来挑战。

5.2. 根据短文内容回答下列问题：

1. 妻子为什么会下岗？

2. 妻子下岗对家庭带来了什么？

3. 丈夫对妻子下岗的态度怎么样？

4. 妻子的态度呢？为什么她那么想？

5. 妻子重新上岗又给家庭带来了什么呢？

6. 丈夫支持不支持妻子的事业？怎么看得出来？

7. 为什么妻子一定要工作？

8. 你觉得这个家庭夫妻关系怎么样？跟传统的家庭关系有什么不同吗？

阅读短文（二）：女人为什么要工作？

大谈男女平等的社会，就说明男女平等还只是希望和愿望。什么时候，我们不必过"三八妇女节 (*Women's Day*)"了，从社会进步的观点看，就真的男女平等了。

不论是西方的女权运动 (*feminist movement*)，还是中国的妇女解放，关键问题是男女平等。平等应该建立在女人的独立之上，这独立包含着女人经济上的独立、精神上的独立、人格上的独立、感情上的独立。经济上的独立是其它一切"独立"的前提 (*premise*)，这一点女人们早已认识到了。

女人经济上的独立靠的是什么？那就是工作，就是赚钱。旧社会的女人很少是职业女性，她们的任务就是"生养持家"。如果说到那时"女人的职业"的话，那就是她的丈夫，失去了丈夫也就等于失了业。没有男人就没有了社会，没有女人就没有了家庭。这是"男主外、女主内"的几千年传统社会现象。好不容易，新时代的女人出来工作了，但随之而产生的问题也不少。从某种程度上说，女人"主内"的任务没有减掉多少，而又增加了半个"主外"的重担，女人的负担不但没轻，反而更重了。

但女人还是要工作的，因为她们要独立。现在社会上虽然有全职太太，但那是富人的权力，一般的家庭做不到。即使能够做到，女人也往往不敢。经济上有依靠，这一点一般的女人都乐于接受，但由此而来的风险女人却接受不了。全职太太一旦成为全职保姆，还谈什么精神独立？全职太太未必有全职爱情，全职太太做不好，就会有"兼职太太"出现，哪来的感情独立？全职太太与社会隔绝，被朋友忘记，被丈夫漠视，怎能说人格独立？所以女人宁可家庭工作两头忙，也不敢冒做"全职太太"的险。

工作着的女人，自立自强自信的女人才是美丽的女人。

5.3. 根据短文内容，回答下列问题：

1. 为什么说"大谈男女平等的社会，就足以说明男女平等还只是希望和愿望"？

2. 妇女解放的核心是什么？

3. 作者认为女人的独立包括哪些方面？

4. "男主外、女主内"是什么意思？

5. 新时代的女人出来工作之后出现了什么问题？

6. 作者认为做全职太太有什么风险？

7. 什么情况下"全职太太"会成为"全职保姆"？

8. "兼职太太"是什么人？

9. 作者的主张是什么？

6. 口语练习

6.1. 讨论题

1. 女性应该工作还是应该回到厨房？

2. 经济基础或者经济能力是否会决定一个人在家庭中的地位？

3. 女性应不应该做专职的家庭妇女？为什么？

4. 妇女的位置应该在哪儿？

5. 如果妻子的工资比丈夫的高，是不是应该由丈夫留在家做"全职家庭主男"？

6. 妇女解放意味着什么？

7. 什么是真正的妇女解放？

8. 在你的国家，妇女解放了吗？请举例说明。

6.2. 辩论题：妇女做全职太太是社会的进步还是倒退？

With a group of classmates, organize a debate about the topic. Each debate team should prepare their arguments ahead of time. Try to guess what the other side's arguments will be. Fill out this table to help you organize:

妇女做全职太太是社会的进步	妇女做全职太太是社会的倒退

You can use this outline to organize the debate:

甲方 (Side 1): Opening statement, 2 minutes

乙方 (Side 2): Opening statement, 2 minutes

甲方 : Main argument, 3 minutes

乙方 : Main argument, 3 minutes

甲方 : Counterargument of 乙方's arguments, 3 minutes

乙方 : Counterargument of 甲方's arguments, 3 minutes

甲方 : Closing statement, 2 minutes

乙方 : Closing statement, 2 minutes

At the end of the debate, everyone in the class should vote on which side won the debate.

7. 写作练习 • 阿兰的故事 (A double-ending story)

7.1. Read the beginning and the two possible endings of this story:

Beginning
阿兰是我大学同学中最漂亮的女生，她不但学习好，性情也不错，是很多男生的梦中情人。大学毕业后，她在一家报社当记者，不久就跟一位年轻有为的进出口公司老板结婚了。结婚后，她辞职回家当了全职太太。

Ending 1	Ending 2
十年后的同学聚会上，阿兰又成了所有女同学羡慕的对象。她仍然是那么漂亮，自信。但又增添了一种持与优雅 (yōuyǎ, elegance)。跟她一起来的儿子就像一个可爱的小王子。听说他刚 7 岁就已经是有名的小钢琴家了。	十年后的同学聚会上，大家几乎认不出这个面容憔悴 (qiáocuì, weary-looking) 的女人了！阿兰说她已经离婚了，儿子也归了他爸爸。现在她还没找到工作。她请同学们帮帮她，随便什么工作都行。因为她实在不想再到职场上去碰壁了。

7.2. Complete the story

Choose one of the endings. What do you think happened during the middle part of the story? Write down an outline and then tell your story to your partner. Answer any follow-up questions your partner may have.

7.3. Writing：阿兰的故事（550-650 字）

Write a composition based on your completion of the middle part of the story. You can also extend the beginning and the ending if needed.

贝贝进行曲

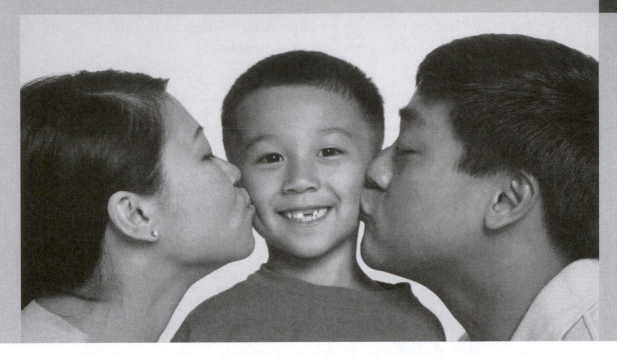

课文提要

The story in this lesson is about a social issue: how to raise an only child in China nowadays. Through the story you will see how Beibei, the only male child in the family, grows into a selfish and self-centered child in the course of five years owing to his indulgent parents. Along the way, you will also read about the parents' attitude towards bringing up their child. Sacrificing their own personal interests, they try very hard to provide the child with material benefits that they never had when they grew up. They also make great investments in the child's intellectual development, hoping the child will grow up to be healthy and intelligent. But the result of their efforts is very disheartening…

阅读前讨论：

1. 看了课文题目和上面的图片，你能不能猜出来这篇课文说的是什么？
2. "贝贝"是什么意思？图片上的孩子看起来怎么样？他的父母呢？
3. "进行曲"是什么音乐？为什么课文用"进行曲"来做标题？
4. 你知道哪些跟儿童教育有关的词语？

自学生词

Match each new word in the left column with its English translation in the right column by guessing the word's meaning from the characters that it is composed of.

	生词	繁体	序号	英文
( )	这会儿	這會兒	1.	sweater
( )	玩具		2.	turn one's head
( )	购物中心		3.	toy
( )	动物园	動園	4.	large scale, big size
( )	毛衣		5.	follow up, catch up
( )	跟上		6.	take a fancy to, take a liking to
( )	转头	轉頭	7.	zoo
( )	看上		8.	shopping center, mall
( )	大型		9.	shop assistant
( )	售货员	貨員	10.	now, at the moment

生词

	简体	繁体	拼音	词性	英文	HSK 等级
1.	进行曲	進	jìnxíngqǔ	*n.*	march (music)	
2.	领	領	lǐng	*v.*	receive	乙
3.	亲	親	qīn	*v.*	kiss	丙
4.	喘气	氣	chuǎnqì	*v.o.*	breathe deeply, pant	丙
5.	掏		tāo	*v.*	dig, scoop out	乙
6.	收获	穫	shōuhuò	*n.*	results, gains; harvest	乙
7.	皱	皺	zhòu	*v.*	wrinkle, furrow (one's brow)	丙
8.	眉头	頭	méitóu	*n.*	eyebrow	丙
9.	舍得	捨	shěde	*v.*	be willing to part with, not begrudge	丙

简体	繁体	拼音	词性	英文	HSK 等级
10. 逗		dòu	*v.*	tease, play with, tantalize	乙
11. 抓		zhuā	*v.*	grab, seize	乙
12. 咸菜		xiáncài	*n.*	salted vegetables, pickles	
13. 吃苦		chīkǔ	*v.o.*	bear hardships, suffer	丙
14. 关键	關鍵	guānjiàn	*n.*	key, the most crucial thing	乙
15. 壮	壯	zhuàng	*adj.*	strong, robust	丙
16. 一辈子	輩	yíbèizi	*n.*	all one's life, lifetime	丙
17. 反正		fǎnzhèng	*adv.*	anyway, anyhow, in any case	乙
18. 赞同	贊	zàntóng	*v.*	approve of, agree with	丁
19. 干脆	乾	gāncuì	*adj.*	clear-cut, straightforward	乙
20. 摸		mō	*v.*	touch, feel	乙
21. 软和	軟	ruǎnhuo	*adj.*	soft and warm	乙
22. 大方		dàfang	*adj.*	generous	丙
23. 看上		kànshang	*v. c.*	take a fancy to, take a liking to	
24. 价钱	價錢	jiàqian	*n.*	price	丙
25. 超支		chāozhī	*v.o.*	exceed one's budget	
26. 咧		liě	*v.*	open one's mouth	
27. 咬牙		yǎoyá	*v.o.*	clench one's teeth	乙
28. 智力		zhìlì	*n.*	intelligence	丁
29. 不停		bùtíng	*adv.*	incessantly	丙
30. 轮	輪	lún	*v.*	take turns	乙
31. 鸽	鴿	gē	*n.*	dove, pigeon	丙
32. 棒		bàng	*adj.*	good, excellent	丙
33. 出息		chūxi	*n.*	prospects, promise, future	丙
34. 奖品	獎	jiǎngpǐn	*n.*	prize, award, trophy	丁
35. 得意		déyì	*adj.*	be pleased with oneself	丙

简体		繁体	拼音	词性	英文	HSK 等级
36.	一旁		yīpáng	*n.*	one side, a side	丙
37.	微笑		wēixiào	*v.*	smile	乙
38.	付出		fùchū	*v.*	pay, expend	丁
39.	心血		xīnxuè	*n.*	painstaking care or effort	丁

成语和惯用语

成语/惯用语	繁体	单字解释	意思
无可奈何 wú kě nài hé	無	无 : no, none 可 : can 奈何 : deal with	be helpless, have no way/choice 例：他们一定要去，我也无可奈何。
理直气壮 lǐ zhí qì zhuàng	氣壯	理 : reason, justice 直 : fair, upright 气 : breath, air, morale 壮 : strong, bold	speaking boldly or confidently, feel confident with justice on one's side 例：别那么理直气壮，你们也有不对的地方。

专有名词 (Proper Nouns)

专有名词	繁体	词性	英文
变形金刚 biàn xíng jīn gāng	變剛	*n.*	transformers (toy, King Kong action figure)

■ 第一读：掌握课文大意

快速阅读课文，看下面三个选择中哪一个最能说明本课主要意思：

1. 贝贝的自私行为
2. 独生孩子的教育问题
3. 父母对孩子的疼爱是无私的

贝贝进行曲

贝贝一岁。

那天，小俩口都领了工资。年轻的妈妈下班回来得特别晚，一到家，立刻把宝贝儿子抱起来，亲了又亲，然后精疲力尽地坐在沙发上。为了给儿子买东西，她跑遍了大半个城市。

这会儿，她一边喘气一边从大包小包里掏出今天的收获来，吃的、穿的、玩的、用的…… 摆满了半张床。年轻的爸爸看了看，皱皱眉头："哇！真舍得买，又花了多少钱？"

"工资去了一半！"她头也没抬，逗着贝贝满床抓玩具。

"哼！到时候没钱买午餐，又得每天带饭吃咸菜。"

"哎呀，咱们吃点苦算什么啊？关键是孩子的营养得跟上。只要我儿子长得壮壮的，玩得开开心心的！"她说，"咱们这辈子反正不行了。"

"这倒也是，"年轻的爸爸赞同道，"咱们这辈子不行了，就看他了，就都投资在儿子身上了！"

贝贝三岁。

在购物中心里。

"请问这件毛衣多少钱？"年轻的妈妈问。

"一百五十元。"售货员回答。

"咱们贝贝穿着一定很好看！"她问儿子，"嘿，贝贝，喜欢不喜欢？"

"喜欢！"儿子回答得很干脆。

"买吧？"她摸摸软和的毛衣，转头问丈夫。

"买吧！"他也很大方。

　　毛衣买好了，他们又来到玩具部。贝贝一眼看上了那个大型的"变形金刚"，一问价钱，三百二。

　　"哇！太贵了，不能买，今天已经超支了。"爸爸说。

　　可是贝贝立刻咧开嘴大哭起来："我要，我要买嘛！"

　　妈妈咬了咬牙，对爸爸说："咳，就算智力投资，给他买吧，我的大衣不买了。"

　　"可是，天冷了，你……"爸爸看着妈妈，无可奈何地说，"哎！那好吧，就给他买吧。我们这辈子不行了，就看他了。"

　　贝贝五岁。

　　在动物园里，贝贝玩得可高兴了。他跑来跑去，小嘴说个不停，好奇地问爸爸妈妈，这种动物叫什么，那种动物叫什么？

　　"贝贝，你知道那是什么吗？"轮到妈妈问他了。

　　"小白鸽。"孩子迅速地回答。

　　"爸爸来考考你，树上有五只白鸽，打死了一只，还剩几只？"

　　"嗯……，一只也没有了，全飞了。"

　　"哟！咱们贝贝真棒！真聪明，长大一定有出息！"爸爸满意地说，"来，给你块巧克力，这是奖品。"贝贝得意地接过巧克力。妈妈在一旁看着聪明的儿子，也不由得微笑起来。

　　"给妈妈一小块吧，贝贝，妈妈也有点饿了。"妈妈说。

　　"不，不给，这是我的，你们不能吃！"

　　"为什么不给？这可是我们买的。"爸爸说。

　　"爸爸妈妈说过，你们吃什么、穿什么都没关系，反正你们这辈子不行了，关键是要让我开开心心的！"贝贝理直气壮地回答。

　　"唉！"妈妈转过脸去，深深地叹了一口气，"没想到，为儿子付出那么多心血，如今，连一小块巧克力都尝不到。"

■ 第二读：细节和理解

1. 领工资那天，年轻的妈妈为什么回来得那么晚？

2. 看到妈妈买的东西，爸爸为什么"皱眉头"？

3. 妈妈说"工资去了一半"时，为什么"头也没抬"？

4. 年轻的爸爸妈妈经济状况好不好？你从什么地方可以看得出来？

5. 为什么年轻的爸爸妈妈总是说"咱们这辈子反正不行了"？

6. 给贝贝买"变形金刚"时，妈妈"咬了咬牙"才决定，这说明了什么？

7. 为什么小贝贝说话总是很"干脆、迅速"？

8. 最后妈妈为什么要"转过身去，深深地叹了一口气"？

9. 你从贝贝"一岁、三岁、五岁"的三个故事里看到了什么？

■ 阅读技巧：理解和运用感叹词

Understanding the Pragmatic Function of Interjections

An interjection is a word used at the beginning of a sentence (usually an exclamation) to express strong, sudden feelings such as fear, surprise, anger, love, or joy. Like the "sentence final particles" discussed in Chapter 11, interjections are frequently used (especially in oral communication) to indicate the emotion or attitude of the speaker/writer towards the situation expressed in the speech, foreshadowing or projecting what will come next in the unfolding discourse. Tones are important for interjections in Chinese: the same interjection with different tones can convey different feelings. Interestingly, the same interjection may also convey different meanings in different contexts with no change of tone. This table lists several commonly used interjections:

常用汉语感叹词

叹词	发音	英文对应词	功能	例句
啊	ā	ah, oh	pleasant surprise, praise	啊！太阳出来了！
	á	huh	pressing a point	啊！你到底去不去？
	ǎ	what	doubt or suspicion	啊！这是怎么回事啊？
	à	oh	sudden enlightenment	啊！我明白了！
哎/唉	ài	oh dear	regret, remorse	哎，又弄错了！
哎呀	āiyā	geez	complaint, impatience, surprise	哎呀，你怎么又来了！ 哎呀！聪聪长这么高了！
哎哟	āiyō	ouch	surprise, agony	哎哟！疼死我了！
哈（哈）	hā	ha	triumph, satisfaction	哈哈！还是我说对了吧？
咳	hài	sigh	sadness, regret, surprise	咳！这件事就别提了。
嘿/嗨	hēi	hey	surprise, drawing attention, showing pride	嘿！你们怎么也来了？ 嘿！你看这孩子多有出息！
嗬	hè	ah	surprise	嗬！这么大的鱼！
哼	hng	humph	dissatisfaction, disbelief	哼！我才不信呢！
嗯	n	um	hesitation	嗯…我能不去吗？
	ń	eh	query, expectation	嗯！你怎么还没去？
	n	okay	answer, response	嗯，我知道了。
哦	ó	really	disbelief	哦，是真的吗？
	ǒ	oh	realization	哦，我想起来了！
哇	wā	wow	surprise	哇！好大的雪啊！
喂	wéi	hello	greeting (on telephone)	喂，请问小王在吗？
哟	yō	oh	slight surprise	哟，是你啊！

Notes:
1. The tones and functions can be very varied according to the discourse context.
2. The English counterparts are given only for reference and analogy. There are no one-to-one equivalencies.

Reading Skill Practice:

1. Like in Chapter 11, the writer of this narrative uses many dialogues to depict the personalities and attitudes of the characters in the story (the father, the mother and their child Beibei). Read the following sentences (with interjections) in the voices of the different characters from this text, and decide from the context which emotion or attitude they express.

爸爸

1. 哇! 真舍得买，又花了多少钱?
   a. surprise
   b. pleasant surprise
   c. doubt or suspicion
   d. complaint

2. 哼! 到时候没钱买午餐，又得每天带饭吃咸菜。
   a. surprise
   b. dissatisfaction
   c. query
   d. disbelief

3. 哇! 太贵了，不能买，今天已经超支了。
   a. surprise
   b. dissatisfaction
   c. query
   d. disbelief

4. 哎! 那好吧，就给他买吧。我们这辈子不行了，就看他了。
   a. sadness
   b. pressing a point
   c. doubt or suspicion
   d. sudden enlightenment

妈妈

5. 哎呀，咱们吃点苦算什么啊? 关键是孩子的营养得跟上。
   a. sudden enlightenment
   b. regret, remorse
   c. complaint, impatience
   d. surprise

6. 嘿，贝贝，喜欢不喜欢?

   a. sadness

   b. drawing attention

   c. surprise

   d. dissatisfaction

7. 咳，就算智力投资，给他买吧，我的大衣不买了。

   a. triumph

   b. sadness

   c. drawing attention

   d. dissatisfaction

8. 哟！咱们贝贝真棒！真聪明，长大一定有出息！

   a. disbelief

   b. realization

   c. slight surprise

   d. sadness

9. 唉！没想到，为儿子付出那么多心血，如今，连一小块巧克力都尝不到。

   a. triumph

   b. sadness

   c. drawing attention

   d. disbelief

贝贝

10. 嗯……，一只也没有了，全飞了。

   a. hesitation

   b. query

   c. triumph

   d. surprise

词汇与句型

1. 舍得/舍不得 • be willing/unwilling to spend (money, time, etc.)
be willing/unwilling to part with (something or somebody)

1. 他们舍不得给自己买衣服，却给孩子买了很多玩具。
   They didn't want to spend any money on their own clothing, but bought a lot of toys for their kid.

2. 他是一位好父亲，无论多忙，都舍得花时间跟孩子们交流。
   He is a good father. He is always willing to spend time communicating with his children no matter how busy he is.

3. 我下个月就要去北京工作了，可是很舍不得在纽约的朋友们。
   I'm going to work in Beijing next month, but I'm not willing to part with my friends in New York.

2. N 也没 V • without even doing...

This phrase is a shortened form of（连）N 也没 V as an emphatic expression, meaning "without even doing …(the least)."

1. "工资去了一半！"她头也没抬，逗着贝贝满床抓玩具。
   "The salary is half gone!" Without even lifting her head, she was playing with Beibei, who was grabbing toys all over the bed.

2. 我昨晚回来筋疲力尽，（连）牙也没刷就睡觉了。
   I came back exhausted last night and went to bed without even brushing my teeth.

3. 他今天早上起床太晚了，（连）脸也没洗就上学去了。
   He got up late this morning and went to school without even washing his face.

3. 反正 • in any case, at any rate, anyway, either way

反 means "the opposite (side)", and 正 means "the right (side)." Their combined meaning is "(no matter whether it's) this way or that way - i.e., either way." A clause with 反正 indicates a presumed situation or fact, and the accompanying clause suggests a result regardless of the positive or negative presumed situation. Either clause may come first. 反正 can be placed before or after the subject of the clause.

1. 我们这辈子反正不行了，就看咱们的儿子的了。
   It's all up with our generation in any case; it will have to depend on our son.

2. 不管你怎么说，反正我不去。
   No matter what you say, I am not going anyway.

3. 我也不知道他究竟多大，反正不到三十岁。
   I don't know how old he is exactly, but at any rate he can't be more than thirty.

4. 这倒是/倒也是/这倒也是 • right; this is actually the case

1. 这倒是个好主意。
   This is actually a brilliant idea.

2. A: 除了智力投资以外，我们也要教育孩子怎样做人。
   B: 这倒也是。
   A: Besides investing in their intellectual development, we also need to educate our kids to grow up decently.
   B: This is certainly true.

3. 你说的倒也是实话。
   What you said is actually the truth.

5. 看 • depend, hinge on

1. 我们都没有办法，这件事就全看你了。
   None of us can do it. Now it all depends on you.

2. 我已经邀请他晚上过来吃饭，就看他有没有时间了。
   I've already invited him to come for dinner tonight. It depends on whether he has time.

3. A: 这件毛衣很漂亮，也不贵。你说要不要买?
   B: 看你了。
   A: This sweater is beautiful and not expensive. Do you think I should buy it?
   B: It's up to you.

6. 看上了 • like, take a fancy to, settle on

1. 我昨天逛街的时候看上一条裙子，可是太贵了。
   When I was shopping yesterday a dress caught my eye, but it was too expensive.

2. 我一眼就看上了那双蓝色的鞋。
   I took a fancy to the pair of blue shoes as soon as I saw them.

3. 说实话，你是不是看上那个女孩了？

Tell me the truth. Do you like that girl?

7. 咬牙 • grit one's teeth; endure with dogged will, bite the bullet

咬牙 is usually used metaphorically as an action of facing a hard or painful situation bravely and stoically, or making a very hard decision. Some similar expressions in English are: steel oneself, brace oneself, pluck up one's courage, etc.

1. 妈妈咬了咬牙说："咳，就算智力投资，给他买吧，我的大衣不买了。"

The mother braced herself and said to the father: "Okay. Let's buy it for him, just as an educational investment. I don't need to buy a coat."

2. 高中最后一年了，我希望孩子们能咬咬牙，挺过去。

This is the last year of their junior high school. I hope the kids can pluck up their courage and survive.

3. 他在长跑比赛中受伤了，但他咬牙跑完了全程。

He got injured in the long-distance race, but he steeled himself and finished the entire race.

8. 吃苦 • stand/bear/suffer hardship

1. 咱们吃点苦算什么啊？关键是孩子的营养得跟上。

What does it matter if we have to suffer a little? The kid's nutrition is the most important.

2. 独生子女一般都不能吃苦。

Only children usually can't stand hardship.

3. 老王过去吃过很多苦。他说人生吃点儿苦也有好处。

Lao Wang has experienced a lot of hardship in the past. He said this experience could actually be beneficial for one's life.

Note: The verb 吃 here means "to receive, stand, bear, endure or suffer." Below are some similar expressions:

吃惊 : to receive shock, to be surprised or shocked

吃亏 : to suffer losses, to be at a disadvantage

吃罚单 : to receive a ticket (fine)

吃红牌 : to get a red card (in sports)

吃黄牌 : to get a yellow card (in sports)

9. 无可奈何 • have no way out; helpless; helplessly

1. 爸爸看着妈妈，无可奈何地说，"哎！那好吧，就给他买吧。"
   The father looked at the mother and said helplessly, "Okay, fine. Let's buy it for him."

2. 他坚持要回上海，我无可奈何地看着他收拾行李。
   He insisted on going back to Shanghai. I had no choice but watch him pack his luggage.

3. 我们无可奈何，只好接受这个事实。
   We have no way out but to accept this fact.

10. V 个…

个 can be used between a verb and its complement to indicate emphasis.

1. 这一对好朋友已经三年没见了，今天一见面就说个不停。
   These two good friends haven't seen each other for three whole years. Today they talked nonstop once they saw each other.

2. 这些菜都是我在院子里种的，今天让你们吃个新鲜。
   All these vegetables are ones that I grew in the yard. Today I'll let you eat them fresh.

3. 我真想期末考试以后能玩个痛快！
   I really hope to enjoy a wonderful time after the final exams!

11. 轮到 • be one's turn

1. 今天轮到我洗碗了。
   It's my turn to wash dishes today.

2. 排队的人那么多，什么时候才能轮到我们?
   There are so many people in line. When will it be our turn?

3. 轮到你了，快去吧!
   It's your turn now. Hurry up!

12. 关键是…… • what really matters is…, the most crucial thing is…

1. 一个人要有所成就，聪明不聪明没关系，关键是得坚持努力。
   A person doesn't have to be smart to succeed. The key is to try persistently.

2. 要教育好独生子女，关键是他们的父母得懂教育。
   The key to appropriately educating the only children is that their parents need to know about education.

3. 要学好中文，关键是什么?
   What is the most important thing in learning Chinese well?

13. 到时候 • when the time comes, then

1. 到时候没钱买午餐，又得每天带饭吃咸菜。
   Then you will have to bring your rice with pickles again, because you won't have any money to buy lunch.

2. 我们问老师考试难不难，她说，"到时候你们就知道了。"
   We asked the teacher whether the exam would be hard or not, and she said, "You will know when the time comes."

3. 你得趁早买飞机票，别到时候买不着了。
   You should buy the plane ticket soon, in case they are sold out when you need it.

14. 理直气壮 • feeling confident with justice on one's side, being bold and assured

1. 他理直气壮地说："我没做错什么！"
   He said confidently, "I didn't do anything wrong!"

2. 得到老板的支持后，他变得更加理直气壮。
   After gaining his boss's support, he became even more confident that he was right.

3. 他不承认自己的错误，反而理直气壮地为自己辩护。
   He refused to admit his mistakes but rather audaciously claimed in his defense that he was right.

语法

■ 中文表被动的方式 ・ Expressing Passivity in Chinese (B)

1. Unmarked Passives

Owing to its unpleasant connotation, the marked passive structure is *much more restricted and less common in Chinese* than in English. The Chinese passive sense is usually implied by the "unmarked passive structures" as long as it is possible to do so without causing confusion.

1.1. Topic-Comment Sentences

The topic-comment sentence is the most commonly used structure for passives in Chinese. In these sentences, the topic is often inanimate (or non-human), and therefore no ambiguity arises as to the relationship between the topic and the verb. For example, in the first sentence below, *the sweater* could not possibly have initiated the action of *buying* itself. All these examples are taken from this lesson:

1. 毛衣买好了。
   The sweater was bought.

2. 吃的、穿的、玩的、用的…… 摆满了半张床。
   Food, clothes, toys and other goods were spread all over half the bed.

3. 工资去了一半！
   The salary is half gone!

4. 这种动物叫什么？
   What was this animal called?

5. 五只白鸽，打死了一只，还剩几只？
   There were five pigeons. One was killed; how many were left?

1.2. "是……的" Structure

The 是…的 construction can also be used as a passive structure to clarify who did something or gave rise to an event, when, where or how, especially when no "adversity" is involved. Verbs that indicate a process of "creating or making" (e.g., 写，画，做，制造，发明 etc.) usually take the 是…的 construction for passives, while verbs indicating a process of destroying (e.g., 打破，烧掉，弄坏，撕碎) are used in the 被 construction.

1. 指南针是中国人 4000 年前发明的。
   The compass was invented by the Chinese 4000 years ago.

2. 今天的晚饭不是保姆做的吧？
   Wasn't today's dinner cooked by the nanny?

3. 这些电视机都是中国制造的。
   These TV sets are all made in China.

4. 这幅画是我中学老师画的。
   This painting was painted by my high school teacher.

5. 这种书是专门为儿童写的。
   This kind of book is written especially for children.

6. 这首诗是一个十岁的小女孩写的。
   This poem was written by a ten-year-old girl.

2. **Discourse Function of the Passive in Chinese**

Chinese does not use passive sentences as often as English, but it has more options for expressing passivity when needed. One of the main pragmatic functions of the passive in Chinese is to emphasize the affected noun (the receiver of the action) by placing it at the beginning of the sentence for discourse coherence (e.g., creating or continuing a topic in discourse). For example:

1. 妈妈：我们刚给你买的变形金刚呢？

   贝贝：变形金刚叫幼儿园的小朋友弄坏了。

   （比较：幼儿园的小朋友弄坏了我的变形金刚。）

2. 老王：你墙上这幅国画很不错啊。

   老李：那当然了。这是齐白石 (*a famous artist*) 画的嘛。

   （比较：齐白石画了这幅画。）

练习

1. 语音

Write pinyin for the following underlined Chinese characters. Pay special attention to their different pronunciations in different contexts.

<u>得</u>意 (　　)　　<u>舍</u>得 (　　)　　<u>干</u>脆 (　　)　　软<u>和</u> (　　)

<u>舍</u>得 (　　)　　宿<u>舍</u> (　　)　　能<u>干</u> (　　)　　<u>和</u>平 (　　)

<u>得</u>跟上 (　　)

2. 词汇句型

2.1. Match the following words by considering their appropriate collocations.

Group One (Verb + Object)			**Group Two** (Adj. + Noun)		
1. 逗	_____	眉头	1. 营养	_____	信息
2. 领	_____	牙	2. 特殊	_____	答复
3. 皱	_____	气	3. 优惠	_____	快餐
4. 喘	_____	孩子	4. 肯定	_____	客户
5. 咬	_____	苦	5. 老	_____	风味
6. 吃	_____	工资	6. 详细	_____	价格

2.2. Match the following words by similarity of their meanings.

Group One			**Group Two**		
1. 亲	_____	健康	1. 赞同	_____	看中，喜欢
2. 掏	_____	大方	2. 看上	_____	旁边
3. 壮	_____	吻	3. 一辈子	_____	没有办法

Group One				Group Two		
4. 棒	_____	重要		4. 一旁	_____	有作为
5. 关键	_____	拿		5. 有出息	_____	同意
6. 舍得	_____	好，不错		6. 无可奈何	_____	一生

2.3. 选择填空 (Choose the most appropriate words to fill in the blanks.)

1. 出息	2. 智力	3. 大方	4. 舍不得	5. 工资
6. 政策	7. 营养	8. 皇帝	9. 玩具	10. 有所作为

中国政府实行的一个家庭只生一个孩子的 _____ 使很多小孩成了家庭中的"小 _____"。虽然年轻的父母 _____ 并不高，可是为了孩子他们花钱很 _____。为了孩子的 _____，他们给他买最贵的食品。父母们自己从来 _____ 吃，舍不得穿，却花很多钱给孩子买 _____，还认为这是 _____ 投资。所有的父母都盼望自己的孩子有 _____，长大以后 _____。

2.4. 用指定的句型完成句子

1. A: 我从来没有做这个工作的经验，恐怕做不好。

   B: _____
   （……算不了什么，关键是……）

2. A: 你可以把你的自行车借给我用一下吗？

   B: 没问题，_____
   （反正）

3. A: 哎呀，离放假只有两个星期了，我还没买回家的机票呢！

   B: 你应该 _____
   （到时候）

4. A: 这个工作虽然很辛苦，但为了挣钱养孩子，我只好咬牙忍受。

   B: _____
   （这倒也是，吃苦）

5. A: 你那么喜欢那件大衣，怎么没买呢?

   B: _____
   （舍不得）

2.5. 选成语填空

a. 无可奈何	b. 争执不休	c. 理直气壮	d. 精疲力尽

1. 我从来没做过这种事，所以我可以 _____ 地说，"这不是我做的！"

2. 中国的"小皇帝"们想要什么就要什么，父母对他们真是 _____。

3. 昨天我从早到晚一共工作了十二个小时，晚上回家时简直是 _____ 了。

4. 看着儿子媳妇一天到晚为孩子的问题 _____，老王也 _____。

3. 语法练习

3.1. 汉译英：**The following are all topic-comment sentences that use the covert passive sense. Pay attention to what happens when you want to express the same meaning in English:**

1. 但家务的责任并没有从肩头卸下去。(L.12)

   _____

2. 家里收拾得井井有条。(L.12)

   _____

3. 所有的检票厅都改成了临时候车室。(L.1)

   _____

4. 中国的教育可以分成基础教育和高等教育。(L.4)

   _____

5. 一个胖乎乎的男婴在北京出生。(L.2)

   _____

6. 她的"快餐中转站"也升级为餐饮公司。(L.7)

   _____

7. 传统的大家庭几乎找不到了。(L.10)

_____

8. 而"小皇帝"妈妈们的地位也提高了。(L.10)

_____

3.2. 英译汉 (Note: Not all of these passive sentences can use 被 in Chinese)

1. That book was written by a famous American writer.

_____

2. That book was bought by the manager of our company.

_____

3. That book was well liked by college students.

_____

4. That book was burned by him during the Cultural Revolution.

_____

5. The letter is not finished yet.

_____

6. The letter is already mailed out.

_____

7. The painting was painted by my teacher.

_____

8. The painting was stolen while my teacher wasn't home.

_____

9. He was taught by a French musician.

_____

10. Are these cars made in China?

_____

11. The chicken soup was cooked by my aunt.

_____

12. The chicken soup was eaten up by my little brother before the guests even arrived.

_____

13. Their house was sold.

_____

14. Their house was sold by her husband while she was away from home.

_____

3.3. Complete the following dialogue according to the cues.

Pay attention to the passive expressions, and use interjections if needed.

小李：嘿！今天还好吗？

小张：_____

Don't even mention it! I was so unlucky!

小李：啊？怎么啦？

小张：_____

My wallet was stolen on the bus.

小李：真的？钱包里没有什么太贵重的东西吧？

小张：_____

About 100 dollars, a credit card and my driver's license.

小李：哎呀！你报警了吗？

小张：_____

Of course. Then they phoned me to say that the pickpocket was caught.

小李：那你钱包找回来啦？

小张：＿＿＿＿＿＿＿＿＿＿＿＿＿＿＿＿＿＿＿＿＿＿＿＿＿＿＿＿＿

＿＿＿＿＿＿＿＿＿＿＿＿＿＿＿＿＿＿＿＿＿＿＿＿＿＿＿＿＿＿＿＿＿

Yes, the wallet was back, but the money was gone. Fortunately, the credit card and the driver's license were not thrown away by the pickpocket.

4. 综合练习

4.1. 选词填空

a. 享有	b. 一是	c. 二是	d. 弱	e. 舍得
f. 独生子女	g. 心血	h. 挑战	i. 有出息	j. 付出
k. 寄托	l. 被	m. 历来	n. 改革开放	o. 压力
p. 吃苦				

现代中国的"小皇帝"

20 世纪 70 年代末，中国发生了两大重要历史事件：＿＿＿ 改革开放，＿＿＿ 人口控制，也就是实行计划生育政策。如今，＿＿＿＿ 已使中国经济飞跃发展，而新一代 ＿＿＿＿ 群也迅速成长起来。到 2008 年，独生子女人数已接近 1 亿人，占全国总人口的 8% 左右。在这么短的时间和这么大的范围内，以这么大的规模 (scale) 出现的独生子女人口群，对于 ＿＿＿＿ 重视儿孙满堂的中国社会来说是一个巨大的 ＿＿＿＿。

1985 年 3 月 18 日，美国《新闻周刊》登了一篇题为《一大群小皇帝》的文章，这是中国独生子女第一次 ＿＿＿＿ 媒体称为"小皇帝"。小皇帝们这样描述自己的生活：我们没有哥哥姐姐的帮助或依靠，也没有弟弟妹妹跟我们玩儿或吵架；我们是父母唯一的孩子，是家庭唯一的后代；我们一出生就 ＿＿＿＿ 优越的生活条件和爸爸妈妈爷爷奶奶的所有关爱；但有时还是感觉孤独。

　　为了让这唯一的孩子长大以后 ＿＿＿＿，家长们很自然地会 ＿＿＿＿ 为他们 ＿＿＿＿ 全部 ＿＿＿＿，因此这些孩子在家庭中处于很核心的地位。有时一个孩子身上会 ＿＿＿＿ 着两辈人、三个家庭的希望，这使他们心理上的 ＿＿＿＿ 很大，想要成功的动力 (motivation) 也较强。但是他们不太能 ＿＿＿＿，也受不了挫折 (setback) 或失败。

　　独生子女长大以后，多半拥有独特 (unique) 的价值观，他们一般选择自己有兴趣的工作，特别是能单独完成并发挥自己独特性的创造性工作。在社会上，由于从小缺少兄弟姐妹的对立竞争，独生子女较容易对别人产生信赖感，也容易获得别人的信任。但是他们生活能力较差、总想依赖他人、自我观念比较强、回报 (repay, reciprocate) 观念比较 ＿＿＿＿。

4.2. 按照上面这篇文章的意思，下面的说法对不对？ (T/F)

＿＿＿＿ 1. 20 世纪 70 年代末，中国发生的两大重要事件包括经济飞跃发展。

＿＿＿＿ 2. 中国历史上从来没有出现过这么多独生子女。

＿＿＿＿ 3. 美国也有很多"小皇帝"。

＿＿＿＿ 4. 到 2008 年，差不多每 12 个中国人中就有一个是独生子女。

＿＿＿＿ 5. 独生子女觉得没有兄弟姐妹的生活是很幸福的。

＿＿＿＿ 6. 独生子女身上的压力很大。

＿＿＿＿ 7. 独生子女的择业观一般比较实际。

＿＿＿＿ 8. 独生子女生活上很独立。

5. 阅读练习

短文一：开学第一天

九月一日是上海市中小学开学的第一天，也是大学新生到校报到的日子。

在一所小学，许多家长站在自己孩子的教室门口。虽然老师已经走进教室，要上课了，但还是有一些家长快步走进教室，有的从孩子嘴里拿下半个面包，有的帮孩子从书包里拿出书来，进进出出，乱得很。老师一次次地请家长离开，但是家长总是不放心自己的孩子，不愿意离开。上课以后，家长又来到教室旁边的操场上，等着孩子下课。小学生们也时常从窗口向操场张望 (*look around*)，不能好好上课。

中学的情况又怎样呢？在一所女子中学宿舍，你可以看到家长们在宿舍里忙前忙后，为孩子整理床铺、打扫房间、洗碗、洗衣服…… 一位老师说，以前有一位家长每天都来学校给女儿送饭，她怕女儿不爱吃学校的饭菜。

在上海一所大学，首先引起你注意的是一辆送新生报到的汽车，有出租车，也有私人汽车。这些车有的是上海市的，也有的是从别的城市来的。走进新生宿舍，你会奇怪地发现，学生们坐在椅子上聊天，而家长们在双层床上爬上爬下，忙着收拾清理…… 一位从东北开车来的家长说，孩子生活能力差，家长实在不放心让他自己来。

看看这些情况，真叫人担心，这些孩子离开父母、进入社会后可怎么生活？

5.1. 根据短文内容，选择最佳答案回答问题：

1. 在上海，九月一日是 _____。
   a. 小学开学的日子
   b. 中学开学的日子
   c. 大学开学的日子
   d. 以上都对

2. 在上海某小学里，家长为什么不愿意离开教室？
   a. 因为他们怕孩子吃不饱。
   b. 因为他们怕孩子没带书。
   c. 因为老师还没到教室。
   d. 因为他们不放心自己的孩子。

3. 下面哪个选项<u>不是</u>上海某女子中学里的情景？
   a. 家长为孩子洗衣服。
   b. 家长为孩子擦窗户。
   c. 家长为孩子整理床铺。
   d. 家长为孩子送饭。

4. 在上海某大学里，人们奇怪地发现，
   a. 家长坐出租车送新生去报到。
   b. 家长从东北开车来上海看望孩子。
   c. 家长在宿舍帮孩子收拾清理，而新生们却坐着聊天。
   d. 家长每天来给孩子送饭，怕孩子不喜欢学校的饭菜。

5. 作者对以上现象的态度是什么？
   a. 很担心这些孩子进入社会后无法独立生活。
   b. 很羡慕这些孩子受到家人的关心和照顾。
   c. 很高兴这些孩子的生活能力不断提高。
   d. 很奇怪这些孩子的生活能力这么差。

6. 以下哪项最好地说明了短文的主题？
   a. 上海中小学开学第一天的情况。
   b. 家长们在学校宿舍忙碌的情形。
   c. 家长过分照顾孩子，影响了孩子的自立能力。
   d. 现在的孩子们很幸福。

5.2. 根据短文内容，回答下列问题：

1. 在上海的小学、中学和大学里，你能发现什么共同的情况？

2. 你认为造成这种现象的原因可能有哪些？

阅读练习二："80 后"这一代

2004 年，一本叫《生于 1980》的长篇小说在大学生中引起了关注。小说用轻松、幽默的笔调，讲述了 1980 年以后出生的这一代独生子女（也称为"80 后"）大学生的生活、恋爱和他们不同于前几代人的内心世界。

小说作者<u>徐兆寿</u> (Xú Zhàoshòu) 是西北某大学的教授，以下是他的创作感受：

"1999 年后入校的大学生都是 1980 年以来出生的独生子女。他们表现出了与前几代人不同的一系列特征，他们普遍缺乏追求精神、心情压抑、恋爱观表现得开放。一方面，他们因为从小就受到家庭的<u>溺爱</u> (spoil) 而自以为是天之骄子，不愿意成为现实中的人；另一方面，他们所成长的年代正是中国改革开放时期，<u>后现代</u> (postmodern) 观念已经在他们心中有了重要位置，他们看待社会的角度与生活方式已经与前几代人完全不一样，未婚同居、反社会、讲求物质生活享受等等都是他们不被社会接受的行为。他们不喜欢过去的生活观，但又没有自己的生活观，所以很<u>迷茫</u> (confused, lost)。他们小时曾是家中的小皇帝，现在则被称为"自私的一代"、"没责任心的一代"、甚至"<u>垮掉的一代</u> (Beat Generation)"。

我原来对独生子女也有这种看法，但跟 80 后学生接触后，我开始觉得这种看法是不公平的。美国上世纪五六十年代也曾把当时的青年称为"垮掉的一代"，但这一代人后来仍然成为社会的主要力量，同样在创造着未来。因此，我现在对 80 后一代也有了不同的认识。他们的确比前几代人更实际、更注重物质的追求与享受。他们崇尚的不再是科学家、作家和思想家，而是像<u>比尔·盖茨</u> (Bill Gates) 式的知识和企业英雄。但我觉得人们对他们的认识是不全面的。其实，他们虽然有着优越的生活环境，但他们并不快乐！他们生活在 80 年代，却被 50 后或 60 后的父母的思想严格控制。而学校教育与现实社会的巨大<u>落差</u> (gap)，更使他们感到迷茫。他们"<u>冷酷</u> (cold and cool)"的表情后面，是一颗渴望爱和交流的心！

"我是怀着一种同情心来写完这本书的。我希望人们能从书中看到 80 后们最真实的内心感受，也希望 80 后这一代人能够从这本书中看到自我的影子而进行反思 (*self-examination*)，从而达成几代人的互相了解和理解。"

5.3. 根据短文内容，选择最佳答案回答问题：

1. "80 后"指的是：
   a. 80 年代后期出生的人
   b. 生活在 80 年代的人
   c. 1980 年以后出生的人
   d. 1980 年出生的人

2. 人们通常认为"80 后"这一代：
   a. 普遍缺乏追求精神
   b. 追求物质生活享受
   c. 从小受到家庭的溺爱
   d. 以上三个都是

3. 以下哪一个说法是正确的？
   a. "80 后"崇拜科学家和思想家
   b. "80 后"比较重视精神生活
   c. "80 后"没有明确的生活观
   d. "80 后"都是天之骄子

4. 以下哪一个<u>不是</u>导致"80 后"迷茫的原因：
   a. 父母对孩子的思想过分严格控制
   b. 学校教育和现实社会脱节
   c. 社会对于"80 后"缺乏理解和同情
   d. "80 后"的物质生活不够优越

5. 以下哪一项<u>不代表</u>作者的观点？
   a. 社会应该试着更好地理解"80 后"
   b. "80 后"是没责任心的一代
   c. "80 后"仍有希望成为社会的主要力量
   d. "80 后"应该对自己进行反思

6. 口语练习

6.1. 小组讨论：

1. 贝贝的爸爸妈妈为他做了很多牺牲，为什么他会让他们失望？

2. 做独生子女有什么好处？有什么坏处？你愿意做独生子女吗？说说你的理由。

3. 父母对孩子过份溺爱会有什么后果？（请举例说明）

4. 贝贝长大后会是一个什么样的人？他结婚成家后会成为怎样的丈夫和父亲？

5. 独生子女政策会给社会带来什么问题？

6. 独生子女政策是不是解决中国人口问题的唯一办法？

7. 新加坡政府在 1984 年提出新的人口政策，这一政策包括两个方面：一是鼓励具有高学历的夫妇一生生育 3 个或 3 个以上子女，并规定这些子女在一年级新生入学报名中享有优先权，有优先进入重点学校的权利。二是鼓励低文化水平的母亲减少生育，这一类妇女如果不到 30 岁就生了 1—2 个孩子，政府就鼓励她们<u>绝育</u> (sterilization)。你知道这是为什么吗？你觉得这个政策有没有道理？为什么？

7. 写作练习（任选一题）(550-650 字)

1. 我的童年

2. 给中国总理的一封信（关于人口政策问题）

3. 给新加坡总理的一封信（关于人口政策问题）

Use at least 15 of the following new vocabulary words and phrases:

喘气	收获	舍得	吃苦	关键
反正	赞同	干脆	大方	看上
价钱	超支	咬牙	智力	不停
轮到	棒	出息	奖品	得意
一旁	微笑	付出	心血	一辈子
无可奈何	理直气壮	舍得 / 舍不得	N 也没 V	到时候

双独家庭

课文提要

"双独家庭" is the product of China's one-child policy, which has had a great effect on the lives of nearly a quarter of the world's population. It is the newest model of the Chinese family, in which husband and wife are each the only child in their own families. (It literally means "two only-child families.") It is estimated that one-child families will account for 71 percent of all the families in Beijing and 73 percent of those in Shanghai by 2035. This first generation of only children, brought up as the apples of their parents' eyes and strongly modern attitudes, are now bringing great changes to the traditional norms of marriage and family in China as they start their own families.

阅读前讨论：

1. 看了课文题目，你能不能解释什么是"双独家庭"？
2. 两个独生子女组成一个家庭会有些什么特点？
3. 有人说孩子在一个家庭的排行顺序 (birth order) 对他们的性格很有影响。你觉得一般来说最大的孩子性格怎么样？最小的呢？中间的孩子呢？没有兄弟姐妹的孩子呢？
4. 你知道哪些跟"家庭"有关的词汇？

自学生词

Match the new words in the left column with the English translation in the right column, by guessing the words' meanings from the characters that compose them.

生词	繁体	序号	英文
(　)　一转眼	轉	1.	maternal grandfather
(　)　双姓	雙	2.	background
(　)　童话	話	3.	total, sum total
(　)　背景		4.	prince
(　)　王子		5.	grandchildren's generation
(　)　外祖父		6.	rational, reasonable
(　)　外祖母		7.	in the days to come; future
(　)　合理		8.	in a second, in a very short time
(　)　日后	後	9.	maternal grandmother
(　)　孙辈	孫輩	10.	double-character surname
(　)　总数	總數	11.	fairy tale

生词

简体	繁体	拼音	词性	英文	HSK 等级
1.　公主		gōngzhǔ	*n.*	princess	
2.　地毯		dìtǎn	*n.*	carpet, rug	丙
3.　是否		shìfǒu	*adv.*	whether or not	丙
4.　结尾	結	jiéwěi	*n.*	ending	
5.　优势	優勢	yōushì	*n.*	superiority	丙
6.　相对	對	xiāngduì	*adv.*	relatively	丙
7.　雄厚		xiónghòu	*adj.*	rich, solid, abundant	丁
8.　稳定	穩	wěndìng	*adj.*	stable	乙
9.　维持	維	wéichí	*v.*	maintain, keep, preserve	丙

简体		繁体	拼音	词性	英文	HSK 等级
10.	溺爱	愛	nì'ài	*v.*	spoil (a child)	
11.	柴		chái	*n.*	firewood	丁
12.	盐	鹽	yán	*n.*	salt	乙
13.	难免	難	nánmiǎn	*adj.*	unavoidable, bound to happen	丁
14.	冲突		chōngtū	*n.*	clash, conflict	丙
15.	依赖	賴	yīlài	*v.*	depend on; rely on	丁
16.	弱		ruò	*adj.*	weak	乙
17.	告终	終	gàozhōng	*v.p.*	end up	
18.	隔		gé	*v.*	separate, be at a distance from, at an interval	乙
19.	属于	屬於	shǔyú	*v.*	belong to	乙
20.	过分	過	guòfèn	*adj.*	excessive	丙
21.	疼爱	愛	téng'ài	*v.*	be very fond of, love dearly	乙
22.	依		yī	*v.*	comply with, yield to	丁
23.	无异于	無異於	wúyìyú	*v.p.*	no different from, the same as	
24.	复制	複製	fùzhì	*v.*	duplicate, reproduce, clone	丙
25.	赡养	贍養	shànyǎng	*v.*	support, provide for	
26.	足够	夠	zúgòu	*adj.*	enough, ample, sufficient	丙
27.	财力	財	cáilì	*n.*	financial resources	丁
28.	陪伴		péibàn	*v.*	accompany	
29.	姓氏		xìngshì	*n.*	family name	
30.	传承	傳	chuánchéng	*v.*	inherit, carry on	
31.	棘手		jíshǒu	*adj.*	thorny, troublesome	
32.	断	斷	duàn	*v.*	break	乙
33.	变通	變	biàntong	*v.*	be flexible; adapt	
34.	组成	組	zǔchéng	*v. c*	form; make up; compose	丙

成语和惯用语

成语/惯用语	繁体	单字解释	意思
与此同时 yǔ cǐ tóng shí	與時	与：with 此：this 同时：the same time	at the same time, meanwhile 例：报上已经登出昨天发生的事件。与此同时，电视台也播出了这条消息。
柴米油盐 chái mǐ yóu yán	鹽	柴：firewood, fuel 米：rice 油：cooking oil 盐：salt	daily necessities, small but basic things in life 例：当领导要关心群众。不要把老百姓的柴米油盐看成是小事。
互不相让 hù bù xiāng ràng	讓	互：each other 不：not 相：mutually 让：yield, give way	neither is willing to give ground 例：这两个国家在领土问题上互不相让，战争就由此而生。

■ 第一读：掌握课文大意

快速阅读课文，看下面三个选择中哪一个最能说明本课主要意思：
1. 中国的独生子女政策
2. 双独家庭的种种问题
3. 独生子女的婚姻家庭

双独家庭

独生子女政策，已经在中国实行差不多 30 年了。一转眼，生于 70 年代末 80 年代初的第一代独生子女，如今都到了该结婚成家的年龄。当"小王子"牵着"小公主"的手，走过红地毯时，他们是否真的像童话故事的结尾所说的那样，从此永远过上了幸福快乐的生活呢？

"双独家庭"有自己的优势，比如，相对雄厚的经济背景，简单的家庭结构等。与此同时，专家们也指出这种家庭结构中出现的种种问题：

一、家庭稳定性问题：据调查，"双独家庭"的稳定性较差，不少婚姻只能维持一两年。原因是第一代独生子女，在成长过程中，被父母过分关心和溺爱，所以他们往往非常依赖父母，独立生活的能力很弱。而且什么事情都以自我为中心，不懂得怎样关心别人。结婚后，他们都不太会照顾对方。至于每天必有的家务事，两个人都不想做，都等着对方做。当浪漫的爱情变成柴米油盐的现实之后，难免会产生冲突。而习惯以自我为中心的"小王子"和"小公主"互不相让，所以只要一有冲突，即使是很小的事，也可能以"离婚"告终。

二、隔代教育的问题："双独夫妇"没有带弟妹的经验，也不太懂怎么照顾别人，为了省心，干脆把孩子的生活教育责任全部推给祖父母或外祖父母，自己则忙事业去了。目前这种隔代教育现象在大城市中越来越普遍，2005 年一项全国调查的结果显示，上海 0-6 岁的孩子中有 50-60% 属于隔代教育；广州占到总数的一半；北京的比例高达 70%。孩子的年龄越小，跟祖父母生活在一起的比例就越高。祖父母对孙辈常常过分疼爱，事事都依着孩子，处处保护孩子，满足孩子的不合理要求，这种教育使孩子缺少独立性，并形成他们以自我为中心的价值观。这样无异于在复制更多的"小皇帝"和"小公主"。

三、赡养老人问题：一对"双独夫妇"的家庭结构由 4 个长辈、夫妻 2 人和 1 个小孩组成，被称为"421 家庭"。两个独生子女小时候独享了父母的爱，长大后也就只有独立承担起对父母的责任。赡养四位老人，负担会很重。即使有足够的财力，也没有时间和精力来陪伴、照顾老人。

四、子女姓氏问题：在中国传统观念中，"姓"是非常重要的，因为家族的传承主要是通过姓氏。"双独夫妇"的孩子姓什么，已经成为棘手的家庭问题。以前，孩子一般都是跟父亲姓，但是现在独生女儿的家庭就会觉得他们的家族断姓了。为了解决这个问题，广州等地提出了一个变通的办法，就是独生子女的孩子可以用父姓，也可以用母姓，或者由父姓母姓组成的双姓，比如张王、赵李等。有人认为，这种双姓方法发展下去，甚至会改变中国的姓名文化。

"双独家庭"是中国刚刚开始大规模出现的婚姻家庭新模式，这种模式必然会对未来社会产生很大的影响。

■ 第二读：细节和理解

1. "双独家庭"是什么意思？

2. 为什么"双独家庭"有比较雄厚的经济背景？

3. 为什么作者称独生子女为"小王子"、"小皇帝"和"小公主"？

4. "双独家庭"稳定性差的主要原因是什么？

5. "隔代教育"指的是什么？

6. "隔代教育"有什么好处？有什么问题？

7. 为什么赡养老人会成为"双独家庭"的一大问题？

8. 孩子跟父亲姓的传统为什么不能被一些"双独家庭"接受？

9. 为什么作者说中国的姓名文化有可能会改变？

■ 根据课文推论：(Making Inferences)

Choose the best inference from the three possible choices for each sentence, and <u>underline</u> the clue(s) that helped you choose.

1. 他们是否真的像童话故事的结尾所说的那样，从此永远过上了幸福快乐的生活呢？
   a. 他们的生活永远幸福快乐
   b. 他们的生活并不幸福快乐
   c. 他们的生活不一定幸福快乐

2. 当浪漫的爱情变成柴米油盐的现实之后，难免会产生冲突。
   a. 当浪漫的爱情变成柴米油盐时，就会产生冲突。
   b. 当浪漫的爱情情变成生活琐事时，就会产生冲突。
   c. 当浪漫的爱情不再存在时，就会产生冲突。

3. 这样无异于在复制更多的"小皇帝"和"小公主"。
   a. 这样做会产生更多被宠坏的独生子女。
   b. 这样做会使独生子女成为"小皇帝"和"小公主"。
   c. 这样做会增加独生子女的数量。

■ 阅读技巧

1. 写出本课结构大纲 ● Construct an outline of the overall structure of this reading.

Based on what you have learned about the Chinese expository essay in Lesson 10 and Lesson 12, briefly outline how the article is organized. Use the following questions as clues.

1. 本文的第一段有什么作用？（参看第十课）

   _____

2. 本文的中心论点 (central point) 是什么？

   _____

3. 你认为作者用的是哪一种论证方式来说明他的论点？是归纳式 ("inductive method") 还是演绎式 ("deductive method")？

   _____

4. 作者用了几个社会现象来说明他的论点？（简单列出这些现象，不必写出细节。）

   _____

   _____

   _____

5. 本文的结论 (conclusion) 是什么？

   _____

2. Understanding Metaphor

A metaphor is the expression of one concept in terms of another concept, where there is some similarity or correlation between the two. Metaphors are used to make expressions more interesting and vivid, and they are often culturally bound. Chinese metaphors bear a strong imprint of the cultural heritage of the Chinese people, i.e. Chinese ideological and philosophical thinking, understanding of the world, social values, and mythical or superstitious beliefs. This is especially apparent in the Chinese language's large collection of metaphorical four-character idioms. For example, 柴米油盐 (fire wood, rice, cooking oil and salt) used to be the basic things a household needed for cooking, so they became a metaphor for "daily necessities or triviality of everyday life", although nowadays they may not be as necessary for people as they used to. Another example is "小皇帝", who used to be the most privileged person in Chinese history. Calling the "only child" 小皇帝 vividly conveys people's concept of this young and spoiled generation.

　　Being able to understand metaphors - to grasp the meaning of expressions from one context with their associated objects and entities in a different context - can greatly enhance your understanding of the Chinese language.

Reading Skill Practice:

The following sentences all contain metaphors. Find out the original and metaphorical meanings of the words used.

1. 当"小王子"牵着"小公主"的手，走过红地毯时，……

    小王子 original meaning: little prince, metaphorical meaning: spoiled only child

    小公主 original meaning: _____, metaphorical meaning: _____

    红地毯 original meaning: _____, metaphorical meaning: _____

2. "双独夫妇"的孩子姓什么，已经成为棘手的家庭问题。

    棘手 original meaning: _____, metaphorical meaning: _____

3. 这样无异于在复制更多的"小皇帝"和"小公主"。

    复制 original meaning: _____, metaphorical meaning: _____

4. 一到家，立刻把宝贝儿子抱起来，亲了又亲。

    宝贝 original meaning: _____, metaphorical meaning: _____

5. 她一边喘气一边从大包小包里掏出今天的收获来。

    收获 original meaning: _____, metaphorical meaning: _____

6. 没想到，为儿子付出那么多心血，如今，连一小块巧克力都尝不到。

    心血 original meaning: _____, metaphorical meaning: _____

7. 女性走回厨房：是进步还是倒退?

    厨房 original meaning: _____, metaphorical meaning: _____

8. 老人也谈起了<u>黄昏</u>恋。

黄昏 original meaning: _____, metaphorical meaning: _____

9. 从大四开始，何英就开始找工作，没想到却到处<u>碰壁</u>。

碰壁 original meaning: _____, metaphorical meaning: _____

10. 那时候的首选肯定是"政府部门和国家机关"，因为那是终身可靠的<u>铁饭碗</u>。

铁饭碗 original meaning: _____, metaphorical meaning: _____

11. 他们的婚姻要由父母决定，讲究的是<u>门当户对</u>。

门当户对 original meaning: _____, metaphorical meaning: _____

12. 如果婚后的现实与婚前的期望产生不可调和的<u>矛盾</u>，他们多数选择离婚。

矛盾 original meaning: _____, metaphorical meaning: _____

13. 我喜欢冒险，不愿<u>平平淡淡</u>过一辈子。

平平淡淡 original meaning: _____, metaphorical meaning: _____

14. 她们的理想生活，就是住在安全的"个人<u>城堡</u>"里。

城堡 original meaning: _____, metaphorical meaning: _____

词汇与句型

1. 一转眼 • in an instant, in a trice, in no time at all

一转眼 can refer to not only an actual short moment, but also a certain period of time that feels like a very short moment.

1. 宝宝刚才还在门外和小朋友玩呢，怎么一转眼就不见了？
Baobao was just playing with his little friends outside the door. How is he gone now just in a second?

2. 一转眼，生于 80 年代初的第一代独生子女，如今都到了结婚成家的年龄。
In no time at all, the members of the first only-child generation, who were born in the early 1980s, have now reached an age for marriage.

3. 今天是毕业典礼的日子，我心里百感交集。好像昨天才走进校园，今天就到了说再见的时候，大学整整四年仿佛只是一转眼的工夫。
Today is my graduation day. All sorts of emotions are welling up in my heart. It seems that I just walked onto campus yesterday, yet today I am about to say goodbye. The four years of university life feel like just the blink of an eye.

2. 从此 • hence, from now on, from then on, since then

1. 他们是否真的像童话故事的结尾所说的那样，从此过上了幸福快乐的生活呢？
Are they going to live happily ever after, just like the ending of every fairy tale?

2. 九年前，贝贝出生了，从此，他就成了全家人的中心。
Nine years ago, Beibei was born. Since then, he has become the center of the whole family.

3. 硕士毕业后，我去了加拿大，他去了美国，我们从此就再也没见过面。
After graduating from our master's program, I went to Canada and he went to the United States. Since then, we have not seen each other.

3. 相对 (adv.) • relatively, in comparison with

1. 大城市的就业机会相对更多，但就业竞争也相对激烈。
There are relatively more employment opportunities in big cities, but the employment competition there is relatively more intense.

2. 相对其他家庭，你们两口的收入已经很不错了。
In comparison with other families, you two have a pretty good income.

相对来说/相对而言 (relatively speaking)

3. 这套公寓相对那套（来说/而言）更宽敞舒适。
This apartment is relatively more spacious and comfortable than that one.

4. 与此同时 • meanwhile, at the same time

1. "双独家庭"有自己的优势，但与此同时，专家们也指出这种家庭结构中出现的种种问题。

   A "double one-child family" has its own advantages, but meanwhile, experts have pointed out certain problems that emerge in such family structures.

2. 随着学龄儿童入学率在全国范围内的增长，升学竞争越来越激烈，与此同时，学生的课业负担也日益加重。

   With the national increase in the enrollment rate of school-age children, the competition of the entrance examination is increasingly severe. At the same time, the burden of schoolwork has become heavier and heavier for the students.

5. 至于 • as for, as to, as far as

至于 is a connective. Presiding at the beginning of the second clause, it is used to introduce another topic, on which comments or views are added in the following part.

1. 小两口在工作上都很有能力，至于家务活，他俩谁也不想管。

   The young couple are both high achievers in their career. As far as household chores, neither of them is willing to take charge.

2. 这个新方法提高了我们的产品质量；至于产量能提高多少要等到年底才知道。

   This new method has raised the quality of our product; as to how much it can increase the production quantity, we won't know until the end of this year.

3. 总经理辞职了，至于谁来接替他，我们都不知道。

   The general manager resigned. As for who will replace him, we don't know.

6. 柴米油盐 • daily necessities, daily trifles, triviality of everyday life

1. 当浪漫的爱情变成柴米油盐的现实之后，难免会产生冲突。

   When the romance of love turns into the reality of daily trifles, conflicts are inevitable.

2. 照顾一个家可不容易。柴米油盐啦，水电啦，都要定期打理，更不要说打扫房间、照顾孩子这些花时间、费体力的活儿了。

   It is not easy to run a household. You have to constantly take care of the daily necessities such as fuel, oil, rice, salt, water and electricity; let alone other time- and energy-consuming chores like cleaning up and childcare.

3. 大到国家的方针政策，小到百姓的柴米油盐，没有什么事是老王不关心的。
From national policies to the daily life of common folks, there is nothing that Lao Wang does not care about.

7. 难免 • difficult to avoid or escape from, unavoidable, inevitable

1. 参加讨论的人这么多，难免会有不同的意见。
There were so many people at the discussion, different opinions were inevitable.

2. 张力第一次自主创业，难免经验不足。
Zhang Li started a business on his own for the first time. Lack of experience is unavoidable.

3. 小两口刚结婚，小吵小闹是难免的。
The young couple just got married. Tiffs here and there are unavoidable.

8. 互不相让 • unwilling to make concessions on either side

1. 小两口一吵架就互不相让。
Once the young couple got into a quarrel, neither would make a compromise to stop.

2. 虽然他们是好朋友，但有了好玩玩具的时候就谁都想要，互不相让。
Though they are good friends, when it comes to some fun toys, they will both fight for them without backing down.

3. 谈判 (negotiation) 双方都为了各自公司的利益而互不相让。
Both parties are bargaining for the profits of their own companies; neither is willing to make concessions.

9. 以……告终 • end in..., end with..., end up doing...

1. "双独家庭"里，夫妻双方处理家庭关系的能力都比较弱，只要一有冲突，即使是很小的事，也可能以"离婚"告终。
In a "double only-child family", both the husband and wife are relatively incapable of handling family relationships. Once conflicts occur, even a trifle can cause the marriage to end in divorce.

2. 由于数据 (data) 丢失，实验以失败告终。
Due to loss of data, the experiment came to nothing in the end.

3. 整场话剧以男主角的一段深情的独白告终。
The whole play ended with an emotional monologue from the male main character.

10. 推 • push; push away/shift (responsibility)

1. "妈妈、爸爸"，聪聪猛然推开门，飞跑进来。
   "Mom! Dad!" Congcong suddenly pushed the door open and dashed in.

2. 他把我从房间里推了出来。
   He shoved me out of the room.

3. 如今很多家庭，夫妻都在忙工作，于是干脆把孩子的生活教育责任全部推给爷爷、奶奶、外公、外婆。
   Nowadays in many families, both the husband and wife are busy with their jobs. Therefore, the responsibilities of raising and educating their children are all pushed onto the grandparents.

11. 无异于 • equal to…, be as much as… （= 等于，就是）

1. 你的沉默，无异于对犯罪行为的默认。
   You silence is no better than giving tacit consent to the criminal offense.

2. 和我讨论计算机编程 (*programming*) 无异于对牛弹琴。
   Talking about computer programming with me is equal to playing a flute before a cow (i.e. casting pearls before swine).

3. 他的评论无异于是在说我们都不够尽力。
   His comment is as much as saying that we didn't try our best.

12. 棘手 • thorny, knotty, difficult to handle

1. "双独家庭"的孩子姓什么，已经成为棘手的家庭问题。
   Which family name is to be chosen for a child of the "double only-child family" has become a knotty family problem.

2. 我这个月有几个棘手的项目要处理，至于你家的派对，我恐怕去不了了。
   I have several tough projects to handle this month. As for the party to be held at your place, I'm afraid that I can't make it.

3. 碰到越棘手的事情，你越要有耐心。
   The more difficult the matter is, the more patient you need to be.

13. 变通 • flexible, accommodating of circumstances

1. 变通是一门艺术，更是一门学问。一个人想要成功一定要学会变通。

   Accommodating is an art, but is also a lot of learning. Anyone who wants to succeed must learn how to accommodate circumstances.

2. 在生意场上，灵活变通是成功的关键。

   In the world of business, flexibility is the key to success.

3. 王伯伯总是守着老规矩，一点也不变通。

   Uncle Wang always sticks to the stale conventions and refuses to change his mind.

语法

1. 现代名词后缀 • Modern Noun Suffixes

Modern noun suffixes are themselves nouns with definite meanings. Grammatically, they are added to an adjective or another noun to form compound noun phrases that convey modern concepts, mostly in the realm of the social sciences. They are called suffixes because they often come from translating suffixes of foreign languages. The following are some commonly used modern noun suffixes.

Suffix	Meaning	Example 1	Example 2	Example 3
- 性	-ity, -ness	稳定性 stability	普遍性 universality	可能性 possibility
- 界	…world	教育界 the educational world	政界 the political world	金融界 financial circles
- 家	-ist	专家 specialist	科学家 scientist	政治家 statesman
- 学	-ics, -logy (subject of study)	物理学 physics	生态学 ecology	心理学 psychology
- 主义	-ism	资本主义 capitalism	社会主义 socialism	女权主义 feminism

Suffix	Meaning	Example 1	Example 2	Example 3
- 观	notion, idea	价值观 values	婚恋观 notions of marriage and love	世界观 world view
- 者	-er	读者 reader	作者 author	初学者 beginner
- 法	law	环境法 environmental law	移民法 immigration law	地方法 bylaw
	method	演绎法 the deductive method	推论法 the inductive method	教学法 teaching method
- 力	power, strength, resource, capacity	财力 financial power	物力 material resource	人力 manpower
- 方	side, party	甲方/乙方 Party A/Party B	女方 the woman's side	双方 both parties
- 族 (new)	clan, kind of people	追星族 star chaser	上班族 career people, office workers	单身族 single people

2. 连词 "则" 的用法 • The Usage of Conjunction 则

则 is a classical Chinese word. In modern Chinese, it is used only in written language as a connective to link two clauses. It usually occurs before the verb in the second clause. 则 can indicate several different kinds of logical relationships, depending on the context.

2.1. 则 Indicating a Contrast

In this sense, its meaning is similar to '却', and it is usually used with "但、不过、而、然而".

1. 这种变化，对他们来说，是一种挑战，而对我们来说，则是一种自由。
   To them, this change is a challenge; but to us, it's kind of freedom.

2. 他们想要一所房子，我们则宁愿住一套公寓。
   They want a house but we rather prefer an apartment.

3. 大家都为毕业后找不到工作着急，而他则相信凭自己的能力找工作不会太难。

Everyone worries about finding a job after graduation, but he believes it won't be too hard for him to locate a job with his abilities.

2.2. 则 Indicating a Necessary Condition or Cause/Result

In this usage, the first clause introduces the cause or condition, and the second clause presents the result. 则 is used in the second clause, equivalent to '就' in vernacular Chinese or 'then' in English. The cue word for the condition or reason '如果，如' is normally unstated.

1. 自己不努力，则父母提供的条件再好也没用。

If one doesn't make his/her own efforts, then whatever one's parents could provide will be useless.

2. 公司再吸引不到好的人才，则应该提高现有待遇。

If our company cannot attract talent any more, then we should improve our present compensation.

3. 在文件下方签名 (*sign*) 则表示您同意接受本公司条件。

Sign at the bottom of the document and you agree to accept our company's terms.

2.3. 则 Indicating a Sequence of Occurrence

1. 暑 (shǔ, *summer*) 往，则冬来。

As summer goes, winter comes.

2. 许多双独夫妇为了省心，把孩子的生活教育推给祖父母，自己则忙事业去了。

Many parents who were brought up as only children have passed the responsibility of their children's livelihood and education on to the kids' grandparents and go on busying themselves with their own careers.

3. 名词重叠 • Noun Reduplication in Mandarin Chinese

Noun reduplication is not as common as verb reduplication or adjective reduplication in Chinese. However, certain nouns (mostly monosyllabic nouns) can be repeated for special purposes. The following examples illustrate the main forms and functions of noun reduplication in Chinese:

3.1. Noun Reduplication Indicating Endearment and Affection

Kinship terms: 妈妈　爸爸　爷爷　奶奶　哥哥　姐姐　叔叔　舅舅　姑姑
Endearing (childish) nouns: 宝宝　贝贝　狗狗　花花　手手　脚脚

3.2. Noun Reduplication Indicating Universality (i.e., "Every" and "All")

AA Type: 天天　年年　岁岁　时时　事事　处处　人人　家家　村村

Note: Nouns reduplicated in this manner are usually used with "都". Examples:

这种事事都依着孩子、处处都保护孩子的教育方法对孩子的成长并没有好处。
It is not good for the wholesome growth of children to cater to their every need and protect them everywhere.

这些独生子女，人人都是"小皇帝"，有矛盾时都互不相让。
Every only child is a little emperor. None of them is willing to give in when conflicts arise.

这个地方真美，家家门前都种着各种各样的花草树木。
This place is beautiful. There are all kinds of plants and trees in front of every house.

自从他们结婚以后，天天都在外面吃饭，从来没有自己做过饭。
They have been eating out everyday since they got married, never cooking a meal themselves.

AABB Type: 家家户户　老老少少　祖祖辈辈　日日夜夜　里里外外

Nouns reduplicated in this type are *symmetrical monosyllabic* words. They can be synonyms (e.g., 家家户户) or antonyms (e.g., 里里外外). Examples:

我们家祖祖辈辈都是农民，从我们这一代起才开始了城市生活。
My family has been peasants for generations. We never lived in the city until our generation.

他们为新公司的发展日日夜夜地工作。
They worked day and night for their new company's development.

为了庆祝新年，家家户户都得把房子里里外外打扫干净。
Every household has to clean inside and outside for the New Year Celebration.

练习

1. 语音

Write pinyin for the following underlined Chinese characters. Pay special attention to their different pronunciations in different contexts.

过<u>分</u>   (   )   <u>背</u>景   (   )   到<u>处</u>   (   )   实<u>行</u>   (   )

<u>分</u>开   (   )   <u>背</u>书包 (   )   <u>处</u>理   (   )   银<u>行</u>   (   )

互不<u>相</u>让 (   )   一<u>转</u>眼 (   )   <u>难</u>免   (   )   负<u>担</u>   (   )

长<u>相</u>   (   )   <u>转</u>动   (   )   困<u>难</u>   (   )   重<u>担</u>   (   )

2. 词汇句型

2.1. Match the following words on the left with the words appropriately associated with them on the right.

Group One (Verb + Object)		**Group Two** (Adj. + Noun)	
1. 溺爱 _____	责任	1. 浪漫的 _____	负担
2. 实行 _____	要求	2. 棘手的 _____	办法
3. 承担 _____	冲突	3. 过分的 _____	爱情
4. 赡养 _____	孩子	4. 普遍的 _____	担心
5. 满足 _____	政策	5. 沉重的 _____	问题
6. 产生 _____	老人	6. 变通的 _____	现象

2.2. 写出下列书面语的口语形式：

Formal	Informal		Formal	Informal
1. 如今			1. 互不相让	
2. 棘手			2. 与此同时	
3. 无异于			3. 陪伴	
4. 与			4. 姓氏	
5. 是否			5. 传承	
6. 告终			6. 日后	
7. 难免			7. 从此	
8. 父母			8. 以……为	
9. 祖父母			9. 例如	

2.3. 选词填空

a. 棘手	b. 推	c. 优势	d. 传承	e. 属于	f. 雄厚	g. 维持	h. 相对来说
i. 变通	j. 溺爱	k. 如今	l. 难免	m. 冲突	n. 稳定	o. 赡养	p. 与此同时

1. 我和这位新同事合不来，他总是把棘手的工作 _____ 给我。

2. 以往讲究 _____ 的婚姻的传统 _____ 已经有了很大的改变，没有爱情的婚姻已经很少有人愿意 _____ 了。

3. 很多民族的早期文化都是通过口头 _____ 下来的。

4. 在家庭会上他们谈论了 _____ 老人的事情。_____，女儿的计划更可行。

5. 他们夫妇俩从小都被家长过分 _____，有 _____ 时互不相让是 _____ 的。

6. 中国近年来经济飞速发展。但 _____，还有很多边远地区 _____ 贫困地区。

7. 她以 _____ 的财力在竞争者中占了 _____。

8. 为了解决这个 _____ 的问题，我想出了一个 _____ 的办法。

3. 语法练习

3.1. Complete the following nouns by adding appropriate noun suffixes according to their English meaning:

-性	-界	-家	-学	-主义	-观	-者	-法	-力	-方	-族

记 _____
journalist

警 _____
the police

创造 _____
creativity

体育 _____
sports world

飞车 _____
car racers

人生 _____
life view

学 _____
scholar

美 _____
the U.S. side

独创 _____
originality

学术 _____
the academia

宠物 _____
pet owners

就业 _____
career view

婚姻 _____
marriage law

乐观 _____
optimism

保鲜 _____
preserving method

脑 _____
brain power

文 _____
literature

银行 _____
banker

贸易 _____
trade law

民族 _____
nationalism

健身 _____
fitness ways

想象 _____
imagination

语言 _____
linguistics

画 _____
artist

3.2. Choose the most appropriate noun reduplication form to replace the underlined part of the following sentences:

a. 字字句句	b. 分分秒秒	c. 时时刻刻	d. 事事
e. 处处	f. 人人	g. 子子孙孙	h. 里里外外
i. 家家户户	j. 天天	k. 男男女女，老老少少	

1. 没有人愿意跟张洋做朋友，他做每一件事都只为自己，不考虑别人。

2. 你刚到外国，到哪儿去都得特别小心，任何时候都要注意安全。

3. 天色晚了，每一家的窗子都亮起了灯光。

4. 几乎每一个人都说独生子女太依赖父母，可我们家的女儿却特别独立。

5. 如果现在不保护环境，我们的所有子孙后代都会受害！

6. 屋子从里到外我都找过了，没找到他要的书。

7. 这几天，这个村所有的人都有一种奇怪的感觉。

8. 要是爷爷和奶奶登记了，聪聪就能<u>每一天</u>都吃到鸡蛋羹了。

9. 他写的这封信，<u>每一个字，每一句话</u>都表达了他对父母的深情。

10. 学生们把<u>所有的时间（每一分，每一秒）</u>都用在准备高考上。

3.3. 根据不同的语境，选用书面语或口语完成下面的句子：

Choose formal or informal expressions to complete the following sentences according to their context:

1. <u>互不相让/谁也不让谁</u>
   A. 昨天我看到两个骑自行车的人吵架，他们都说是对方的错，_____。
   B. 据报道，两位总统候选人竞争激烈，_____。

2. <u>父母/爸爸 妈妈   子女/孩子   棘手/很难</u>
   A. 独生子女的孩子是用 _____ 姓还是 _____ 姓已经成为了一个 _____ 的问题。
   B. 年轻的 _____ 告诉我们，现在每家都只生一个，所以 _____ 到底应该跟谁姓是一个 _____ 的问题。

3. <u>无异于/等于</u>
   A. 没有新闻自由，报纸 _____ 一张废纸（*wastepaper*）。
   B. 现在找工作这样难。我看啊，这毕业就 _____ 失业了。

4. <u>如此/这么   是否/是不是</u>
   A. 老龄化的问题 _____ 严重，政府 _____ 应该考虑取消独生子女政策？
   B. 你说，雨下得 _____ 大，我们 _____ 应该取消明天的爬山比赛？

5. <u>姓氏/姓</u>
   A. 只要我的孩子身体健康，聪明活泼，他 _____ 什么都没关系。
   B. 日本的 _____ 是世界上最多的，有 20 多万个。中国只有 4600 多个。

6. <u>传承/传</u>
   A. 他说的这个消息不是真的，请大家不要再 _____ 下去了。
   B. 中国民营企业创业者正面临着如何把企业 _____ 给第二代人的现实问题。

7. <u>祖父母/爷爷奶奶</u>
   A. 孙子女对 _____ 有无赡养义务？
   B. 我小时候最喜欢去 _____ 家里玩儿。

4. 综合练习

4.1. 选词填空

a. 柴米油盐	b. 流行	c. 无异于	d. 财力	e. 推	f. 组成
g. 难免	h. 隔代	i. 过分溺爱	j. 负担	k. 是否	l. 依赖
m. 陪伴	n. 足够	o. 孙辈	p. 无奈		

中国式"丁克"夫妻

"丁克 (DINK)"本是指双收入，无孩子，追求生活享受的年轻夫妇。但在中国传统家庭观与年轻人的新婚恋观的结合下，却 _____ 了独特的中国式"丁克"家庭：一些年轻夫妇生孩子后，把孩子 _____ 给自己的父母照顾，而他们自己则成为"双收入、有子女、仍享受二人世界"的新式丁克一族。

为父母生孩子

晚上，刘小可一边吃<u>零食 (snack)</u>，一边躺在沙发里看电视，她的先生李刚则在另一间屋子里专心玩电脑<u>游戏 (games)</u>。他们四岁半的儿子从出生以来一直和爷爷奶奶生活在一起，所以小夫妻俩每天回到自己的小家后仍然过着"二人世界"。小可说，"不是我 _____ 父母，是工作压力太大，竞争激烈，一不小心就 _____ 有下岗的危险，所以我没心情管家里 _____ 的事情，也没时间 _____ 孩子。而且，他从小就跟他爷爷奶奶住在一起，只听他们的话，我说什么他都不听。所以只好让父母带算了。其实我们并不想要孩子，可是父母一定要我们生一个，这个孩子 _____ 是为他们生的。"

永远的父母心

给子女带小孩的这些父母现在大多退休在家了。一位铁路退休职工陈先生说："我们老两口每月都有退休金，有 _____ 的 _____ 和精力给儿子、媳妇减轻点 _____，这是我们做父母唯一能帮他们的了。再说，我们自己也想抱孙子啊。"对子女 _____，对他们生活能力不放心也是他们照顾 _____ 的主要理由之一。给女儿带孩子的方大妈感慨地说："让我女儿自己带孩子，我哪能放心呢？她会干什么啊？她从小就什么都不会干，自己还是个孩子呢。"

已为人父母的"孩子"

文文今年 27 岁，不满三岁的女儿豆豆一直由爷爷奶奶或姥姥姥爷带。她说："虽然做了母亲，可是我心里觉得自己还是个孩子，我还是像以前一样爱听 _____ 音乐、看动画片，喜欢吃零食。"说起女儿，她显得很 _____。"孩子不跟我，也不听我的。每天晚上只肯跟姥姥睡，我有时也想带她睡，可是刚一躺到她身边，她就哭着叫姥姥。"当问到她 _____ 担心这种 _____ 教育会让孩子长大以后跟他们感情不深的时候，文文说："应该不会吧，孩子长大了，自然知道谁是自己的父母，血缘 (blood relationship) 关系是不会改变的。"你要是问豆豆："你家住哪儿啊？"小豆豆会回答："我爷爷家住城东，我姥姥家住城西，我家在哪儿呢？我不知道。"

4.2. 按照上面这篇文章的意思，下面的说法对不对？(T/F)

_____ 1. 本文所说的中国式"丁克"家庭指的是双收入，无子女，享受二人世界的夫妇。

_____ 2. 刘小可的儿子从来没有和她生活在一起。

_____ 3. 刘小可起初不想要孩子的原因是工作压力太大。

_____ 4. 许多父母一边工作，一边给子女带小孩。

_____ 5. 方大妈认为女儿没有能力自己照顾孩子。

_____ 6. 文文的女儿豆豆晚上只喜欢和母亲睡。

_____ 7. 中国式的"丁克"家庭造成了子女和父母感情不深的现象。

_____ 8. "已为人父母的'孩子'"的意思是很多人年纪很轻便有了孩子。

5. 阅读练习

阅读短文（一）
"王子和公主"的生活

　　白文和王丽都是家里的独生子女，刚结婚时，两人还是像长不大的孩子。每天下班后，他们还是像谈恋爱时那样，手牵着手去外面的餐厅吃饭。饭后，他们或者去看电影，或者去和朋友聚会。两个人的小日子过得很开心。

　　可是慢慢地，他们不得不开始面对现实。从小到大，两个人都从来没做过家务事，所以他们的小家总是又脏又乱，可是谁也不愿意动手收拾，反而你怪我、我怪你，常常争执不休。小两口工资也不算太少，可他们属于典型的"月光族"，每月还不到发工资的那天，钱包就空了，到最后连吃饭都成了问题。于是，白文怪王丽太会花钱，不会过日子；王丽则说："都怪你没本事，赚不到大钱！"最后，夫妻俩只好去各自父母那儿"借"钱。

　　一天，白文生病了，请假在家里休息。王丽下班回来，问白文好些了没有？尽管很不舒服，但白文还是说，"没事"。王丽给他倒了一杯水，送上了几片药，然后就换衣服准备出门，说是和朋友约好了出去买东西。看着妻子穿得漂漂亮亮地出了门，越走越远，白文突然觉得有些伤心。他想起结婚前与父母生活在一起的情形。那时候，自己只要有什么地方不舒服，父母就会急得团团转，忙前忙后地照顾他。可现在……

　　晚上10点多，王丽才回家。回来后，她高兴地一件件试穿着自己刚买的衣服，还不停地问白文这个好不好看、那个好不好看。白文终于<u>忍不住</u> (*can't bear*) 了，向王丽大骂起来："你怎么这么<u>没心没肺</u> (*heartless*)？我生病在家，你却跑出去玩。现在回来，又只管试你那几件破衣服，还问个没完……"

　　没等白文说完，王丽也大声叫起来："你不是说自己没事了吗？再说，就算我陪在你的身边，你的病就能好吗？说我没心没肺，你才没心没肺呢，我生病的时候你不是也跟朋友在外面整晚喝酒吗……？"王丽大哭着跑开了。白文也无力地<u>垂</u> (*droop*) 下头……

5.1. 根据短文内容，选择最佳答案回答问题：

1. 白文和王丽有什么共同之处？

  a. 他俩都是独生子女。

  b. 他俩以前都没做过家务。

  c. 他俩都不会照顾别人。

  d. 以上都是。

2. 文中的"月光族"指的是什么？

  a. 挣不到大钱的人。

  b. 经常为钱吵架的人。

  c. 把每个月工资全部花光的人。

  d. 喜欢在中秋节看月亮的人。

3. 关于白文和王丽，下面哪句话是正确的？

  a. 白文觉得王丽花钱太多，王丽觉得白文赚钱太少。

  b. 白文喜欢花钱旅游，王丽喜欢花钱买衣服。

  c. 他们俩的工资很少，只好花父母的钱。

  d. 他们俩刚结婚时就经常吵架。

4. 在白文生病的时候，他为什么那么生气？

  a. 因为他觉得王丽回家太晚。

  b. 因为他觉得王丽买衣服花了太多钱。

  c. 因为他不得不自己倒水吃药。

  d. 因为他生病时，王丽不像父母那样关心照顾他。

5. 你认为白文和王丽婚姻关系中的主要问题是什么？

  a. 白文不喜欢王丽花钱买衣服。

  b. 王丽对白文的感情不深，不愿意照顾他。

  c. 白文对王丽的要求太高，不给她自由。

  d. 两个人都比较自我中心，不懂得付出。

6. 以下哪个选项最好地说明了短文的主题？

　　a. 白文和王丽像两个长不大的孩子。

　　b. 年轻的夫妻往往争吵不断。

　　c. 独生子女的婚姻面临很多挑战。

　　d. 白文的父母非常宠爱他。

5.2. 按照这篇文章的意思，下面的说法对不对？ (T/F)

_____ 1. 白文和王丽刚结婚就常常吵架。

_____ 2. 白文和王丽都不会做家务，所以他们家里很乱。

_____ 3. 白文常常生病，所以赚钱不多。

_____ 4. 两人结婚后常常在饭店吃饭。

_____ 5. 王丽回家后没有问白文病怎么样。

_____ 6. 白文觉得父母比妻子对他好。

_____ 7. 王丽为白文买了几件衣服，问他好不好看。

_____ 8. 王丽生病的时候白文对她很关心。

阅读短文（二）
中国的"421 家庭"

　　"421 家庭"指的是独生夫妇生孩子后的家庭结构：4 个父母长辈、他们夫妻 2 人和 1 个小孩。在不久的将来，中国四世同堂式的家庭"<u>金字塔 (pyramid)</u>"将迅速变成"倒金字塔"的家庭结构，"421 家庭"将成为中国社会新的家庭主流。随着新家庭模式的出现，整个中国传统家庭关系也将被改变。

刘娜是一家电脑公司的白领，她和她先生都是独生子女。他们的家庭由 4 个长辈、1 个小孩和他们 2 人组成，是典型的 421 家庭。孩子一生下来就交给了老人带。刘娜说："趁父母身体情况还好的时候，生下孩子可以给他们照顾。如果等个三五年，到时又要照顾父母又要照顾孩子，就麻烦了。"这是目前 421 家庭中的"2"的普遍想法，上有老、下有小，一个家庭的倒金字塔结构，令"2"们不得不早做打算。

与刘娜的家庭相比，陈正林家的经济条件就差多了。陈正林每天在城里东奔西跑地为不同的电视机用户安装、维修；而他的妻子每天有 8 个小时要站在超市工作。陈正林每周一到周四把孩子放在自己的父母家照看，周五到周日则把孩子带到妻子父母家。"如果不这么平均分配时间把小孩给双方父母，他们还会不高兴呢。要是我们两个年轻人能够自己带小孩就好了，但我们得工作挣钱啊，要不就养不起小孩了。"

压在陈正林心头的，不仅是"养不起孩子"的忧虑，还有"养不起父母"的担心。他和妻子的父母都是下岗工人。这就意味着在未来几年或十几年内，他们可能要面临照顾至少 4 个老人的情况。陈正林常常为此感到担忧，他说："如果有个兄弟姐妹就好了，最好有一两个哥哥。"现在夫妻俩忙着挣钱不仅仅是为了孩子、为了自己的小家庭，也是为老人们的养老作准备。

中国现在 60 岁以上老人已经接近 1.3 亿，成为世界上拥有老人人口最多的国家。为了应对老龄化，上海、北京、广州等大城市已经开始鼓励双独夫妻再生育第二个子女。然而，调查显示，双独夫妇很少有意愿再生第二个孩子。工作压力大、子女养育成本高及生育观念转变是主要原因。

5.3. 根据短文内容，选择最佳答案回答问题：

1. "421"家庭指的是：

    a. 四个子女、两个老人和一个小孩

    b. 四个老人、一对夫妻和一个小孩

    c. 四个小孩、一对夫妻和一个老人

    d. 以上都不是

2. 为什么说随着新家庭模式的出现，整个中国传统家庭关系也将被改变？

    a. 新家庭模式只有一个小孩，所以孩子成了整个家庭的中心

    b. 新家庭模式中的第二代既要负担父母又要养育子女，压力很大

    c. 随着新家庭模式的出现，社会老龄化越来越严重

    d. 以上三个都对

3. 从文章中我们可以推断出刘娜 _____

    a. 不喜欢照顾孩子

    b. 不愿意照顾父母

    c. 很早就生了孩子

    d. 又要照顾父母又要照顾孩子

4. 陈正林想要兄弟姐妹的原因是：

    a. 他觉得作为独生子女十分孤单

    b. 他希望能够有人分担照顾父母的义务

    c. 他的父母希望有很多子女

    d. 以上都不对

5. 下面哪个不是双独夫妇不愿意再生第二个孩子的理由？

    a. 他们觉得生养一个孩子需要太多钱

    b. 他们担心父母太老不能帮他们照顾孩子

    c. 他们的生育观念跟长辈们的不一样

    d. 他们的工作压力太大

6. 以下哪一项最好地概括了双独夫妇的生活状态？

　　a. 双独夫妇不愿意生育子女

　　b. 双独夫妇的父母通常帮助他们照顾子女

　　c. 双独夫妇都想要兄弟姐妹

　　d. 双独夫妇上有父母，下有子女，生活压力很大

5.4. 请根据短文内容，画出"金字塔"和"倒金字塔"的家庭结构图：

　　　　　　————————————　　　　　　　————————————

　　　　　　　　　金字塔　　　　　　　　　　　　　倒金字塔

6. 口语练习

讨论题

1. 人们对独生子女的看法都不太好。你觉得这是一种偏见 (bias) 还是有根据的？你有没有跟独生子女交往的经历？如果有，请你谈谈你对他们的印象。

2. 这篇课文主要谈的是双独家庭模式的弱点。你觉得这种家庭模式也有什么优势？

3. 这篇课文最后说，"双独家庭模式必然会对未来社会产生很大的影响。"请你谈谈这种新家庭模式会在下面几个方面对社会带来什么影响：

　　a. 家庭关系（夫妻关系、父母与子女关系、祖父母与儿女及孙子女关系、夫妻的父母两家关系）

　　b. 赡养老人

　　c. 家庭姓氏

　　d. 其他？

4. 中国式的丁克家庭有什么特点？这种家庭在你们国家有没有？多不多？为什么？

5. 421 家庭的危机应该怎样解决？只靠小夫妻二人挣钱够不够？钱能不能解决 421 家庭的所有问题？

7. 写作练习（550-650 字）任选一题

A. 变化中的现代家庭

B. 双独家庭模式对未来社会的影响

Required vocabulary and expressions:

1. Use at least 10 of the following new vocabulary:

无异于	互不相让	是否	难免	优势	相对	雄厚
稳定	维持	过分	溺爱	依赖	告终	属于
复制	赡养	陪伴	传承	棘手	变通	组成

2. Use at least 5 of the following connectives:

如果……就……	一方面……	另一方面……
尽管……还是……	至于……	因为……所以……
一是……，二是……	不但……而且……	另外，……比如……
无论……都……	即使……也……	从此，……
既……又……	与此同时……	对……来说……
……则……		

离婚潮

课文提要

Since China began its market reforms in the late 1970s, the number of people getting divorced has soared. The dramatic rise of the divorce rate reflects a deeper change in society. In traditional China, family was given top emphasis, while the quality of the marriage tended to be neglected. In such circumstances, families often became a cage for people in unhappy marriages, and getting a divorce was practically impossible. Now more importance is being given to the real content of marriage rather than its outer form. In 2003, the government streamlined the divorce process in response to citizens' complaints. It also dropped the onerous requirement that couples needed approval from their employers to divorce. For many older couples trapped in loveless marriages, the new law has meant an exit without the shame of seeking permission. But younger couples are less concerned about shame and more interested in whether the marriage provides enough money and sex. If a younger person is unhappy over these issues, he or she is less likely than prior generations to simply bear it.

China now has divorce lawyers, divorce counselors, prenuptial agreements and private detective agencies that photograph cheating spouses in the act. Several television shows about divorce have become popular among all age groups.

阅读前讨论：

1. "离婚潮"是什么意思？根据这个题目，猜猜这篇课文会讲什么？
2. 离婚对谁最不利？为什么？
3. 你觉得什么样的婚姻不应该维持？
4. 你知道哪些跟"离婚"有关的词汇？

自学生词

Match the new words in the left column with the English translation in the right column, by guessing the words' meanings from the characters that compose them.

	生词	繁体	序号	英文
( )	单亲	單親	1.	remarry
( )	缺失		2.	ex-husband
( )	重组	組	3.	external
( )	再婚		4.	alone, by oneself
( )	婚外情		5.	reconstruct, recompose
( )	前夫		6.	legal, legitimate
( )	成双成对	雙對	7.	single parent
( )	卡拉 OK		8.	extramarital affair
( )	外在		9.	not get along well
( )	不和		10.	again and again, repeatedly
( )	合法		11.	self-esteem
( )	再三		12.	in a pair, in pairs
( )	独自	獨	13.	Ministry of Civil Affairs
( )	民政部		14.	karaoke
( )	自尊		15.	lack, miss

生词

简体		繁体	拼音	词性	英文	HSK 等级
1.	成功		chénggōng	*v.*	succeed	乙
2.	羡慕		xiànmù	*v.*	admire, envy	乙
3.	不已		bùyǐ	*adv.*	endlessly, incessantly	
4.	偶然		ǒurán	*adj.*	accidental, unexpected	丙
5.	追问	問	zhuīwèn	*v.*	question closely	丁
6.	承认	認	chéngrèn	*v.*	admit, acknowledge	乙
7.	经历	經歷	jīnglì	*v.*	go through, experience	乙
8.	变故	變	biàngù	*n.*	unforeseen event or change	
9.	抚养	撫養	fǔyǎng	*v.*	foster, raise, bring up	丁
10.	渐渐	漸	jiànjiàn	*adv.*	gradually, by degrees	乙
11.	悲伤	傷	bēishāng	*adj.*	sad, sorrowful	丁
12.	俱乐部	俱樂	jùlèbù	*n.*	club	乙
13.	加入		jiārù	*v.*	join	丙
14.	成员	員	chéngyuán	*n.*	member, members	丙
15.	认可	認	rènkě	*v.*	approve of, endorse	丁
16.	灾难	災難	zāinàn	*n.*	disaster, catastrophe	丙
17.	羞耻		xiūchǐ	*n.*	shame	丁
18.	许可	許	xǔkě	*v.*	allow, permit	丁
19.	解除		jiěchú	*v.*	remove, relieve, get rid of	丁
20.	尽力	盡	jìnlì	*v.o.*	do all one can, try one's best	丙
21.	劝说	勸說	quànshuō	*v.*	persuade, advise	乙
22.	延续	續	yánxù	*v.*	continue, go on, last	丁
23.	资产	資產	zīchǎn	*n.*	property, estate; capital	丙
24.	阶级	階級	jiējí	*n.*	social class	丁
25.	情调	調	qíngdiào	*n.*	~~save worry, avoid worry~~	乙
26.	民众	眾	mínzhòng	*n.*	masses, common people	丁

简体		繁体	拼音	词性	英文	HSK 等级
27.	人士		rénshì	*n.*	person, personage, public figure	丙
28.	包容		bāoróng	*v.*	pardon; forgive; tolerate	丁
29.	因素		yīnsù	*n.*	factor, element	乙
30.	发觉	發覺	fājué	*v.*	find, detect, discover	丙
31.	不良		bùliáng	*attr.*	bad, harmful, unhealthy	丁
32.	后果	後	hòuguǒ	*n.*	consequence	丙
33.	权利	權	quánlì	*n.*	right, privilege	丙
34.	手续	續	shǒuxù	*n.*	procedures, formalities	乙
35.	简化	簡	jiǎnhuà	*v.*	simplify	丁
36.	导致	導	dǎozhì	*v.*	lead to, bring about	丙
37.	闪电	閃電	shǎndiàn	*n.*	lightning	丙
38.	式		shì	*n.*	type, style	丁
39.	吵架		chǎojià	*v.o.*	quarrel or argue vehemently	丙
40.	拥有	擁	yōngyǒu	*v.*	possess, have, own	丁
41.	继父母	繼	jìfùmǔ	*n.*	stepparents	丁
42.	潜在	潛	qiánzài	*attr.*	latent, hidden, potential	丁
43.	阴影	陰	yīnyǐng	*n.*	shadow	丁

地名

简体		繁体	拼音	词性	英文
1.	韩国	韓國	Hánguó	*p.n.*	Republic of Korea
2.	新加坡		Xīnjiāpō	*p.n.*	Singapore
3.	亚洲	亞	Yàzhōu	*p.n.*	Asia

成语和惯用语

成语/惯用语	繁体	单字解释	意思
突如其来 tū rú qí lái	來	突如：突然 其：a function word, no translation here 来：come	突然发生，出现 例：我们的假期旅游计划被这个突如其来的意外全部打破了。 Our vacation plan was completely ruined by this sudden accident.
天长地久 tiān cháng dì jiǔ	長	天：sky 地：earth 长：long 久：lasting, enduring	enduring as long as the sky and earth 例：祝我们的友谊天长地久！ （也可以说"地久天长"） May our friendship be ever-lasting!

课文

■ 第一读：掌握课文大意

快速阅读课文，看下面三个选择中哪一个最能说明本课主要意思：

1. 一个婚外恋导致离婚的故事
2. 中国的离婚潮现象
3. 离婚对社会的影响

离婚潮

　　陈红今年 42 岁，是上海一家进出口公司的管理人员。她曾经家庭幸福、事业成功，让许多人羡慕不已。她从没想到过"离婚"这个词会跟自己有什么关系。直到去年有一天，陈红偶然发现丈夫手机中有一个经常出现的电话号码，而且这个号码总是出现在自己出门后的几分钟。再三追问之下，丈夫承认了婚外情。经历了这个突如其来的变故，陈红离婚了。

　　刚离婚时，陈红心里很难受，尤其是想到自己要独自抚养 11 岁的女儿，而前夫却跟另一个女人成双成对。几个月之后，她渐渐走出了悲伤。今年情人节时，她参加了离婚者俱乐部的活动，与其他几十位离婚者一起跳舞、唱卡拉 OK。她还加入了一个有 9.1 万名成员的离婚者网站，希望再找男朋友。她说："虽然我以前选错了人，但不等于这一辈子就再没有机会了。"

　　离婚，在中国实行改革开放以前，就已经是合法的，但却不被社会普遍认可。那时人们认为，离婚给家庭带来的是灾难和羞耻。要求离婚的夫妇，除了要面对来自各方面的责备和压力以外，还必须先得到工作单位的许可，才能真正解除婚姻关系，而工作单位及亲友则常常会尽力劝说，使婚姻关系延续下去。那时候，爱情并不是婚姻关系中的重点；反而常常被认为是"资产阶级情调"。自 20 世纪 70 年代末以来，随着社会与经济的发展，政府对民众个人生活的控制不断放松，人们的婚姻观念也因此渐渐改变。社会对离婚和单身人士有了更多的包容和认可。离婚的人越来越多。国家民政部发布的统计报告显示，2008 年，全国共有 227 万对夫妻办理离婚手续，比上一年增加 17 万对。如今，离婚在中国成了一种普遍的社会现象。中国现在的离婚率已超过日本、韩国、新加坡等离婚率较高的亚洲国家。有人甚至开玩笑说，以前人们见面时互相问的是"吃了吗？"，而现在流行的问候语已经成了"离了吗？"

　　据调查，离婚率越来越高的原因有以下几点：第一，过去人们选择婚姻伴侣时重视的是对方的经济条件、家庭社会地位、长相等外在因素；而现在，人们更重视的是感情。结婚后，双方发觉感情不和时，往往会用离婚来结束婚姻。第二，女性现在的经济条件和社会地位一般和男性都差不多高，她们不再像上一代女性那样，担心离婚的不良后果。她们觉得自己有能力和权利追求幸福的生活。第三 2003 年政府对离婚手续的简化，导致了一种新的社会婚姻现象那就是"闪电式结婚"和"闪电式离婚"。报纸曾经报道过年轻人早上结婚中午吵架，下午离婚的事情。用他们的话说："不求天长地久，只求曾经拥有。"

　　离婚率增高也带来了很多不好的后果：比如，在单亲家庭里，父母一方的缺失影响到孩子的成长和对婚姻的看法；在重组家庭里，存在着孩子与继父母、或两家孩子之间的潜在矛盾；在离婚者中，不少人长期走不出孤独的阴影；另外，再婚者的离婚率也在逐年上升。

　　有关专家认为，中国的离婚潮，具有社会进步的意义，体现了女性自我意识和女性社会地位的提高。也说明人们在物质生活水平提高以后，对精神生活的期望值也相应提高。从某种程度上讲，这是迅速走向现代化的中国社会必然出现的现象。

■ 第二读：细节和理解

A．根据课文内容回答下列问题：

1. 2007 年中国共有多少对夫妻办理离婚手续？

2. 政府对离婚手续的简化是从哪一年开始的？

3. 陈红离婚的主要原因是什么？

4. 陈红是怎么走出离婚的阴影的？

5. 以前离婚夫妇需要面对哪些压力？

6. 导致现代中国人婚姻观念改变的原因是什么？

7. 中国离婚率增高的原因是什么？

8. 现在人们选择婚姻伴侣时的标准和以前有什么不同？

9. 离婚率增高会带来什么负面影响？

10. 为什么再婚者的离婚率也在逐年上升？

B．根据课文推论 (Making Inferences)：

Choose the best inference from the three possible choices for each sentence, and underline the clue(s) that helped you choose.

1. 离婚，在中国实行改革开放以前，就已经是合法的，但却不被社会普遍认可。
   a. 在中国，离婚曾经是不合法的。
   b. 以前离婚虽然合法，但是整个社会都不认可这种行为。
   c. 以前离婚虽然合法，但是只有一小部分人认可这种行为。

2. "不求天长地久，只求曾经拥有。"
   a. 长久的爱情是不可求的。
   b. 只要曾经拥有爱情，即使短暂也没有关系。
   c. 拥有爱情就是要长长久久地在一起。

3. 在重组家庭里，存在着孩子与继父母、或两家孩子之间的潜在矛盾。

    a. 重组家庭中的矛盾很激烈。

    b. 所有的重组家庭都存在矛盾。

    c. 重组家庭有可能产生矛盾。

■ 阅读技巧：归纳文章要点

Reading Skills: Outlining Main Ideas

Outlining the main ideas of a reading requires readers to engage in a careful in-context evaluation of both the big picture and the minute details, the logical relationships between them, and the text structure that organizes them. Being able to successfully outline the main ideas of a reading will enhance your reading comprehension processes.

Reading Skill Practice: Outlining Main Ideas

A. **There are six paragraphs in 离婚潮. Below are six statements of main ideas of these paragraphs, but they are not in the right order. Rearrange them by filling in the correct number of the corresponding paragraph for each, based on your understanding of the reading:**

_____ 陈红离婚后的生活

_____ 专家对离婚潮的看法

_____ 离婚的不良后果

_____ 陈红离婚的经历

_____ 离婚率升高的原因

_____ 中国社会离婚现象的改变

B. **Below is a list of the main details supporting the above main ideas in** 离婚潮**. They are not in the right order. Write out the correct numbers of the paragraphs these details appear in. Use the text to check your answersif necessary.**

_____ 陈红曾经有一个幸福的家庭

_____ 离婚对孩子有不良影响

_____ 陈红加入了离婚者俱乐部，希望再找男朋友

_____ 随着社会和经济发展，中国人婚姻观念渐渐改变

_____ 中国的离婚潮，主要具有社会进步的意义

_____ 陈红的先生有婚外情

_____ 人们对婚姻期望值的改变

_____ 陈红离婚了

_____ 妇女地位和观念的改变

_____ 陈红渐渐走出了悲伤

_____ 政府离婚政策的改变

_____ 重组家庭有潜在矛盾

_____ 以前中国人离婚很难

_____ 刚离婚时陈红很难过

_____ 现在离婚现象很普遍

_____ 离婚给有的离婚者带来痛苦

C. Now fill in the outline with the information above. (The first paragraph has been done for you as an example.)

Paragraph	Main Idea	Supporting Details
Paragraph 1	陈红离婚的经历	陈红曾经有一个幸福的家庭
		陈红的先生有婚外情
		陈红离婚了
Paragraph 2		
Paragraph 3		
Paragraph 4		
Paragraph 5		
Paragraph 6		

词汇与句型

1. 潮 • tide, trend

1. 随着移民潮的不断涌入，加拿大社会变得越来越多元化。
   With the continuous influx of tides of immigrants, Canadian society has become more and more diverse.

2. 在新一波的留学潮中，美国大学校园里增加了许多亚洲面孔。
   With the new tide of studying abroad, the number of Asian faces on American university campuses has increased.

3. 他出生于第二次世界大战后的婴儿潮时期。
   He was born in the baby boom period after the Second World War.

2. 偶然 • accidental, unexpected

1. 陈红偶然发现丈夫手机中有一个经常出现的电话号码。
   Chen Hong happened to find there was a frequently occurring phone number in her husband's cell phone.

2. 因为这个偶然的机会，她找到了理想的对象，走出了孤独的阴影。
   By this pure chance, she found an ideal lover and walked out of the shadow of loneliness.

3. 出现这种问题绝不是偶然的。
   The occurrence of such things is by no means fortuitous.

3. 再三 • repeatedly, over and over again

1. 再三追问之下，丈夫承认了婚外情。
   After repeated close inquiry, her husband admitted the extramarital affair.

2. 经过再三考虑，这对夫妻决定搬到美国去。
   After repeated consideration, this couple decided to move to the United States.

3. 他再三劝儿子维持他的婚姻关系。
   He tried over and again to persuade his son to maintain his marriage.

4. 突如其来 • arise suddenly or unexpectedly

1. 经历了这个突如其来的变故，陈红离婚了。
   Chen Hong got a divorce after this unforeseen event.

2. 我不知道如何回答这个突如其来的问题。
   I don't know how to answer this unexpected question.

3. 他们突如其来的离婚决定使孩子们非常震惊。
   Their sudden decision to divorce shocked their children.

5. 尤其 • especially, particularly

1. 离婚在中国成了一种普遍的社会现象，尤其在大城市。
   Divorce has become a common social phenomenon, especially in big cities.

2. 我喜欢游泳，尤其喜欢在大海中游泳。
   I like to swim, especially in the sea.

3. 我喜欢各种各样的水果，尤其是葡萄。
   I like various kinds of fruit, especially grapes.

6. 认可 • approve, confirm, authorize

1. 离婚虽然是合法的，但却不被社会普遍认可。
   Although divorce was legally allowed, it was not commonly accepted by society.

2. 他们的恋爱关系已经被双方家人认可。
   Their relationship has been approved by both families.

3. 这是一所官方认可的学院。
   This is an officially accredited college.

7. 情调 • feeling, sense, sentiment

1. 那时爱情并不是婚姻关系中的重点；反而常常被认为是"资产阶级情调"。
   At that time, love was not the priority of marriage. On the contrary, it was often condemned as "capitalist sentiments."

2. 这家法国餐厅充满了浪漫的情调。
   This French restaurant is full of romantic atmosphere.

3. 她的诗歌有一种简单的乡土情调。
   Her poetry has a simple rural sentiment.

8. 包容 • accept, tolerate, forgive, contain, hold, include

1. 社会对离婚和单身人士有了更多的包容和认可。
   Society has become much more tolerant and inclusive towards divorced and single people.

2. 谢谢你包容我的弱点。
   Thank you for tolerating my weaknesses.

3. 加拿大是个包容性的国家，接纳各种外来文化。
   Canada is an inclusive country; it embraces various outside cultures.

9. 导致 • lead, cause, result in

1. 政府对离婚手续的简化，导致了一种新的社会婚姻现象。
   The government's simplifying the process of divorce led to a new social phenomenon in marriage.

2. 父母离婚可能会导致孩子们消极的婚姻观。
   Parents' divorce may lead to their children's negative view of marriage.

3. 两国之间的矛盾最终导致一场战争。
   The conflict between these two countries finally resulted in a war.

10. 闪电式 • as fast as lightning, as fast as a whirlwind

1. 他俩一见钟情，谈了一场闪电式恋爱但两周后就分手了。
   They fell in love at first sight and had a whirlwind romance. But within two weeks, they broke up.

2. 敌人对我们发起一场闪电式攻击，但是没有成功。
   The enemy launched a lightning attack on us, but didn't succeed.

3. 法国总统昨天对北京做了闪电式访问，他下午一点到达北京，晚上八点离开。
   The French president had a whirlwind visit to Beijing yesterday afternoon. He arrived in Beijing at 1 p.m. and left at 8 p.m.

11. 重组 • recombine, reconstruct, reorganize

1. 在重组家庭里，存在着孩子与继父母、或两家孩子之间的潜在矛盾。
   There exist potential conflicts between the children and the stepparents, or between children of the two families in the reconstructed family.

2. 上级研究决定，下一步要对公司进行重组。
   The higher authorities decided that the next step is to restructure the company.

3. 公司重组以后，员工的工作效率明显提高。
   After the company reorganization, the employees' work efficiency has increased noticeably.

12. 潜在 • potential, latent

1. 一般来说，闪电结婚的夫妇互相不够了解，因此婚姻中存在潜在危机。
   Generally speaking, couples who had a whirlwind wedding don't know enough about each other; therefore, there is a potential crisis in their marriage.

2. 这位老师很会发现学生们的潜在才能。
   This teacher is very good at discovering students' latent talents.

3. 对我们来说，最重要的任务就是吸引潜在的投资者。
   For us, the most important task is to attract potential investors.

语法

1. 形容词副词后缀：然

然 is a classical word. It can be used as an adjective or adverb suffix, meaning "the like (…的样子, 这样, 那样)." the main meaning of the adjective or the adverb depends on the first character it is attached to. For example: 显 means "apparent, obvious"; so 显然 means "obviously." 飘 means "float in the air"; so 飘飘然 means "smug, self-satisfied, and complacent (as if being carried away and floating in the sky)." Below are some commonly used adjectives/adverbs with the suffix 然：

突	sudden	突然	adj./adv.	sudden, suddenly, abruptly
自	self, nature	自然	adj./adv.	natural, naturally
偶	by chance	偶然	adj./adv.	accidental, fortuitous, accidentally
当	should	当然	adj./adv.	as it should be, certainly
必	must, certainly	必然	adj./adv.	inevitable, inevitably, certain, certainly
忽	fast, sudden	忽然	adv.	suddenly; all of a sudden
猛	fierce, quick	猛然	adv.	suddenly, abruptly
安	peace, safe	安然	adv.	peacefully, safely, at ease
仍	still, yet, remain	仍然	adv.	still, as usual, remain the same
果	fruit, result	果然	adv.	really, as expected, sure enough

In this list, 忽然，猛然，安然，仍然，果然 can only be used as adverbs, but 突然，自然，偶然，当然，必然 can be both adjectives and adverbs.

2. 不已

已 means "to end, to stop." 不已 is used after disyllabic verbs to intensify the meaning, indicating "cannot stop doing, do something endlessly." The resulting compounds are like four-character idioms which are only used in the written language. For example:

1. 她曾经家庭幸福、事业成功，让许多人羡慕不已。
   She used to be the envy of many people, with her happy family life and successful career.

2. 这样的婚姻使他痛苦不已。
   Such a marriage makes him feel endless pain.

3. 听到儿子考上名校清华大学，他激动不已。
   He couldn't contain his excitement when he heard the news that his son was admitted to the famous Tsinghua University.

Other useful expressions with 不已:

赞叹不已　praise again and again, praise endlessly

感动不已　be overwhelmingly moved

头痛不已　feeling an endless headache

后悔不已　be overcome with regret, cannot stop regretting

伤心不已　be in deep sorrow

3. 近义词 • Synonyms

A synonym is a word that has the same or almost the same meaning as another word.

There are very few *identical synonyms* (同义词) in Chinese. They usually come from dialects or loan words. For example:

地瓜/白薯 (sweet potato)

电脑/计算机 (computer)

动画/卡通 (cartoon)

Most synonyms in Chinese are "*partial*" or "*near*" *synonyms* (近义词) which are synonymous in certain contexts but not in others. There are semantic, stylistic, regional, or other differences between them.

Synonyms offer us variety in our expression and make our language more interesting and less repetitive. However, not knowing the subtle differences between them will result in inaccurate or incorrect use. We cannot exhaust this topic in one lesson, but we are going to provide some basic knowledge of Chinese synonyms so as to help you learn how to differentiate them for appropriate usage in different contexts. If you pay close attention to vocabulary as you read or listen to authentic materials, you will gradually gain a better understanding of which word to use in which context.

The majority of Chinese synonyms have a shared character (e. g., 表示/表白忽然/突然/猛然，认可/许可，抚养/赡养) that contributes common meaning components to the synonyms.[1] The characters that are different usually give the words different connotations or stylistic senses.

For example: 许可 and 认可 both include 可, which means "to approve." But 许 (allow, permit) and 认 (recognize, acknowledge) make the two words different in the sense that 许可 is approval or permission given by an authority, while 认可 is approval or acknowledgement given by either authoritative or non-authoritative sources. The following sentences show how they are used differently.

认可/许可

1. 离婚，在中国改革开放以前，就已经是合法的，但却不被社会普遍认可。

2. 要求离婚的夫妇，……必须先得到工作单位的许可，才能解除婚姻关系。

---

[1] There are also some synonyms with completely different characters. For example: 原因/缘故，美丽/漂亮。

抚养 vs. 赡养 （抚: nurture, foster; 赡 support, provide for [elders]）

1. 他们把他当亲生孩子抚养。

2. 一对独生夫妇将承担赡养四位老人的重担。

Synonyms can be different in their **affective meanings** (their positive or negative connotations.) For example, 成果, 结果 and 后果 all include 果 (fruit, result). But 成果 (accomplishment) is a positive word, while 结果 (result) is neutral, and 后果 (consequence) is negative.

1. 这本书体现了他十多年研究的成果。

2. 我们不知道这样做会有什么结果，但只要我们尽力了，就心满意足了。

3. 只注意发展经济而不注意保护环境已经给我们带来了严重的后果！

Many synonyms are differentiated by their **stylistic differences** (formal or informal). They have the same meaning but are used in different contexts. For example: 拥有 (possess) can only be used in a formal context, while 有 (have) can be used in all contexts.

1. 这个国家拥有丰富的自然资源，应该发展很快。

2. 我有一个哥哥，两个妹妹。

Similar examples are 不已 (incessantly), 不休 (endlessly [negative]) and 不停 (unceasing).

1. 他们的幸福生活让人羡慕不已。

2. 夫妻之间要互相包容，为一点小事就争执不休只会导致不良后果。

3. 你看这雨下个不停，我们别去了吧。

There are other differences involved with synonyms such as their grammatical usage, word collocations, etc.,In order to become a fully proficient reader and writer, you should pay special attention during reading and writing to which synonyms you are reading or using.

练习

1. 语音

Write pinyin for the following underlined Chinese characters. Pay special attention to their different pronunciations in different contexts:

<u>曾</u>经（　　） 　　<u>难</u>受（　　） 　　<u>尽</u>力（　　） 　　<u>重</u>视（　　） 　　长<u>相</u>（　　）

姓<u>曾</u>（　　） 　　灾<u>难</u>（　　） 　　<u>尽</u>量（　　） 　　<u>重</u>组（　　） 　　<u>相</u>信（　　）

2. 词汇与句型

2.1. 词语搭配 Match the following words by considering their appropriate collocations.

Group One
(Verb + Object)
_____

1. 解除　_____　手续

2. 加入　_____　真相

3. 放松　_____　俱乐部

4. 简化　_____　别人

5. 追问　_____　控制

6. 指责　_____　婚姻

Group Two
(Adj. + Noun)
_____

1. 潜在　_____　阴影

2. 孤独的　_____　变故

3. 不良　_____　家庭

4. 突如其来的　_____　因素

5. 外在　_____　能力

6. 重组　_____　后果

Group Three
(Adv + Verb)
_____

1. 渐渐 _____ 维持

2. 尽力 _____ 发现

3. 再三 _____ 拥有

4. 偶然 _____ 认可

5. 曾经 _____ 追问

6. 普遍 _____ 改变

Group Four
(Noun+ Adj.)
_____

1. 家庭 _____ 严重

2. 事业 _____ 难受

3. 感情 _____ 成功

4. 离婚率 _____ 幸福

5. 心里 _____ 增高

6. 后果 _____ 不和

2.2. 选词填空

a. 延续	b. 继父	c. 拥有	d. 认可	e. 再三
f. 婚外情	g. 天长地久	h. 简化	i. 追问	j. 重组
k. 偶然	l. 情调	m. 包容性	n. 突如其来	o. 导致
p. 承认	q. 逐年	r. 手续	s. 后果	t. 渐渐地
u. 伤心不已				

1. 丈夫 _____ 的离婚要求，让她 _____。

2. 他向妻子 _____ 保证，自己并没有 _____。

3. 昨天我 _____ 发现了一家很有 _____ 的意大利饭馆。

4. 他的提议还没有得到校方的 _____。

5. 80 后"不求天长地久，只求曾经 _____"的心态 _____ 近年离婚率增高。

6. 我在一个 _____ 家庭中长大，我的两个妹妹都是 _____ 的孩子。

7. 你知道为什么"Auld Lang Syne"这首歌被翻译成"友谊 _____"吗？

8.在我们再三 _____ 下，他才 _____ 那件事是他做的。

9.春节的庆祝活动一般会 _____ 半个月。

10.加拿大是个 _____ 的国家，欢迎各种外来文化。

11.三十年前，大部分中国人还没有考虑到环境污染的严重 _____。

12.我们学校最近 _____ 了申请奖学金的 _____。

13.上海的离婚者俱乐部 _____ 增多。

14.他 _____ 适应了国外的生活。

2.3. 用要求的词汇或句型翻译下面的句子：

1. Yu Li used to have a great job that was coveted by everyone. However, she had to stay home to be a full time homemaker after her son was born. Now she can't find any job that suits her and she feels deeply regretful.（不已）

    _____

    _____

2. I have considered it over and over again and decided not to take that job.（再三）

    _____

3. The government simplified the divorce procedure. The numbers of "whirlwind weddings" and "whirlwind divorces" are therefore growing very fast.（因此）

    _____

    _____

4. Xie Wen is a literature enthusiast. He cherishes a special interest in 19th century English literature.（尤其）

    _____

5. Lao Zhang's daughter made her own decisions on her marriage and career. <u>Instead</u> of feeling bad (about not being consulted), Lao Zhang was happy about his daughter's being so capable and independent.（反而）

_____

_____

6. I'm willing to take responsibility for any <u>consequences caused</u> by this decision.（导致，后果）

_____

7. The weather forecast says that high-temperature days will <u>continue for</u> another week.（延续）

_____

3. 语法

3.1. 下面的句子应该用哪个由"然"构成的词填空？

a. 当然	b. 仍然	c. 必然	d. 突然	e. 忽然
f. 自然	g. 竟然	h. 显然	i. 果然	j. 安然
k. 猛然	l. 偶然			

1. 一直等到妈妈回来，孩子才 _____ 入睡。

2. 出门时天气还好好的，谁知道 _____ 下起了大雨，我们只好赶快跑回家。

3. 虽然经历了那么 _____ 的变故，阿兰 _____ 对生活充满了信心。

4. 陈红的父母根本不能认可她不生孩子的想法。他们说："结了婚，_____ 要生孩子，这是很 _____ 的事。既然不要孩子，那为什么要结婚呢？"

5. 环境污染 (_pollution_) 是工业化发展的 _____ 结果吗？

6. 昨天我在公共汽车上，_____ 碰到了一个老同学。他 _____ 还是 10 年前的那个老样子。当时他站在公共汽车上 _____ 睡着了，_____ 是太累了。

3.2. 用"＿＿不已"完成下列句子：

伤心不已	兴奋不已	羡慕不已	惊叹不已	后悔不已

1. 这些精美的艺术作品，使参观者 ＿＿＿＿＿＿。

2. 失去了这次机会，他 ＿＿＿＿＿＿。

3. 年轻的妈妈被迫与孩子分离，她 ＿＿＿＿＿＿。

4. 他们家的孩子又聪明又可爱，让朋友们 ＿＿＿＿＿＿。

5. 听说明年工资将增加 20%，所有的员工都 ＿＿＿＿＿＿。

3.3. 下面的句子用哪一个近义词比较合适？

1. 不休/不停/不已
   a. 她的父母常常为了生活小事而争吵 ＿＿＿＿＿，让她痛苦 ＿＿＿＿＿。
   b. 聪聪很好奇，走到哪儿小嘴都问个 ＿＿＿＿＿。

2. 抚养/赡养
   a. 许多农民工的孩子由于父母在外打工，从小由爷爷奶奶 ＿＿＿＿＿ 长大。
   b. 想想小时候父母对我们的照顾，现在我们有什么理由不好好 ＿＿＿＿＿ 父母？

3. 猛然/忽然/突然
   a. 万玲下夜班后一个人回家，＿＿＿＿＿ 路旁树林里走出一个人把她吓了一跳。
   b. 这 ＿＿＿＿＿ 的消息让她惊呆了。
   c. 他从梦中 ＿＿＿＿＿ 惊醒，发现刚才发生的一切都不是真的。不由得松了一口气。

4. 认可/许可
   a. 为了得到父母和老师对自己的 ＿＿＿＿＿，芳芳一直在努力要考进年级前三名。
   b. 未经领导的 ＿＿＿＿＿ 不能随意不上班。

5. 权力/权利
   a. 为了维护顾客的正当 ＿＿＿＿＿，商店设了一个消费者服务处。
   b. 政府官员一定得正确使用自己手中的 ＿＿＿＿＿。

6. 有/拥有/享有

a. _____ 一个完美的伴侣是许多人年轻时最大的希望。

b. 杨振宁在物理方面的研究使他在国际上 _____ 很高的声誉。

c. 每个人都 _____ 梦想，但坚持一个梦想并最终实现它却是很难的。

7. 发现/发觉

a. 她突然 _____ 身后有脚步声。

b. 世上不缺少美的事物，但缺少 _____ 美的眼睛。

8. 后果/结果

a. 有些年轻人学着抽烟，但是他们不知道抽烟的 _____ 很严重。

b. 有的学生一天到晚做功课，考试的 _____ 却很不理想；有的学生看上去学得随随便便，考出的成绩却反而很好。

4. 综合练习

4.1. 选词填空

a. 后果	b. 指责	c. 情调	d. 维持	e. 过分	f. 渐渐
g. 与此同时	h. 无异于	i. 发觉	j. 再三	k. 难免	l. 变通
m. 经历	n. 解除	o. 羡慕不已	p. 闪电式		

试离婚

"试离婚"是指夫妻双方在已准备离婚的情况下，在生活上先"离"一段时间。相当于给婚姻一个试验 (trial) 期，再决定是离还是不离。

李刚和张然是一对结婚快两年的夫妻。李刚的稳重 (steady)、张然的活泼曾经是两个人相互吸引并走上婚姻红地毯的原因。可随着新婚的甜蜜期一过，两人之间的差异就 _____ 显现出来了。李刚觉得张然想问题不够深刻，处事太随便；而张然则觉得李刚想问题 _____ 复杂，

不知 _____。两人性格不同 _____ 吵架，吵烦了，就觉得生活没有浪漫 _____，感情没有寄托。两个人都觉得自己选错了人，想要离婚。

不过，他们没有马上 _____ 婚姻，而是选择了"试离婚"。他们规定在"试离婚"期间，两人可以有自己的生活，也互不<u>干扰</u> (interfere) 对方生活，并且不能让双方的父母、同事、朋友知道。

分开的最初几天，他们俩各自尽情地享受着早就令他们 _____ 的单身贵族的生活：张然下班后可以逛街一直逛到深夜；而李刚也可以和朋友喝酒聊天到天亮都不用担心回家后要面对的 _____……自由的感觉真的太棒了！

然而，自由的单身生活给这对小夫妻带来的兴奋和刺激并没有 _____ 多久。两个星期后，他们开始想念和惦记对方。李刚的朋友们都说他最近看上去越来越不开心，他怀念张然的开朗笑声。_____，张然也常常在工作和生活中想起聪明能干的李刚的好处。_____ 了三个月的试离婚日子后，平静下来的夫妻两人同时 _____，在他们心里，对方还是像从前一样重要。经过 _____ 考虑，他们又都回到了自己的小家。两人都认为，是"试离婚"挽救了他们的婚姻。

"试离婚"的做法 _____ 是给夫妻感情一个冷静期和<u>过渡</u> (transition) 期。它的好处是可以让夫妻双方以冷静、认真的态度对待婚姻，给他们一个反思自己、反思这段婚姻的时间，重新检查两人关系，以避免在一时<u>冲动</u> (on impulse) 的情况下 _____ 离婚的不良 _____。至于那种真正不能挽救的婚姻，"试离婚"也能给双方一段心理准备的时间，让他们在真正告别这段婚姻时，有一个比较<u>平和</u> (mild, moderate) 的心态。

在"闪电式离婚"流行之时，"试离婚"说不定还真能挽救一些没有完全破碎的婚姻。

4.2. 按照上面这篇文章的意思，下面的说法对不对？(T/F)

_____ 1. "试离婚"就是离婚的一个试验期。

_____ 2. 李刚和张然性格的差异曾经是他们互相吸引对方的地方。

_____ 3. 他们吵架的原因是：李刚觉得张然不够活泼，而张然觉得李刚不够稳重。

_____ 4. 在试离婚期间，夫妻可以像单身男女一样生活。

_____ 5. 李刚和张然都很喜欢试离婚的自由生活。

_____ 6. 李刚和张然的父母不同意他们试离婚。

_____ 7. 经过了三个月的试离婚后，李刚和张然能冷静地考虑他们的关系了。

_____ 8. 试离婚的好处就是可以避免离婚的不良后果。

_____ 9. 如果没有试离婚，李刚和张然可能会因离婚而后悔。

_____ 10. 试离婚不能挽救所有的婚姻。

5. 阅读练习

阅读短文（一）
"闪婚"和"短婚"

3 秒钟可以走两米，现在的年轻人却说，3 秒钟足够爱上一个人；5 分钟可以喝一杯咖啡，现在的年轻人却说 5 分钟足够谈一场恋爱；13 小时可以坐飞机从中国飞到美国，现在的年轻人却说，13 小时足够确定伴侣结一次婚。

27 岁的小汤与 28 岁的小黄，认识 7 小时就决定结婚了。今年 8 月 1 日上午 8 时，小汤在网上聊天室 (chat room) 向一位叫小黄的姑娘讲了他的失恋经历。小黄说："他失恋了，就全部告诉我，这么实在 (honest) 的人，现在可不多了。"下午 3 点，小汤又在网上跟小黄聊天说："我当时特别喜欢唱《你到底爱谁》，尤其是'求求你给个机会'那句。"小黄说："我可以给你个机会。"于是，他俩约好第二天中午见面，去登记结婚。3 天后，就结婚了。

这就是"闪婚族"的观念。"闪婚"就是说从相识到结婚的时间非常短，就像闪电一样快。现在，人的生命越来越长，从恋爱到婚姻的过程却越来越短。网恋、一夜情、"闪婚"等现象在一些大中城市出现，"闪婚族"认为，现代社会的恋爱、婚姻是一种个人行为，自己的感觉最重要，合适就结婚，不合适就离婚。

"闪婚"现象也带来了"短婚"和"闪离"。2006 年，北京共有 24,952 对夫妻离婚，其中五分之一结婚不到 3 年，三分之一在结婚 5 年内离婚；有 970 对结婚不到 1 年就离婚，有 52 对结婚还不到 1 个月就离婚。在这些离婚夫妻中，"80 后"占了相当大的比例。而在这些"80 后"离婚者中，有 90% 夫妻双方都是独生子女。

与上一代不同的是，面对离婚，他们不吵不闹，表现得很平静，离婚后，还可以像朋友一样来往。在这些年轻人眼中，离婚已不是悲剧 (tragedy)，反而似乎是社会进步的表现。

5.1. 根据短文填写下列数据：

北京 2006 年离婚者婚史				
离婚总数	结婚不到 1 月	结婚不到 1 年	结婚不到 3 年	结婚不到 5 年
24,952 对				

5.2. 根据短文内容，选择最佳答案回答问题

1. 上面的数据说明，
   a. 离婚夫妻中，"80 后"占了相当大的比例。
   b. 离婚者中，有 90% 夫妻双方都是独生子女。
   c. "闪婚"现象带来了"短婚"和"闪离"。
   d. 以上都对。

2. 关于小汤和小黄，下面哪项<u>不正确</u>？
   a. 他俩是在网上聊天时认识的。
   b. 小汤特别喜欢唱《你到底爱谁》。
   c. 小汤比小黄大一岁。
   d. 他俩决定结婚时还没见过面。

3. 根据短文内容，"闪婚族"指的是 _____
   a. 逃避 (escape) 结婚的人。
   b. 决定结婚的速度像闪电 (lightning) 一样快的人。
   c. 从恋爱到婚姻的过程不到 3 天的人。
   d. 很快结婚也很快离婚的人。

4."闪婚"现象造成什么后果？

　　a. 夫妻结婚后不久就离婚。

　　b. 一夜情现象增多。

　　c. 离婚后的人还可以像朋友一样来往。

　　d. 人的生命越来越长。

5. 这一代离婚的年轻人与上一代人有什么不同？

　　a. 面对离婚，他们不吵不闹，表现得很平静。

　　b. 离婚后，他们还可以像朋友一样来往。

　　c. 他们认为，离婚不是悲剧，而是社会进步的表现。

　　d. 以上都是。

阅读短文（二）
中国近代 4 次离婚潮

近半个多世纪以来，中国经历了 4 次"离婚潮"。

第一次：1950 年至 1956 年

当时第一部《婚姻法》刚刚实行，许多传统式婚姻关系，如一夫多妻、包办婚姻 (arranged marriage) 等因而解体 (breakup)。此外，一些干部进城后，纷纷跟原来的农村妻子离婚。这两个因素造成了中国近代史上的第一次离婚大潮，据统计，1951 年到 1956 年期间全国大约有 600 万对夫妇离婚。

第二次：文化大革命

文化大革命这一时期的离婚大多是出自政治原因。在文革期间，成千上万的人被打成"阶级敌人 (enemy)"。他们的妻子或丈夫在"与阶级敌人划清界线 (dividing line)"的压力下，不得不离婚。也有一些人为了子女的命运和前途，被迫离婚。据统计，这十年中"政治离婚"的夫妻高达 180 万对。

第三次：80 年代

第三次离婚潮发生于 80 年代，是在文革结束以后。文革这一特殊时期，由于政治原因出现了大量凑合家庭，夫妻关系不是靠感情建立起来的，被称为"文革婚姻"。还有一种情况则是<u>上山下乡</u>[2]的政策造成的。文革中，千百万城市青年被下放到农村，其中一些人在农村结婚成家。文革后由于各种各样的原因，很多知青婚姻解体。

第四次：21 世纪初

近年来出现的第四次离婚浪潮是社会、经济、道德各方面变化的综合反映。国家民政部发布的《2008 年民政事业发展统计报告》显示，2008 年，全国平均每 4 对夫妻结婚之时，就有一对夫妻分手。而大城市和经济发达省市，离婚率比全国平均数字更高。跟以前三次离婚潮不同的是，这一次离婚潮大部分是女方首先提出离婚。官方的一项调查表明，在广东省，女方提出离婚的情况占到 70%。女方提出离婚的最主要理由是丈夫"婚外情"。此外，家庭矛盾不可调和、家庭经济原因、双方个性问题都是离婚因素。值得注意的另一个现象是：由于家庭<u>暴力</u> (*violence*) 的因素导致离婚的数量有了十分明显的上升，而家庭暴力问题在过去则是另一个很少有人有勇气讨论的<u>禁区</u> (*forbidden zone*)。

5.3. 根据短文内容，选择最佳答案回答问题

1. 第一次离婚潮产生的原因是：
   a.《婚姻法》的实行
   b. 旧式婚姻关系的解除
   c. 干部和农村妻子离婚
   d. 以上都是

2. 文化大革命时期夫妻离婚的主要原因是：
   a. 夫妇感情不和
   b. 子女要求父母离婚
   c. 迫于政治压力
   d. 子女的命运不好

---

[2]知识青年上山下乡：A movement under a directive from Mao Zedong, then leader of China, of "going to mountain areas and the countryside" set off on December 12, 1968. 17 million urban youth went or were forced to go to work in the countryside and mountainous areas during the years from 1968 to 1980. Ironically, although 知识青年 referred to young people with education, the vast majority of those who migrated had only received elementary to high school education.

3. "文革婚姻"指的是：

　　a. 文革结束以后的婚姻

　　b. 经历了文革的婚姻

　　c. 文革期间的凑合婚姻

　　d. 文革期间结束的婚姻

4. 以下哪种说法是正确的?

　　a. 第四次离婚潮的原因是妻子有婚外恋。

　　b. 2008 年全国的离婚率是 25%。

　　c. 在中国，女性提出离婚的情况占 70%。

　　d. 家庭暴力一直都是人们讨论的热点。

5. 这篇短文的主题是：

　　a. 中国的离婚率的改变

　　b. 中国的离婚潮现象及其形成原因

　　c. 中国一共有四次离婚潮

　　d. 中国每次的离婚潮都不相同

6. 口语练习

6.1. 讨论题

1. 离婚率增高是社会进步还是落后的表现?

2. 课文说中国以前离婚很不自由，但是为什么又出现过几次"离婚潮"?

3. 如果一对夫妻已经没有感情，应不应该为了孩子而维持婚姻?

4. 对孩子来说，是留在一个父母天天吵架的家庭好还是生活在离异的家庭好?

5. 有人说"没有爱情的婚姻是不道德的婚姻"，这种婚姻不道德在什么地方?

6. 有人说"离婚的父母是自私的父母"，请说说这些父母自私在什么地方?

7. 如果一个人已经离过几次婚，他/她再婚的结果会怎样?

8. 为什么现在提出离婚的大多是女性？这说明了什么？

9. 重组家庭会有些什么样的潜在矛盾？怎样才能避免这些矛盾发生？

10. 谈谈你对"试婚"的看法。

6.2. 辩论题：离婚率上升是社会进步还是落后的表现？

With a group of classmates, organize a debate about the topic. Each debate team should prepare their arguments ahead of time. Try to guess what the other side's arguments will be. Fill out this table to help you organize:

离婚率上升是社会进步的表现	离婚率上升是社会落后的表现

You can use this outline to organize the debate:

甲方 (Side 1): Opening statement, 2 minutes

乙方 (Side 2): Opening statement, 2 minutes

甲方 : Main argument, 3 minutes

乙方 : Main argument, 3 minutes

甲方 : Counterargument to Side 2's arguments, 3 minutes

乙方 : Counterargument to Side 1's arguments, 3 minutes

甲方 : Closing statement, 2 minutes

乙方 : Closing statement, 2 minutes

At the end of the debate, everyone in the class should vote on which side won the debate.

7. 写作练习（550-650 字）

作文题：（任选一题）

离婚对孩子的影响。

离婚潮对社会的影响。

什么样的婚姻是不应该维持的婚姻？

Write an expository essay on one of the topics above. Use the following table to create an outline of the main ideas and supporting details. You can alter the structure of the essay if needed. Try to use as many new words and expressions as possible.

Topic of Essay: _____

Paragraph	Main idea	Supporting Details
Paragraph 1	Introduction	
Paragraph 2		
Paragraph 3		
Paragraph 4		
Paragraph 4	Conclusion	

中国经济发展动态

课文提要

China, which was at a very low level of economic development before 1949, has become one of the world's major economic powers with a greatly improved overall standard of living. Especially in the years following reform and opening-up in 1978, China's economy developed at an unprecedented rate, and that momentum has held steady into the twenty-first century. The secure job in state run businesses, or so-called "Iron Rice Bowl" has been one of the casualties of China's transition to a market economy, while private business has become the fastest-growing sector of China's economy, expanding at an annual rate of 20 percent. China's GDP is growing by 10 percent a year. Industrial production is galloping ahead at an annual rate of 17 per cent. Its economy is now the second-biggest in the world, behind only the United States, and there are predictions that it will assume the top spot as early as 2020.

China's explosive growth has come at a price, however. The growing gap between rich and poor, corruption among government officials, and staggering environmental problems are just a few of the big challenges that China is facing.

阅读前讨论：

1. 据你所知，中国经济发展经历了什么变化？
2. 从哪些方面可以看出中国经济的发展？请举例说明。
3. 经济的繁荣会对社会产生什么影响？
4. 你知道哪些跟"经济、经济发展"有关的词语？

自学生词

Match new words in the left column with the English translation in the right column, by guessing the words' meanings from characters that compose them. (The first one is done for you).

	生词	繁体	序号	英文
( )	安全感		1.	national economy
( )	失业	業	2.	values
( )	国民	國	3.	businessman, merchant
( )	个体	個體	4.	Hong Kong, Macao, and Taiwan
( )	商品经济	經濟	5.	open a business
( )	商人		6.	be unemployed, lose one's job
( )	开张	開張	7.	commodity economy
( )	知识分子	識	8.	people of a nation
( )	国民经济	國經濟	9.	individual, individuality
( )	港澳台	臺	10.	sense of security
( )	价值观念	價觀	11.	intellectual

生词

	简体	繁体	拼音	词性	英文	HSK 等级
1.	动态	動態	dòngtài	n.	trend, development, situation	丁
2.	悄悄		qiāoqiāo	adv.	gently, softly, stealthily	乙
3.	国营	國營	guóyíng	attr.	state-run	丙
4.	指标	標	zhǐbiāo	n.	target, quota	丙

	简体	繁体	拼音	词性	英文	HSK 等级
5.	收购	購	shōugòu	v.	purchase, buy	丁
6.	销售	銷	xiāoshòu	v.	sell, market	丁
7.	效率		xiàolǜ	n.	efficiency	乙
8.	体制	體	tǐzhì	n.	system of organization	丁
9.	非		fēi	adv.	not, no, non-, un-	丙
10.	其		qí	pron.	(classical) he, she, it, his, her, its	丙
11.	经商	經	jīngshāng	v.o.	engage in trade, be in business	丁
12.	涌现	現	yǒngxiàn	v.	emerge in large numbers	丁
13.	发挥	發揮	fāhuī	v.	bring into play, give free rein	乙
14.	股票		gǔpiào	n.	stock, stock certificate	丁
15.	上市		shàngshì	v.o.	go (appear) on the market	
16.	规模	規	guīmó	n.	scale, scope, extent	乙
17.	类型	類	lèixíng	n.	type, category	丙
18.	交易		jiāoyì	n.	deal, trade, transaction	丙
19.	繁荣	榮	fánróng	adj.	flourishing, prosperous	乙
20.	纯	純	chún	adj.	pure	丙
21.	多余	餘	duōyú	adj.	superfluous, extra, unnecessary	丙
22.	存		cún	v.	save, deposit	乙
23.	物质	質	wùzhì	n.	matter, substance, material	乙
24.	一向		yīxiàng	adv.	all along, the whole time, constantly	丙
25.	轻视	輕視	qīngshì	v.	despise, look down on	丙
26.	民谣	謠	mínyáo	n.	folk rhyme, folklore	
27.	灵活	靈	línghuó	adj.	flexible	乙
28.	心目		xīnmù	n.	mind, mind's eye	
29.	奇迹	跡	qíjì	n.	miracle	丙
30.	平衡		pínghéng	adj.	balanced	丙
31.	差距		chājù	n.	gap, disparity	丁
32.	腐败	敗	fǔbài	adj.	corrupt, rotten, decadent	丁
33.	污染		wūrǎn	v./n.	pollute, contaminate, pollution	乙
34.	机遇	機	jīyù	n.	opportunity	丁
35.	难怪	難	nánguài	adv.	no wonder	丙

成语和惯用语

成语/惯用语	繁体	单字解释	意思
翻天覆地 fān tiān fù dì		翻：turn over 天：the sky 覆：overturn 地：the earth	turn the world upside down, earthshaking, a tremendous change 例：像这样翻天覆地的变化一定会产生深远的 影响。 Such an earthshaking change must have far-reaching effects.
养家糊口 yǎng jiā hú kǒu	養	养：support 家：family 糊口：survive with only porridge, keep body and soul together	manage to support one's family 例：他们家以前很穷。全家人就靠他父亲一人 教书养家糊口。 Their family used to be very poor. The whole family depended on his father's teaching job to survive.
前所未有 qián suǒ wèi yǒu		前：以前 所：grammatical particle 未有：没有	unprecedented 例：我们正面临前所未有的挑战。 We are facing unprecedented challenges.
欣欣向荣 xīn xīn xiàng róng	榮	欣欣：thriving 向：towards 荣：flourishing	thriving, flourishing, growing more prosperous 例：各行各业都欣欣向荣。 Every trade is thriving.
雨后春笋 yǔ hòu chūn sǔn	後筍	雨后：after rain 春：spring 笋：bamboo shoots	(of good things) spring up like bamboo shoots after rain 例：新建的高楼大厦就像雨后春笋一般立了 起来。 New high-rises have sprung up like bamboo shoots after rain.
日新月异 rì xīn yuè yì	異	日：day 新：new 月：month 异：different	flourish [change] with each passing day 从传统到现代，从书本到网络，外语学习方式 日新月异。 From traditional to modern, from using books to internet, the ways we learn foreign languages are constantly changing.
突飞猛进 tū fēi měng jìn	飛進	突：dash forward 飞：fly 猛：fierce, vigorous 进：advance	advance swiftly and vigorously, make remarkable progress 汽车制造业的科技发展突飞猛进。 The science and technology of automobile production has made remarkable progress.

成语/惯用语	繁体	单字解释	意思
重文轻商 zhòng wén qīng shāng	轻	重 : value highly 文 : man of letters, scholar, liberal arts 轻 : hold in contempt 商 : commerce, merchant	look up to scholars and down on merchants 例 : 在中国数千年历史中，重文轻商始终是主流思潮。 For thousands of years in Chinese history, it was always the mainstream ideological trend to look up to scholars and down on merchants.

课文

■ 第一读：掌握课文大意

快速阅读课文，看下面三个选择中哪一个最能说明本课主要意思：

1. 中国经济的走势和发展
2. 中国经济体制的改革
3. 中国经济的发展及其影响

中国经济发展动态

中国自 1978 年改革开放与发展私有经济以来，发生了翻天覆地的变化。国民经济欣欣向荣，人们生活水平不断提高，中国人的传统社会价值观念和就业选择也悄悄地改变。

改革以前，中国企业基本上都是国营企业，实际上是在政府控制下的"生产单位"，没有独立性，更没有创造性。它们的生产指标由政府统一规定，产品由政府统一收购、统一销售，利润由政府统一分配。对很多人来说，工作只是"吃大锅饭[1]"，"干好干坏一个样，干多干少一个样"，所以国营企业的效率非常低。这种情况导致了 70 年代末的经济体制改革。

---

[1]大锅饭: eat from the same big rice pot: a distribution system started in 1958 when the People's Commune Movement tried to transform China quickly from a socialist system to a communist system. Organized along paramilitary and labor-saving lines, the communes had shared kitchens where everyone ate in the canteen, the same as everyone else. Later the phrase became a metaphor of egalitarian treatment of enterprises and individuals, regardless of their performance.

在改革期间，政府在政策和法律上，明确地认可了非国有经济市场的地位，并对其采取保护政策。非国有经济在这段时间实现了突破性的发展，个人经商、大型私人企业和中外合资企业如雨后春笋般涌现出来。中国人被压抑多年的生产力和创造力终于得到发挥。公司股票上市的规模也不断扩大，更有了各种类型的交易市场。国家建设日新月异，经济发展突飞猛进。从 1978 年到 2008 年，中国经济一直保持着 10% 的年平均增长率。

繁荣的商品经济大大提高了中国人的收入水平和生活水平。从 1978 到 2008 年，中国人均纯收入增长了 6 倍。消费市场内容更加丰富、质量全面提高。中国人住房条件明显改善，私人汽车也正在快速进入百姓家庭。现在人们不仅把多余的钱存在银行里，还在股票市场和房地产市场投资。与此同时，人们的社会价值观念也有了很大的改变。中国人一向"重文轻商"，知识分子受人尊敬，商人却被人看不起。而现在，商人的社会地位达到了前所未有的高度，他们的生活水平也远远超过知识分子，成为人们羡慕的对象。现在"经商"不但不再被人轻视，反而成为新一代人的追求。社会上甚至流传起"十亿人民九亿商，还有一亿要开张"的民谣。

经济发展也改变了人们的择业观。上世纪 50 年代到 80 年代期间，中国人最向往的就是能有一个国有单位里稳定的"铁饭碗"。那时，有了"铁饭碗"才有安全感。但是在今天的中国人心目中，"铁饭碗"已经渐渐失去了价值。90 年代以来，经济市场的需要为人们创造了比较灵活的就业市场，也为人们提供了多样化的工作。所以工作不再只是为了养家糊口，更重要的是为了实现事业上的理想，并过上高质量的生活。因此，兴趣、收入及发展前途成了一般人选择职业的第一考虑，而稳定性就没有过去那么重要了。

2009 年，中国国内生产总值 (GDP) 达到世界第三位。（虽然在人均生产总值方面，中国仍然排在 100 名之后，仍属于发展中国家。）中国在创造经济奇迹的同时，也产生了经济发展不平衡，贫富差距增大，政府官员腐败，环境污染等等问题。要解决这些问题，中国还有很长一段路要走。难怪有人说，中国经济现在是处在一个"机遇前所未有，挑战也前所未有"的时代。

■ 第二读：细节和理解

A．根据课文内容回答下列问题：

1. 改革以前的中国企业有什么特点？

2. 改革以后的中国企业有什么变化？

3. "非国有经济" 指的是什么？

4. "重文轻商" 是什么意思？

5. 经济繁荣以后人们的生活发生了什么改变？

6. 中国人对商人这一职业的看法是怎样改变的？

7. "铁饭碗" 指的是什么？有什么特点？

8. 为什么 "铁饭碗" 在今天的中国人心中已经渐渐失去了价值？

9. 现在的中国人的择业特点是什么？

10. 中国经济面临哪些挑战？

B．根据课文推论：

Choose the best inference from the three possible choices for each sentence, and underline the clue(s) that helped you choose.

1. 对很多人来说，工作只是 "吃大锅饭"，"干好干坏一个样，干多干少一个样"，所以国营企业的效率非常低。

   a. 国营企业的效率非常低是因为所有的人都在一个大锅里吃饭。

   b. 国营企业的效率非常低是因为大家的工作都一样。

   c. 国营企业的效率非常低是因为工作努力的人得不到应该有的报酬。

2. 社会上甚至流传起"十亿人民九亿商，还有一亿要开张"的民谣。
   a. 民谣的意思是现在中国每个人都想经商。
   b. 民谣的意思是现在中国有十亿人口经商。
   c. 民谣的意思是现在中国有十九亿人口经商。

3. 但是在今天的中国人心目中，"铁饭碗"已经渐渐失去了价值。
   a. 现在"铁饭碗"越来越便宜。
   b. 现在"铁饭碗"已经不能再吸引人。
   c. 现在"铁饭碗"越来越少。

■ 阅读技巧：写文章摘要

Reading Skills: Summarizing Main Ideas

Being able to determine the important and less important ideas in a text is an essential reading skill. The act of summarizing entails rethinking what you have read, prioritizing ideas and then conveying them in a more condensed manner. Summarizing requires readers to review information effectively and communicate precisely. This skill can be utilized for your future reading, note-taking and writing. Previewing, skimming and reading carefully for the main idea and details will all help you prepare a good summary.

The length of the summary depends on the length of the original article and your needs. It can be a few sentences, one short paragraph or a few paragraphs.

写段落大意 • Summarizing a Paragraph

A paragraph summary should be one to two sentences long. It should express the main idea of the paragraph in a simple way. Often this is already stated by the author in the topic sentence of the paragraph. However, sometimes you may need to simplify or add to the topic sentence to make a good summary. If the author didn't write a topic sentence, you need to skim the paragraph and decide what the main idea is.

Example: Re-read the first paragraph of 中国经济发展动态 and the summary below. Notice how most of the details of the paragraph are left out of the summary. Only the most important ideas are kept in the summary.

Original Paragraph: 中国自 1978 年改革开放与发展私有经济以来，国民经济欣欣向荣，人们生活水平不断提高，中国人的传统社会价值观念和就业选择也悄悄地发生了变化。

Summary: 中国改革开放发展了国民经济，人们生活水平与价值观念都有了变化。

Now summarize the rest of the paragraphs in the article. Write your summaries (one or two sentences each) in the spaces below. When you have finished, compare your summaries with another student's.

Paragraph 2: _____

_____

Paragraph 3: _____

_____

Paragraph 4: _____

_____

Paragraph 5: _____

_____

Paragraph 6: _____

_____

Reading Skill Practice: Summary of the article

Writing the summary of the article should be easy after you have completed the Reading Skill Practice Exercises above. Use the key words below to write a summary of 中国经济发展动态. Write about five to six sentences.

改革开放	非国有经济	经济发展	生活水平
社会价值观念	择业观	挑战	

_____

_____

_____

_____

词汇与句型

1. 动态 • (n.) developments, tendency, trends (adj.) dynamic, in motion

1. 在对自然风光的描写中，静态描写和动态描写都是必不可少的。
   To portray natural scenery, depictions of static objects and objects in motion are both indispensable.

2. 需要注意的是，地势地形不是一成不变的，而是处于不停的动态发展中的。
   It is important to keep in mind that topography is not fixed and static, but in a process of endless dynamic development.

3. 本栏目向您报道世界各地的最新文化动态。
   Our program reports for you the latest developments in cultural news from around the world.

2. 雨后春笋 • (of new things) spring up like bamboo shoots after rain

This is a metaphoric idiom usually used with 如……般 as an adverbial phrase to describe things emerging (like bamboo shoots) on a large scale and at a fast speed.

1. 80年代到90年代期间，个人经商、大型私人企业和中外合资企业如雨后春笋般涌现出来。
   During the 80s and 90s, small individual private businesses, large private enterprises and Sino-foreign joint venture enterprises burgeoned enormously.

2. 自从政府大规模投资建房以后，新公寓和办公楼就如雨后春笋般迅速建起来。
   Since the government made a vast investment in housing, new apartment buildings and office buildings have been mushrooming rapidly.

3. 随着就业竞争的日益激烈，各类职业高中如雨后春笋般纷纷出现。
   With the increasingly severe employment competition, various vocational high schools sprang up like bamboo shoots.

3. 体现 • (v.) embody, incarnate, reflect (n.) embodiment

1. 商品经济从2000年起加速发展，不但体现在增长速度上，还体现在广度上。
   The rapid growth of the commodity economy since 2000 was manifested not only in the speed of its growth, but also in its breadth.

2. 这首诗体现了作者对大自然的向往和热爱。
   This poem expresses the author's yearning and love for Nature.

3. 如今，环保意识的提高已被认为是社会文明的体现。
   The raising of environmental awareness is now regarded as a reflection of social civilization.

体现 vs. 表现

体现 is the embodiment of a concept or attitude by an object, thing, or phenomenon, but

表现 is more about human beings' subjective showing or acting.

4. 在危险面前，平时矜持的约翰反而表现得非常勇敢。
   In time of danger, John, who was usually reserved and shy, acted very bravely.

5. 令我不快的是，她总是喜欢在别人面前表现自己。
   What bugs me is that she always likes to show off in front of others.

4. 个体…… ● individual; individual-run... (in contrast to state-owned)

1. 一般来说，个体企业的运营成本比大型企业低很多。
   Generally speaking, the operating costs of an individual proprietor are much lower than that of a large-scale enterprise.

2. 我想尝试做个体户，自己既当老板又当伙计，灵活也自由。
   I am thinking of trying to run a self-employed business, owned and operated all by myself; [I would have] more freedom and more flexibility.

3. 爸爸从前在国有企业工作，后来辞职干起了个体（户）。
   Father used to work in a state-owned enterprise, and then he resigned and became an individual proprietor.

5. 经商…… ● run business, engage in business

1. 现在"经商"不但不再被人轻视，反而成为新一代人的追求。
   Nowadays, "running a business" is not despised by people any more, but on the contrary, it is being pursued among the new generation.

2. 小赵很善于经商。他经营的快餐店开张不到一年，利润就突破 30 万。
   Xiao Zhao is very good at business. His fast-food restaurant has only been open for less than a year, yet its profit has exceeded ¥300,000.

3. 乔治来中国经商多年，结交了不少商界的朋友。
   George has been doing business in China for years. He has made quite a few friends in the business world.

6. ⋯⋯制（制度）· ...system

1. 我市的股份制企业相对去年增长了 8%。
   The number of joint-stock enterprises in our city increased by 8% compared to last year.

2. 一夫一妻制在世界许多国家都是由法律确定的。
   Monogamy is mandated by law in many countries.

3. 有人说恢复私有制是中国经济发展的真正源泉，你同意吗？
   Some people say that the reestablishment of the private ownership system in China is the real source of China's economic growth. Do you agree?

7. 更⋯⋯ · more…, even more…, what's more

1. 你再不停止，后果会更严重。
   If you don't stop now, the outcome may be worse.

2. 打电话的人不可能是小赵，更不可能是小王，因为小王一直和我在一起。
   Xiao Zhao can't be the one who made the phone call. Xiao Wang is even less possible, because Xiao Wang was with me the whole time.

3. 由于父母的溺爱，很多独生子女不但缺乏独立生活的能力，而且在困难和挫折面前心理素质较差，更养成了以自我为中心、不尊重长辈的个性。
   Due to parents' overindulgence, many only children not only lack independent living abilities, but also are psychologically unable to deal with difficulty and failure. What's worse, they are typically self-centered and disrespect elders.

8. 一向 · constantly, all along, earlier on, lately

1. 妈妈一向舍不得花钱，总是尽量省下来存在银行里。
   Mom has been hesitant to spend money all along. She always tried to save and deposit it in the bank.

2. 提高就业率一向是我省的工作重点之一。
   Increasing the employment rate has always been one of the focuses of work in our province.

3. 不知道为什么我这一向心情很不好。
   I don't know why I have been in such a bad mood lately.

一向 vs. 一直

1. 一向 and 一直 both mean "always, consistently, all along" during a period from the past to the present. In this sense, they are interchangeable. For example:

   他一向很独立。（= 他一直很独立。）

   我妈妈身体一向很好，可是昨天忽然病倒了。（= 我妈妈身体一直很好，可是昨天忽然病倒了。）

2. When the focus is on the time frame (i.e., lately, earlier on), only 一向 can be used. In this case, 这 or 前 is usually used with 一向. When the focus is on the continuous, consistent action or state, only 一直 can be used. 一直 also means "straight forward", but 一向 doesn't have this meaning. For example:

   你这一向口语进步很快。(not 一直)
   You have made big progress in oral proficiency recently.

   昨天晚上他看书一直看到晚上十一点。(not 一向)
   He was reading up to 11pm last night.

   从这儿一直往前走就是火车站。(not 一向)
   Walk straight ahead and you will reach the train station.

Collocations:

	前/这~	~很好	~热情	~工作到半夜	~不放心	~咳嗽	~往前走
一向	✔	✔	✔	x	x	x	x
一直	x	✔	✔	✔	✔	✔	✔

9. 重 A 轻 B • regard A as superior to B, value A more than B

重文轻商/重文轻武/重文轻理/重理轻文/重男轻女

1. 中国人"重文轻商"的传统观念到 80 年代才开始动摇。
   The traditional Chinese notion of regarding intellectuals as superior to businessmen started to shake in the 80s.

2. 中国古代曾一度重文轻武、重文轻理，如今随着国家和社会对科技的日益重视，学校教育重理轻文的趋势越来越明显。
   In ancient China, literature was valued more than martial arts and science. At present, as the country and society have attached more and more importance to science and technology, the tendency to value science more than liberal arts has become increasingly salient in school education.

3. 21 世纪的今天，传统的"重男轻女"观念仍对女性的就业有所影响。
   In today's twenty-first century, the traditional notion of valuing male more than female still has an influence on women's employment.

10. 前所未有 • unprecedented

1. 改革以来，由于经济迅速发展，商人的社会地位提高到前所未有的地步。
   Since the beginning of the economic reform, the social status of businessmen has been raised to an unprecedented level because of the rapid economic development.

2. 经济全球化为某些企业创造了前所未有的发展机遇。
   Economic globalization has provided unprecedented opportunities for the development of some enterprises.

3. 今年我校的毕业生就业率为 90%，这在我校历史上是前所未有的。
   This year, the employment rate of our school's graduates is 90%, which is unprecedented in our school's history.

11. 养家糊口 • bring home the bacon, support one's family financially

1. 就业不再只是为了养家糊口，更重要的是为了实现事业上的理想抱负，并过上高质量的生活。
   Seeking employment is not only for bringing home the bacon. More importantly, it is for realizing one's career ideals and ambitions and living a life of high quality.

2. 父亲去世后，为了养家糊口，哥哥不得不放弃学业，去城里找了份工作。
   After Father's death, to support the whole family, my elder brother had to drop out of school and went to the city to find a job.

3. 对小王来说，在餐馆打工只是份暂时养家糊口的工作，不是一辈子的事业。他的职业理想是成为一名优秀的画家。
   For Xiao Wang, working at the restaurant is just a temporary job to bring home the bacon, not a life career. His career dream is to become an excellent artist.

12. 难怪 • no wonder

1. 窗户都打开了，难怪风这么大！
   All the windows are open, no wonder it's so windy!

2. 难怪找不到人，都开会去了。
   No wonder you can't find anybody here; they're all away at a meeting.

3. 她是新来的，难怪我不认识她。
   She's new here. No wonder I don't know her.

13. 非…… • non-, un-, in- (negation marker)

1. 80 年代到 90 年代期间，政府在政策和法律上，明确地认可了非国有经济市场的地位，并采取保护政策。
   During the 80s and 90s, the market of the non-state-owned [i.e. privatized] economy was recognized and protected by governmental policies and laws.

2. 为了方便非专业读者理解，缩写词汇在书中第一次出现时需要完整拼写。
   To make it accessible for non-professional readers, acronyms need to be spelled out when they first appear in the book.

3. 这种打招呼方式只适合非正式场合。
   Such ways of greeting are only suitable for informal occasions.

语法

1. 书面否定词 • Literary Markers of Negation

You already know that the most familiar negation markers in Chinese are 不, 没 (有), and 别. But there are some other characters in Chinese that can also mark negation. They are originally classical words, but are still used in modern Chinese language, especially in a formal context. They can function almost like the English negative prefixes (e.g., il-, im-, in-, ir-, non-, un-, dis- etc.) to form verbs, nouns, adjectives, adverb, conjunctions, and idiomatic expressions such as 成语. Some of the words or expressions formed by them have been so conventionalized that we no longer associate them with their classical origin. For example, 非常 is composed of 非 (not) and 常 (usual, common), which means "unusual, uncommon" and is frequently used in spoken Chinese.

These negation markers are also used in public signs, notices, advertisement and formal documents. For example, a sign "请勿 (not) 入内" tells you not to enter or trespass, while an official form will probably request you to make a choice between 是 (yes) or 否 (no). Knowing the meanings and functions of literary negative markers will help you extend your vocabulary and learn the formal style of Chinese language.

The following table lists some frequently used literary negation markers:

否定词	意思	例			
非	不、不是	非法 illegal	非官方消息 unofficial news	非城市居民 non-city residents	非人待遇 inhuman treatment
无	没有、不	无能 incapable	无理 unreasonable	无比 incomparable	无论 no matter
未	没、不	未成年 underage	未婚 unmarried	未来 future	未定 undecided
否	不	是否 is...or not?	能否 can...or not?	可否 may...or not?	否则 otherwise	否定 negate
勿	不要	请勿入内 do not enter	请勿吸烟 no smoking		

2. 成语（一）• Idioms/Set Phrases (A)

成语 ("set phrases") are a type of Chinese idiomatic expressions, most of which consist of four characters. They are all terse, concise and expressive. Many of them contain profound philosophy and interesting, entertaining stories calling for deep thought. Appropriate application of 成语 in speaking and writing can greatly enhance the vividness and effectiveness of your expression. They are mostly used in written Chinese but can also be employed in oral communication, which can increase the degree of formality and elegance. (However, the effect can only be achieved with appropriate use.)

The meaning of a 成语 usually surpasses the sum of the meanings carried by the four characters, as 成语 are intimately linked with the classical literature, story or historical fact from which they were derived. Often the four characters reflect the moral behind a story rather than the story itself (e.g., 对牛弹琴、画蛇添足、自相矛盾).

On the other hand, some 成语 are free of metaphorical nuances because they are not derived from a specific occurrence in history; rather, they are concise in their original meaning and could be understood by an individual familiar with formal written Chinese.

The typical features of 成语 are:

▶ **Form:**   **condensed four-character set phrase**

▶ **Meaning:**   **surface meaning (+ idiomatic/metaphorical meaning)**

▶ **Use:**   **metaphorical or extended implication for vividness and effectiveness**

Based on how they are formed, 成语 can be divided into three categories: story-based idioms, analogous idioms, and structural idioms.

典故性成语 (Story-Based Idioms)

A story-based idiom involves an allusion to a historical event or literary text. You need to know the surface meaning (the story behind it) to understand the implied meaning or moral (寓意 yùyì) of the idiom before you can use it.

Example:	自相矛盾 (self, each other, spear, shield)
Meaning:	**surface meaning:** a seller of spears and shields boasted that his spears were the sharpest in the world and could penetrate anything, and then added that his shields were the toughest in the world and couldn't be penetrated by anything. People asked, "What would happen if you threw one of your spears at one of your shields?"
	Idiomatic meaning: one argues against oneself, or is inconsistent with oneself
Usage:	used to imply "self-contradiction or being self-contradictory"

例：　他肯定是在说谎，因为他前后说的话自相矛盾。

　　　He must be lying, because what he said is self-contradictory.

比喻性成语 (Analogous Idioms)

These idioms apply analogous strategies to create visual imagery explaining certain ideas or describing certain states. In order to to understand these metaphorical expressions, you should understand how to interpret their figurative turns of phrase. These metaphorical idioms are sometimes used together with phrases such as "如……般"，"像……一样".

Example:　　雨后春笋 (rain, after, spring, bamboo shoots)

Meaning:　　spring up like bamboo shoots after rain

Usage:　　　metaphorical image to describe the way of things emerging (like bamboo shoots, or mushrooms in the West) at a large scale and fast speed.

例：　80 年代后，非国有企业如雨后春笋般涌现出来。

　　　Non-state-owned enterprises have sprung up like bamboo shoots after rain since the 80s.

结构性成语 (Structural Idioms)

Structural idioms are pretty straightforward. Their meanings can be understood directly from the four characters that compose them. The following examples are from the lessons in this book:

子孙满堂　　having a house full of children and grandchildren

重男轻女　　look up to men and down on women

传宗接代　　have a son to carry on the family line

从一而终　　follow one (the only) husband to the end/death

三口之家　　a family of three (people)

Usually, the four characters of most idioms are fixed. They cannot be replaced by other characters (hence the term "set phrases"). However, some idioms, particularly the structural idioms, may have a semi-variable structure in which two characters are fixed, but the others are variable. For example:

一 X 所 X	一无所有 have nothing	一无所知 know nothing	一无所获 gain nothing
互不 X X	互不相让 no concessions to each other	互不干扰 do not disturb each other	互不理睬 do not greet each other
自 X 自 X	自言自语 talk to oneself	自高自大 arrogant	自作自受 suffer on one's own account
无 X 无 X	无缘无故 without reason	无声无息 soundless	无忧无虑 light-hearted, free of worry
千 X 万 X	千变万化 ever-changing	千军万马 millions of troops	千言万语 innumerable words

练习

1. 语音

Write pinyin for the following underlined Chinese characters. Pay special attention to their different pronunciations in different contexts.

增长（　　）　　　知识分子（　　　）　　　发展（　　）　　　扩大（　　）

长处（　　）　　　分别　　　（　　）　　　头发（　　）　　　大夫（　　）

2. 词汇句型

2.1. Match the following words on the left with the words appropriately associated with them on the right.

Group One (Verb + Object)		
1. 提高	_____	价值
2. 失去	_____	条件
3. 创造	_____	水平

Group Two (Adj. + Noun)		
1. 翻天覆地的	_____	发展
2. 欣欣向荣的	_____	机遇
3. 突飞猛进的	_____	工作

Group One (Verb + Object)			**Group Two** (Adj. + Noun)		
4. 扩大	_____	理想	4. 前所未有的	_____	经济
5. 改善	_____	规模	5. 养家糊口的	_____	观念
6. 实现	_____	奇迹	6. 重文轻商的	_____	变化

2.2. 写出下列词语的近义词：

涌现 _____   多余 _____   机遇 _____   看不起 _____

2.3. 写出下列词语的反义词：

城镇 _____   轻视 _____   失业 _____   提高 _____

2.4. 选择填空 (Choose the most appropriate words to fill in the blanks.)

a. 机会	b. 追求	c. 纯	d. 一向	e. 心目中
f. 污染	g. 价值观念	h. 发挥	i. 多余	j. 羡慕
k. 灵活	l. 平衡	m. 稳定	n. 悄悄地	

1. 这个年轻人家庭幸福，工作上也有所作为，我很 _____ 他。

2. 中国的开放政策使人们有更多的 _____ 学习外国先进的科学技术。

3. 很多农民工为了 _____ 更好的生活，离开了自己的家乡。

4. 虽然他已经大学毕业了，但在父母的 _____，他还是个孩子。

5. 这个地区一向不 _____，国家之间常常发生战争。

6. 很多成语体现了中华民族的传统 _____。

7. 发生那件事以后，他 _____ 回国了，没有告诉任何人。

8. 我们的教育应该充分 _____ 孩子们的想象力和创造力。

9. 这个工厂排出的废水 _____ 了周围的环境。

10. 她 _____ 不喜欢这种社交活动。今天她来这里完全是为了你。

11. 学生应该 _____ 运用学过的知识。

12. 事实证明我们的担心是 _____ 的。

13. 他第一年办公司 _____ 收入就突破了 100 万元。

14. 中国东部与西部的发展很不 _____。

3. 语法练习

3.1. 用合适的否定词（非、无、否、未、勿）填空：**(Each word may be used more than once)**

1. 为什么美国有这么多 _____ 法移民?

2. 学校规定 _____ 成年学生不得饮酒。

3. 你们完全可以拒绝他们的 _____ 理要求。

4. 中国的经济发展离不了 _____ 国有企业的贡献。

5. 他不知道自己今年是 _____ 能考上研究生。

6. 一场自然灾害让大家看清楚了这个领导人的 _____ 能。

7. 这个俱乐部为 _____ 婚青年举办了"情满七夕"的联谊晚会。

8. 机场内请 _____ 吸烟。

9. 病人出院日期 _____ 定，还需观察一段时间。

10. _____ 婚生子女应不应该享有同样的权利?

3.2. 成语典故

Find the stories behind the following four story-based idioms by using a dictionary or an online resource (e.g., http://www.chengyu.org or http://www.zdic.net/cy). Summarize the stories and the implied meanings in the spaces provided below:

1. 对牛弹琴

典故 _____

_____

寓意 _____

2. 杞人忧天

典故 _____

_____

寓意 _____

3. 胸有成竹

典故 _____

_____

寓意 _____

4. 拔苗助长

典故 _____

_____

寓意 _____

3.3. Match the analogous idioms to their extended meanings:

1. 脸红心跳   _____   巨大的变化

2. 欣欣向荣   _____   很不好意思，很紧张

3. 天之骄子   _____   两家的社会地位很相配

4. 柴米油盐   _____   大量涌现的新事物

5. 天长地久   _____   非常繁荣的景象

6. 门当户对   _____   日常生活很普通但必需用品

7. 翻天覆地   _____   很长很长的时间

8. 雨后春笋   _____   享有特殊地位和待遇的人

3.4. Based on the meanings of the phrases, write out the corresponding structural idioms.

1. 以前从来没有过的 ＿＿＿＿＿＿

2. 互相都不肯让步 ＿＿＿＿＿＿

3. 重视男的，轻视女的 ＿＿＿＿＿＿

4. 非常自由，没有任何束缚 ＿＿＿＿＿＿

5. 一点儿都没感觉到 ＿＿＿＿＿＿

6. 非常累，一点精力都没有了 ＿＿＿＿＿＿

7. 很有兴趣，非常高兴 ＿＿＿＿＿＿

8. 非常有条理，有秩序 ＿＿＿＿＿＿

9. 没有一点办法 ＿＿＿＿＿＿

10. 觉得自己很有道理，所以说话很有气势 ＿＿＿＿＿＿

11. 在同一个时候 ＿＿＿＿＿＿

12. 突然来到 ＿＿＿＿＿＿

13. 每天都有新事物出现，每个月都不一样 ＿＿＿＿＿＿

14. 非常大非常快的进步 ＿＿＿＿＿＿

15. 有很大的成就 ＿＿＿＿＿＿

3.5. Fill in the blanks with appropriate idioms:

第一组：

a. 门当户对	b. 天长地久	c. 雨后春笋	d. 翻天覆地	e. 自由自在
f. 有所作为	g. 天之骄子	h. 互不相让	i. 柴米油盐	j. 重男轻女

1. 终于放假了！孩子们可以 _____ 地玩儿了！

2. 他们两人 _____ ，最后只好闹到法院要离婚。

3. 大学生曾经是中国人心目中的 _____ 。那是因为以前大学生太少。

4. 不要小看这些 _____ 的小问题，如果处理不好也会导致家庭的大矛盾。

5. 你希望有一场很热烈但是短暂的爱情，还是很平淡，可是 _____ 的爱情？

6. 现在还有人找对象很注重对方的家庭背景，要求 _____ 。

7. 自从改革开放以来，中国发生了 _____ 的变化。

8. 过去短短十年里，成千上万的私人企业如 _____ 般涌现出来。

9. 很多招聘单位 _____ ，所以女生找工作难上加难。

10. 每个父母都希望自己的孩子长大后 _____ 。

第二组：

a. 日新月异	b. 拔苗助长	c. 不知不觉	d. 筋疲力尽	e. 兴致勃勃
f. 井井有条	g. 对牛弹琴	h. 杞人忧天	i. 胸有成竹	j. 无可奈何

1. _____ 一年又过去了！可我年初下的决心都没做到！明年再来吧！

2. 他连续工作了三天三夜，已经累得 _____ 了。

3. 这次比赛他 _____ 。因为他已经为此练了三个月了。

4. 他学的不是这个专业，跟他讨论这个问题实在是 _____ 。

5. 他非常喜欢这种活动，所以我们一打电话他就 _____ 地来了。

6. 新经理到来后，所有工作都安排得 _____ ，工作效率也大大提高了。

7. 他总是担心这，担心那，一天到晚放不下心，真是 _____ 。

8. 买不到飞机票，小马只好 _____ 地留在家里。

9. _____ 的科技发展，为人们生活带来了很多便利。

10. 那种不顾学生能否接受，只顾增加课程考试的教学方法，无异于 _____。

4. 综合练习

4.1. 选词填空

民工潮

a. 奇迹	b. 控制	c. 体制	d. 繁荣	e. 规模	f. 前所未有
g. 突飞猛进	h. 群体	i. 轻视	j. 贡献	k. 解放	l. 非
m. 差距	n. 成千上万	o. 安全感	p. 突破		

"民工潮"是改革开放以来中国大地上出现的 _____ 的人口流动现象。是中国历史上，也可能是世界历史上 _____ 最大，速度最快的一次移民 (*migrate, immigrate*) 行动。

从50年代初以来，中国实行的是城乡二元 (*binary*) 体制。农村的生活水平与城市的生活水平 _____ 很大，而农村人口进入城市要受到很大的限制，所以农民实际上是国家的"二等公民"。

改革开放后，中国的经济 _____ 开始向商品经济转变，城市建设 _____，需要大量的劳动力。于是 _____ 的农民开始涌进城市。他们远离亲人和家乡，工作在环境最危险的工地和厂矿，从事着城里人不愿做的各类服务行业。然而，就是这样一个群体，他们用血汗创造出了中国经济 _____。中国近18年来经济增长的16%是由农民工创造的。到90年代中后期，农民工流动的数量每年以800万至1000万的速度增加，最多时总数 _____ 了1.4亿。

农民工为城市建设的日新月异做出了这么大的 _____。然而他们得到的却总是最小的回报 (repay)。农民工被认为是工作时间最长，工资最少，_____ 最低，待遇最差的劳动 _____。他们的农民身份和农村口音，又使他们常常受到城里人的 _____。由于他们的 _____ 城市居民身份，被带到城里的子女多年都无法到当地学校上学，而更多农民工的子女则被留在农村由爷爷奶奶抚养长大。这些情况直到近些年才得到社会的重视。

随着越来越多农村劳动力进城务工，国家也逐步放松了对农民进城就业的 _____，为农民的身份转变创造了条件。民工潮是中国农村改革史上的一个新现象。它让大批农民从土地中 _____ 出来，实现了人这种生产力在城市和农村之间的自由流动。中国的城市化进程因此而加快。农民工以他们的汗水和毅力 (willpower)，在创造 _____ 社会的同时，也在改变着他们自身的命运。

4.2. 按照上面这篇文章的意思，下面的说法对不对？(T/F)

_____ 1. "民工潮"是世界历史上最大的一次移民行动。

_____ 2. 在以前，农村人口进入城市非常困难。

_____ 3. 改革开放以后农民涌进城市的原因是政府放松了对农民工的控制。

_____ 4. 农民工从事的职业通常是城里人看不上的。

_____ 5. 农民工的工资虽然很低，待遇也不好，但是工作很稳定。

_____ 6. 城里人常常看不起农民或农民工。

_____ 7. 大多数农民工孩子被留了在乡下。

_____ 8. 农村人口的自由流动加快了中国城市发展的速度。

4.3. 英译汉

1. She has always been an independent woman. She does everything according to her own interests, regardless of other people's views. (一向)

   _____

2. At the same time that he was seeking a job in the post office, he also sent applications to some graduate schools, hoping to continue his education on a higher level. (在……的同时)

   _____

3. Although the country's legal system has many problems, it is being improved gradually. (体制，改善)

   _____

4. Under the circumstances of increasingly intense employment competition, many university graduates chose to pursue postgraduate education in order to increase their chances to find a job. (日益，扩大)

   _____

5. Because of the establishment and improvement of the recycling system, environmental protection in our city has made breakthrough progress in the past five years. (系统，突破性)

   _____

6. The world seems to pay close attention to the latest economic developments of China. (关注，动态)

   _____

7. This picture is the work of a nine-year-old girl. It depicts a new type of car in the future she imagined. What's more interesting is that the whole picture is made up of natural flowers. (更……的是)

   _____

8. More and more young people invested their extra money in the stock market or real estate, rather than saving it in the bank. (多余，存)

   _____

9. There are many differences in values between the elder and younger generations. (差异，价值观念)

   _____

5. 阅读练习

阅读短文（一）回国印象

近十年来，我经常回中国去看望父母和朋友。刚刚带着一家人在广州待了半个月回来。总的感觉是中国变化得太快了。

比起两年前，房价贵了不少。两年前我看中了一套三房一厅的公寓，就在我父母的楼下，房子很漂亮，要价五十五万。我当时还觉得贵，没买下来，如今类似的房子比两年前至少要高一倍的价钱才能买到。

路上汽车多了很多。我弟弟一家三口人，就有两辆汽车，现在中国自己造的汽车越来越多，有的也很便宜。小型汽车，只要 三、四万人民币就可以买到。只是随着汽车增多，交通、空气也越来越差了。上海、北京、广州等大城市路上堵车 (*traffic jam*) 的情况，比南加州 (*California*) 还厉害。那儿天空常常是灰的。

广州的地铁，起价才两元，坐上去感觉很好，非常现代化。但有些人还没学会先下后上的习惯，上车下车的人挤在一起，互不相让。科技比文明先行了一步。

到处都在建设：建住宅、建商场、建桥梁、建高速公路。令人难以相信的建设速度正在飞快地改变这个国家。曾经熟悉的城市却让我每次回去都找不到路。我爸爸说，就是住在这个城市里的人，也需要不断重新认路。一个星期不去路边转弯处的小店买菜，可能再去时已经找不到了，原来的菜店附近变成了一个建筑工地，几个月后就建起一座大楼。

对我来说，在中国生活，真的很方便。街上是数不清的餐馆、食品店、理发店和药店。要出门，公共汽车、地铁，都很方便。若不想等，就坐的士 (*taxi*)，如果换成美元来考虑，一点都不贵。的士司机一般都很友好，很乐意聊天。走进超市，吃的用的，无所不有。外国品牌，尽管可能是在中国生产的，一般也要贵百分之五十。进口水果一般比国产水果贵一倍，尽管国产水果看上去更新鲜。

报纸杂志的可阅读性提高了很多。评论<u>时政</u> (*current affairs*) 的文章也不少。到处都有<u>网吧</u> (*Internet café*)，但我在美国常看的很多网站都看不到了，包括中文和英文的<u>维基百科</u> (*Wikipedia*)。我十四岁的儿子最喜欢维基百科，有事没事都要往那里查一下。在中国让他痛苦了半个月。

5.1. 根据短文内容，选择最佳答案回答问题：

1. 以下哪个选项说明"中国变化得太快了"？
   a. 房价涨了不少
   b. 路上汽车多了不少
   c. 城市建设飞速发展
   d. 以上都是

2. 在广州，一套三房一厅的公寓现在大概要卖多少钱？
   a. 3、4 万
   b. 110 万
   c. 68 万
   d. 55 万

3. 根据短文，城市建设主要包括
   a. 建工厂、建地铁站、建飞机场
   b. 建水果店、建餐馆、建菜市场
   c. 建报社、建杂志社、建新闻社
   d. 建住宅、建商场、建桥梁和高速公路

4. 作者为什么说在中国生活真方便？
   a. 因为超市里吃的用的都有
   b. 因为街上有很多餐馆、食品店、理发店和药店
   c. 因为出门有很多公共汽车、地铁和出租汽车
   d. 以上都是

5. 根据短文内容，下面哪个选项<u>不正确</u>？
   a. 国产水果的价格是进口水果的一半
   b. 超市里"外国品牌"的商品也可能是中国生产的
   c. 我儿子在中国时两个半月不能查维基百科
   d. 人们文明行为的进步速度没有科技进步的速度快

6. 以下哪项最好地说明了这篇短文的主题？
   a. 中国近年来的变化非常快
   b. 在中国生活非常方便
   c. 中国的房价上涨得很快
   d. 我很喜欢读中国的报纸和杂志

阅读短文（二）中国的贫富差距

美林国际银行 (*Merrill Lynch*) 与凯捷顾问公司 (*Cap Gemini*) 联合发布的全球财富报告显示，由于经济危机，2008 年全世界富豪 (*rich and powerful, high net worth individuals*) 人数减少了 15%，但中国富豪人数却反而上升，并首次超过英国，跃居全球第四位。其实，中国富豪人数并不代表所有国民富裕程度，它反而反映了一个社会问题 —— 中国贫富差距问题。

经过 30 年的改革开放，中国的经济发展日新月异，与此同时，中国的贫富差距也越来越大 – 富人越来越富，穷人越来越穷。中国社会科学院李培林指出，1990 年，中国最高收入的 20% 的人跟最低收入的 20% 的人的收入差距是 4 倍。到了 2006 年，这个差距已经增长为 18.2 倍。一方面，根据中国国家统计局数字，2008 年中国仍然有 8000 万贫困人口年收入在 1067 元人民币（不到 200 美元）以下，而另一方面上海却出现了世界级富人区，那里最贵的一栋房子售价达到 1.3 亿元人民币，相当于 12 万贫困人口一年的收入。

《中国青年报》和新浪网曾联合进行了一项民意调查，在五万多名受调查者中，高达 98.3% 的人说，和十年前相比，贫富差距更大了。84.6% 的人认为，目前的这种贫富差距已经到了无法让人接受的地步。经济高速增长的好处能否公平地分配给全体人民？这已是当今社会越来越关心的话题。

5.3. 按照上面这篇文章的意思，下面的说法对不对？(T/F)

_____ 1. 2008 年全世界富豪人数减少了是因为经济危机。

_____ 2. 中国富豪人数上升说明中国人越来越富有。

_____ 3. 2008 年英国富豪人数是世界第四位。

_____ 4. 经济改革造成了中国的贫富差距。

_____ 5. 中国的贫困人口每天平均收入不到一美元。

_____ 6. 上海的富人每年收入相当于 12 万贫困人口一年的收入。

_____ 7. 大多数中国人无法接受这种贫富差距。

_____ 8. 贫富差距增大是一个很严重的社会问题。

6. 口语练习（讨论题）

1. 你羡慕什么人？为什么？

2. 你看不起什么人？为什么？

3. 对你来说，什么人应该受到尊敬？为什么？

4. 没有铁饭碗是好事还是坏事？请说出理由。

5. 如果你最近去过中国，谈一谈你看到的中国经济发展的情况。

6. 中国的经济发展使中国人的思想有了什么改变？为什么会改变？

7. 你们国家最近的经济变化给人们的生活和思想带来了什么变化？请举例说明。

8. 中国进城打工的农民工跟美国的移民有什么相似的地方？有什么不同的地方？

9.有人反对贫富差距太大的现象，怀念以前中国实行的吃大锅饭的<u>平均主义</u>(egalitarianism)，你觉得中国是否应该回到吃大锅饭的经济体制？

10.在你们国家有没有贫富差距的问题？是什么原因造成的？

11.贫富差距的问题应该怎样解决？

7. 写作练习（字数：600-700）

作文题：（任选一题）

A:经济腾飞的中国。

B: 贫富差距的问题应该怎样解决？

C:没有铁饭碗是好事还是坏事？

Required vocabulary and expressions:

1. Use at least 10 of the following new words and phrases:

效率	体制	个体	经商	涌现	发挥	规模
类型·	繁荣	一向	轻视	灵活	心目	奇迹
平衡	差距	腐败	污染	机遇	翻天覆地	养家糊口
前所未有	欣欣向荣	雨后春笋	日新月异	突飞猛进	重文轻商	

2. Use at least 5 of the following connectives:

自……以来	不仅……还……	如果……就……
不但不……反而……	与此同时……	尽管……还是……
难怪……	更重要的是……	而……　　一方面……另一方面……

个人投资：股票与房地产

课文提要

Beginning in 1978, China's Reform and Opening Up Policy initiated fast economic development, providing unprecedented opportunities for people to engage in financial investment, especially in real estate and the stock market. Even though the stock market in China is young (it was started in the early 1990s), tens of millions of Chinese people have become familiar with investing in stocks, creating the interesting "all nation stock market" phenomenon. Trading by individual investors accounts for about sixty percent of market volume (compared to five percent in the United States). Many have tasted the glory of getting rich, as Deng Xiaoping once said that "to get rich is glorious," a famous phrase that boosted a series of reforms in China in the past three decades. At the same time, several bear markets have also given many people a taste of risk.

This lesson and the supplementary readings provide stories about how people try to get rich by private investment in the special "market socialism" of contemporary China.

阅读前讨论：

1. 个人投资包括哪些项目？
2. 股票投资有什么好处和坏处？
3. 房地产投资有什么好处和坏处？
4. 你觉得股票和房地产投资哪个更加保险？为什么？
5. 你知道那些跟投资有关的词汇？

自学生词

Match each new word in the left column with its English translation in the right column by guessing the word's meaning from the characters that it is composed of.

	生词	繁体	序号	英文
( )	熊市		1.	for this reason
( )	牛市		2.	original price
( )	升值	昇	3.	millionaire
( )	原价	價	4.	multiplication, redouble
( )	商谈	談	5.	appreciate, increase in value
( )	百万富翁	萬	6.	overall, full-scale
( )	倍增		7.	bear market
( )	全面		8.	discuss, negotiate
( )	总数	總數	9.	bull market

生词

	简体	繁体	拼音	词性	英文	HSK 等级
1.	合伙		héhuǒ	v.o.	form a partnership	丁
2.	心动	動	xīndòng	v.	be interested, be attracted	
3.	参与	參與	cānyù	v.	partake, participate in	丁
4.	谨慎	謹	jǐnshèn	adj.	prudent, careful, cautious	丙
5.	观察	觀	guānchá	v.	observe carefully, watch	乙

简体	繁体	拼音	词性	英文	HSK 等级
6. 股市		gǔshì	*n.*	stock market	
7. 行情		hángqíng	*n.*	prices of goods on the market	
8. 大不了		dàbuliǎo	*adv.*	at the worst	
9. 股		gǔ	*m(n)*	share of a company	丙
10. 炒股		chǎogǔ	*v.o.*	speculate in stocks	
11. 体会	體會	tǐhuì	*v.*	realize	乙
12. 暴		bào	*adj.*	sudden and violent	丙
13. 跌		diē	*v.*	fall, drop	乙
14. 沮丧	喪	jǔsàng	*adj.*	discouraged, depressed	
15. 绝望	絕	juéwàng	*adj.*	despairing, hopeless	丁
16. 反弹	彈	fǎntán	*v.*	(of price or stock) rebound	丁
17. 富裕		fùyù	*adj.*	well off, rich	丙
18. 探亲	親	tànqīn	*v.o.*	go home to see family	丁
19. 惊讶	驚訝	jīngyà	*adj.*	surprised, amazed	丙
20. 装修	裝	zhuāngxiū	*v.*	fix up (a house), renovate	丙
21. 富翁		fùwēng	*n.*	rich man, man of wealth	丙
22. 保险	險	bǎoxiǎn	*adj./n.*	sure, safe, insurance	丙
23. 房东	東	fángdōng	*n.*	landlord, landlady	丁
24. 直线	綫	zhíxiàn	*n.*	straight line	丁
25. 利息		lìxī	*n.*	interest	丁
26. 成本		chéngběn	*n.*	costs	丙
27. 收益		shōuyì	*n.*	profit, gain	丁
28. 与其	與	yǔqí	*conj.*	rather than, better than	丙
29. 市郊		shìjiāo	*n.*	suburb	乙
30. 出售		chūshòu	*v.*	sell	丁
31. 筹	籌	chóu	*v.*	prepare, plan	
32. 资金	資	zījīn	*n.*	fund, capital	
33. 预	預	yù	*adv.*	in advance, beforehand	

简体		繁体	拼音	词性	英文	HSK 等级
34.	尚未		shàngwèi	*adv.*	not yet	丁
35.	盈利		yínglì	*v.o.*	make a profit	丁
36.	经纪商	經紀	jīngjìshāng	*n.*	broker, agent, dealer	丁

成语和惯用语

成语/惯用语	繁体	单字解释	意思和例句
省吃俭用 shěng chī jiǎn yòng	儉	省：sparing 吃：eat 俭：thrifty 用：spend	pinch and save 例：她省吃俭用才为儿子存够了学费。 She pinched and scraped, and finally saved enough money for her son's tuition.
吃苦耐劳 chī kǔ nài láo	勞	吃：bear 苦：hardship 耐：endure 劳：hard work	endure hardship and work hard 例：他工作能吃苦耐劳，经理很喜欢他。
寸土如金 cùn tǔ rú jīn		寸：an inch 土：land 如：like 金：gold	(of land) as expensive as gold 例：香港是个寸土如金的地方，房子很贵。 Hong Kong is a place where an inch of land is worth an inch of gold. The houses are very expensive.
变化无常 biàn huà wú cháng	變無	变化：change 无：no 常：constant	constantly changing, changeable 例：这里春天的天气变化无常。 The weather here in spring is very changeable.

课文

■ 第一读：掌握课文大意

快速阅读课文，看下面三个选择中哪一个最能说明本课主要意思：
1. 股票投资风险很大
2. 房地产投资更能赚钱
3. 老万和弟弟的个人投资史

个人投资：股票与房地产

八十年代初，老万和弟弟合伙开了一家维修公司，专门维修各单位的旧楼房。两个人工作上吃苦耐劳，生活上省吃俭用，十年后，在银行里有了一笔不小的存款。

九十年代初，市场上开始出现股票交易。老万的朋友中，有不少人买卖股票赚了钱，老万和弟弟看了不禁心动，也想投资股票市场。问题是他俩都不懂股票，所以一时不敢参与。后来经过跟朋友的多次商谈，又谨慎观察了一阵股市行情，两个人终于决心试试看。在投资股票市场之前，他们先做好了心理准备：就当这次是学习经验，大不了把钱全部输光。

有了心理准备后，两人就从银行提出一部分存款去买股票。开始时，他们选了一只便宜的股票，买进300股。没想到四个月以后，这只股票每股比原价涨了20元，老万和弟弟炒股的信心大增，于是他们把银行里的存款全部提了出来，投资在股票上。三年后，他们赚了将近70万元。但是他们也体会到，在股票市场中赚钱实在风险太大。股市行情一时暴涨，一时大跌，等你绝望时，它又全面回弹。熊市牛市，变化无常，处理得不好就可能把辛辛苦苦赚来的钱都丢掉。为此，他们虽然日子过得比以前富裕多了，但心情却更加焦虑和紧张。

九十年代中，老万的伯父春节期间从香港回上海探亲。饭后聊天时，伯父谈起香港的房地价，说那真是"寸土如金"，一套普普通通的公寓就要上百万元。老万惊讶地说："那拥有一套公寓的人，不就是百万富翁了吗？""是啊，"伯父说，"如果上海也像香港的话，你们现在的这套住房，没有百万，也有几十万了。"

伯父的话打动了老万的心。他想，他和弟弟的工作是维修旧楼房，他们对房屋结构很熟悉，对房屋装修也很有经验。何不尝试买一两套旧房，装修后租出去呢？也许这样做会比股市投资保险得多。于是，伯父一走，老万和弟弟就将股票卖掉，再向银行贷款，在市区内买了两套两室一厅的旧房，装修后租给别人，自己做起房东来了。

两年过去了，人们的生活越来越好，对居住条件的要求也越来越高，房价直线上升。老万和弟弟的两套普普通通的房子，一下子价值倍增。老万和弟弟算了一下，他们那两套房子，除去装修和利息成本后，还可以收益近百万元，而且房价在一段时间内只会涨不会跌。两人将情况分析过后，觉得与其买房投资，不如建房投资。于是将原有的房子卖掉，然后在市郊买了一大块地，建了新房出售，两年后收益两千多万元。

这种具有稳定性而利润又高的商业方式，使许多人像老万兄弟那样投资于房地产业。有的人通过筹资甚至贷款买下他们认为会升值的房产；有的人用较少的预付款买下尚未建好的新房，等房价上升后再出售盈利；更有的人趁着房地产热当起房地产经纪商来了。房地产市场的兴起，使许多人考虑到长期投资的可能性。在人均所得越来越高的情况下，投资性买房也会越来越多。

A. 根据课文内容回答下列问题：

1. 老万和弟弟的生意是如何起步的？

2. 刚开始的时候，老万兄弟是怎么炒股的？

3. 后来他们炒股的方式和以前有什么不同？

4. 老万兄弟为什么决定退出股市？

5. 老万兄弟为什么会想到投资房地产？

6. 兄弟俩一开始是怎么投资房地产的？

7. 两年以后他们的房地产投资有什么改变？

8. 为什么许多人都选择房地产投资？

9. 他们是如何投资房地产业的？

B. 根据课文推论：（Making Inferences）

Choose the best inference from the three possible choices for each sentence, and <u>underline</u> the clue(s) that helped you choose.

1. 为什么"开始时，他们选了一只便宜的股票，买进 300 股"？
   a. 因为他们买不起贵的股票
   b. 因为他们不想冒太大的险
   c. 因为便宜的股票才会上涨

2. 如果上海也像香港的话，你们现在的这套住房，没有百万，也有几十万了。
   a. 香港的房子没有上海的值钱
   b. 上海和香港的房子都很贵
   c. 上海的房子没有香港的贵

3. 两人把情况分析过后，觉得与其买房投资，不如盖房投资。
   a. 买房投资比建房投资更赚钱
   b. 建房投资比买房投资更赚钱
   c. 建房投资不如买房投资

■ 阅读技巧：学会思考与提问 Critical Reading Skills: Asking Questions

Critical reading implies that a reader is actively and constructively engaged in the process of reading, continually relating what a person knows to what he or she is trying to make sense of. The role of background knowledge and the reader's ability to draw upon it are essential to critical thinking and learning. One of the critical reading skills is formulating questions before, during, and after reading.

The ability to ask questions is a test of your understanding of the reading material. Asking good questions depends upon your ability to pick out the most important ideas, focus on the construction of the argument, identify potentially weak links in the evidence, and make associations with other knowledge that you have already acquired, that is, to make comparisons between texts. Out of this question-asking process, you will develop your own point of view on the material — a key to successful reading.

After you read the text, you should step back from the details of the material and ask some questions. Some sample questions for this text could be:

1. 是什么大环境给了中国人个人投资的机会？

2. 这个机会是不是公平地给了所有人？

3. 什么人在个人投资方面有优势？

4. 是不是所有投资者都像课文中的老万兄弟俩一样成功？

Now, write three good questions that you can discuss with your classmates. Your questions should focus on *ideas* presented in this chapter, not just facts.

1. _____

2. _____

3. _____

词汇与句型

1. 合伙 • form a (business) partnership, partnership

1. 我和妹妹合伙开了一家花店。
   I entered into a partnership with my younger sister to start a florist shop.

2. 我们三年前开始合伙，现在生意越做越好。
   We started our partnership three years ago. Now our business is growing.

3. 私营企业的模式可以分为三种：独资企业、合伙企业、有限责任公司。
   Private enterprises can be divided into three types: solely owned enterprises, partnership firms, and companies with limited liability.

2. 参与 • participate in, have a hand in, involve oneself in

1. 那个公司参与了中国西部的开发。
   The company participated in the development of western China.

2. 我不想参与他们的投资计划。
   I don't want to involve myself in their investment plan.

3. 因为他的参与，我们赢了那场篮球赛。
Because of his participation, we won the basketball game.

参与 vs. 参加

参与 and 参加 can be used to mean "participating in certain activities." However, they differ in certain ways:

1. 参加 can be used to mean "joining an organization," while 参与 cannot be used in this way.

2. 参加 can be used in both formal and informal contexts, while 参与 can only be used in a formal or written context.

Collocation:

	旅行团	会议	选举	组织	工作	活动	讨论	比赛
参加	✔	✔	✔	✔	✔	✔	✔	✔
参与	x	x	x	x	x	✔	✔	✔

例 ：

他参加了公司扩大投资计划的讨论。（✔ 他参与了公司扩大投资计划的讨论。）
我们参加了一个旅行团去北京旅游。（x 我们参与了一个旅行团去北京旅游。）

3. 心动 ● be interested, be attracted to

1. 看着姑娘的照片，他禁不住心动了。
Looking at the girl's picture, he couldn't help being attracted to her.

2. 听说邻居投资房地产赚了大钱，我也心动起来。
Upon hearing that my neighbor earned a great amount of money, I started to get interested as well.

3. 看见很多朋友都准备出国旅游，他们也心动了。
Seeing their friends getting ready to travel abroad, they became interested too.

4. 大不了 ● if worse comes to worst, nothing serious

1. A: 爸爸今天也许不能来接我们了。
   B: 没关系，大不了我们走回家去。
   A: Dad probably can't come pick us up today.
   B: No big deal. At the worst, we would walk home.

2. 医生说，我的病没什么大不了的，休息几天就好了。
    The doctor says that my sickness is not serious. I'll be fine after a few days' rest.

3. 这不是什么大不了的成就，我不想接受记者的采访。
    This is not some important achievement. I don't want to accept the reporter's interview.

5. 提 + 存款（款，现金，etc.）• withdraw (money)

1. 因为自动提款机坏了，银行里很多人排队等着提款。
    Because the ATMs are broken, many people line up in the bank waiting to make a withdrawal.

2. 去看电影前，我得先去提些现金。
    I need to withdraw some cash before going to see the movie.

3. 他昨天从我们账上提了 500 美元。
    He withdrew 500 US dollars from our bank account.

6. 炒 + 股（票），房，• play (the market), invest

1. 爸爸每天忙着炒股，没时间跟我们在一起。
    Dad is busy playing the stock market every day without spending time with us.

2. 老王炒股已经炒了很多年了，一定赚了不少钱。
    Lao Wang has been making investments in the stock market for years. He must have made a lot of money.

3. 他把所有的股票都卖掉，准备开始炒房。
    He sold all his stocks and got ready to invest in real estate.

7. 一时 • for a short while, temporary, momentary

1. 问题是他俩都不懂股票，所以一时不敢参与。
    The problem was that they knew nothing about the stock market, so for a while they didn't dare to involve themselves in that area.

2. 我以前一定见过他。可他叫什么名字我一时想不起来。
    I must have seen him before. But I can't recall his name offhand (at the moment).

3. 这首歌曾风行一时。
    The song was very trendy at one time.

8. 一时 A 一时 B · now..., now...; one moment..., the next...

1. 这只股票不太稳定，一时上涨，一时下跌，让妈妈很紧张。
   This stock is not very stable, now rising, now falling, which makes Mom really nervous.

2. 她的情绪变化无常，一时高兴，一时难过，真让人难以捉摸。
   Her mood changes constantly, now happy, now sad, which is really unpredictable.

3. 妹妹一时想学电脑，一时想学会计，还没选定她的专业。
   My younger sister sometimes wants to study computers and sometimes wants to learn accounting. She hasn't decided on her major yet.

9. ……不……就是……? · isn't that...?

1. 那个房地产经纪商不就是你以前的房东吗？
   Isn't that real estate agent your former landlord?

2. 那两套房子不就是你长期投资的开始吗？
   Aren't the two apartments the beginning of your long-term investment?

3. 看，那不就是你最喜欢的影星吗？
   Look! Isn't that your favorite movie star?

10. 没有 A 也有 B · (even) if it's not as much as A, then it's at least B

1. 他这次出差时间挺长，没有一个月，也有二十几天。
   He went on this business trip for quite a long time. If it was not a month, then it was at least more than twenty days.

2. 今天真热，没有三十七度，也有三十五度。
   It's really hot today. If the temperature is not as high as 37 degrees, then it's at least 35 degrees.

3. 他投资房地产赚了很多钱，没有三千万，也有两千万。
   He earned a lot of money through real estate investment. If it was not as much as 30 million, it was at least 20 million.

11. 何不 · why not（为什么不）

1. 这种商业方式具有稳定性，利润又高，何不考虑投资呢？
   This business model is both stable and highly profitable. Why not consider investing?

2. 你们的收入越来越高，何不买一所居住条件更好的房子？
    Your income has been increasing. Why not buy a house with better conditions?

3. 如果炒股使你的生活充满焦虑，何不尝试更具稳定性的投资呢？
    If investing in the stock market fills your days with stress, why not try some more stable investments?

12. 与其 A 不如 B • better B than A (A 不如 B)

1. 我觉得，与其向亲戚借钱，不如向银行申请贷款。
    I think it's better to apply for a loan from a bank than borrow money from relatives.

2. 老张决定，与其投资股市，不如投资房地产。
    Old Zhang decided that it is better to invest in real estate than in the stock market.

3. 我们刚搬到这个城市。太太认为，与其租房住，不如向银行贷款买房。
    We just moved to this city. My wife believes that it's better to get a loan from a bank to buy a house than to rent a house.

13. V + (于 phrase) • (do something) in a certain area (literary) (Review of 于 in Lesson 8)

1. 他把每月收入的百分之三十投资于股市。
    He invested one third of his monthly salary in the stock market.

2. 他一生致力于保护野生动物的工作。
    He devoted his whole life to the work of wildlife protection.

3. 大学毕业后，她就服务于一个环境保护组织。
    She served in an environmental protection organization right after she graduated from university.

14. 尚未 • not... yet (literary)

1. 医生们尚未查出得这种病的原因。
    The doctors haven't established the causes of this illness.

2. 他们尚未决定是否买那份保险。
   They haven't decided if they'll buy that insurance.

3. 王先生想把这所房子卖掉，只是尚未找到合适的买主。
   Mr. Wang wants to sell this house, but he hasn't found a suitable buyer yet.

15. 上 + Number • up to...

The numbers following "上" can only be "百，千，万".

1. 香港的房地价真是"寸土如金"，一套普普通通的公寓就要上百万元。
   The real estate in Hong Kong is extremely expensive. An ordinary apartment will sell for as much as a million HK dollars.

2. 地震以后，成千上万的人失去了自己的家。
   After the earthquake, thousands of people lost their homes.

3. 这家公司发展很快，今年聘用了上千名新职工。
   This company is developing very fast. It hired up to a thousand new employees this year.

语法

1. 成语（二）• Idioms/Set Phrases (B)

In the last chapter, we introduced the basic features and categories of 成语. However, it's one thing to learn to understand these expressions in Chinese text, but a completely different thing to learn to actively use them in your own writing or speech. A deeper knowledge of the structure of these idiomatic expressions may help you master them better.

1.1. The Structure of 成语

Although most 成语 consist of only four characters, their structures may be quite complicated. The number of character combinations is almost unlimited, and the ways of combining them very flexible. The table below illustrates major structures of 成语:

Type	Combination	Examples			
Parallel Structure	NV+NV	脸红心跳	头昏脑胀	脸红心跳	
	NA+NA	天长地久 理直气壮	精疲力尽 门当户对	日新月异	门当户对
	VN+VN	重文轻商 养家糊口	重男轻女 吃苦耐劳	翻天覆地 传宗接代	
	AN+AN	粗心大意			
	AV+ AV	突飞猛进	省吃俭用		
Non-Parallel Structure	N+VO	愚公移山	杞人忧天		
	Prep. N+V	应运而生	由此而来	从一而终	
	Adverbial +V	突如其来	前所未有	互不相让	无可奈何
	Attributive + N	天之骄子	一家之主	雨后春笋	
	V+O	有所作为			
	V+C	一分为二	争执不休		
	Adv. +VO	井井有条	欣欣向荣		

1.2. The Use of 成语

In actual use, the internal structures of 成语 do not necessarily determine how these units will function. Many of them can be used in a very flexible way. For example:

吃苦耐劳是中华民族的传统美德。(used as a noun)

这些农民工吃苦耐劳，为城市建设做出了很大的贡献。(used as a verb)

我们只想聘用能吃苦耐劳的职工。(used as an adjective)

However, some 成语 have more fixed grammatical roles. For example, 天之骄子 usuallyfunctions as a noun, while 互不相让 is mainly a verb. The following are some typical functions of 成语 and their respective grammatical rules.

1.2.1. As a Predicate • Subj.（就/真/实在）是 XXXX

One of the main functions of 成语 is as a predicate after 是. Sometimes adverbs such as 真 or 实在 can be used before 是 for emphasis. In literary text, 无异于 can replace 是.

他们昨天工作到半夜，实在是<u>精疲力尽</u>了。

这个公司的这种做法无异于<u>重男轻女</u>。

1.2.2. As a Verb • Subj.（应该/要/会/可以 / 必须）XXXX

他们每月工资不多，所以必须<u>省吃俭用</u>。

小夫妻吵起架来互不相让，父母也<u>无可奈何</u>。

Note: When a 成语 functions as a verb, it usually cannot take an object. If necessary, we must use a preposition such as 对、为、把, etc. to introduce the object before the verb. For example (sentences with the mark * are incorrect):

既然聪聪也来了，奶奶就<u>把鸡蛋羹</u>一分为二，一人一半。
* 既然聪聪也来了，奶奶就一分为二鸡蛋羹，一人一半。

聪聪不听话，爷爷真是<u>对他</u>无可奈何。
* 聪聪不听话，爷爷真是无可奈何他。

这对夫妻总是<u>为了孩子</u>的事情争执不休。
* 这对夫妻总是争执不休孩子的事情。

1.2.3. As an Attributive • XXXX 的 N

It is said that almost every 成语 can be used as an attributive to modify a noun. When 成语 is used to modify a noun, it must use 的.

现在还有多少人追求那种<u>天长地久的</u>爱情？

这个<u>突如其来的</u>变故让小王特别伤心。

1.2.4. As an Adverbial or Complement • XXXX 地 V or V 得 XXXX

When 成语 modifies a verb, it must use 地. As a verb complement, it must use 得.

他<u>理直气壮</u>地说："这不是我的错！"

这几天考试考得<u>头昏脑胀</u>，真该好好休息一下了。

成语 give a broad palette of colors to illuminate the Chinese language. They build a connection to cultural roots, history and traditions and also enable communication that reaches below the surface of thought, touching on metaphysical and philosophical discourses. When used *properly*, they can contribute immensely to the lucidity of a piece of writing or to the quality of a conversation, as they are evidence of a person's advanced command of the language. We'll end this introduction with an English idiom: "Practice makes perfect." （熟能生巧）

2. "将" 作介词 • 将 as a Preposition

We have learned 将 as an adverb before. It is followed by a verb, meaning "will." For example: 据我估计，小王上个月买进的股票，价值将增涨两倍。However, when 将 is followed by a noun, it becomes a preposition, which is the equivalent of 把. The difference between 将 and 把 is that the former is literary, the latter colloquial.

1. 请将正式文件送交总经理。
   Please send a formal document to the general manager.

2. 公司决定将这栋旧楼推倒重建。
   The company decided to demolish this old building and build a new one.

3. 小林将银行里的存款都提了出来，投资在房地产上。
   Xiao Lin withdrew all his deposit money from the bank, and invested it in real estate.

3. "何" 的用法

3.1. 何 is a classical interrogative pronoun, meaning "which, what." It can form classical (formal) question words such as:

何处 （which place = 哪儿）

何人 （which person = 谁）

何时（what time = 什么时候）

何事（which thing = 什么事/什么）

为何（for what reason = 为什么）

如何（like what = 怎么样/怎样）

3.2. Like all question words, 何 can also used to form rhetorical questions to add stress or emphasis to the tone. These rhetorical questions are more formal than their colloquial counterparts.

1. 有何不可？（有什么不可以呢？ = 当然可以）
   用自己的钱买股票投资，有何不可？
   How come a person can't invest in the stock market with his/her own money?
   (or: What's wrong with investing in the stock market with a person's own money?)

2. 有何不同？（有什么不一样？ = 完全是一样的）
   这种做法与重男轻女有何不同？
   What's the difference between this behavior and gender discrimination?

3. 何不……呢？（为什么不……呢？ = 应该……）
   如果那些西药没有效果，何不试一试中药呢？
   If the Western medicine has no effect, why not try some Chinese medicine?

练习

1. 语音

Write pinyin for the following underlined Chinese characters. Pay special attention to their different pronunciations in different contexts.

大不<u>了</u>（　　）　　　<u>行</u>情（　　）　　　反<u>弹</u>（　　）　　　参<u>与</u>（　　）

看完<u>了</u>（　　）　　　<u>行</u>李（　　）　　　子<u>弹</u>（　　）　　　<u>与</u>其（　　）

2. 词汇句型

2.1. Match the following words on the left with the words appropriately associated with them on the right.

Group One (Verb + Object)			Group Two (Noun + Noun)		
1. 吃	＿＿＿	股	1. 股市	＿＿＿	准备
2. 提	＿＿＿	利	2. 人均	＿＿＿	贷款
3. 炒	＿＿＿	资	3. 房屋	＿＿＿	所得
4. 探	＿＿＿	款	4. 银行	＿＿＿	行情
5. 盈	＿＿＿	亲	5. 心理	＿＿＿	装修
6. 投	＿＿＿	苦			

2.2. 选词填空

a. 将	b. 何不	c. 心动	d. 合伙
e. 大不了	f. 没有……也有……	g. 与其……还不如……	h. 一时
i. 提	j. 尚未	k. 专门	l. 参与
m. 不就是	n. 一时……一时……	o. 信心大增	p. 炒
q. 于			

1. 为了节约成本，两个公司 ＿＿＿ 做起了生意：一个 ＿＿＿ 负责生产食品，另一个负责销售食品。

2. 越来越多的学校开始鼓励学生 ＿＿＿ 各种不同的社会活动，因为仅仅能考出好分数的学生并不是社会需要的人才。

3. 既然这幅油画让你如此 ＿＿＿，＿＿＿ 将它买下来呢？

4. 得到老师的鼓励后，她 ＿＿＿＿＿，决心要在这次比赛中得到好成绩。

5. 做什么事情都应该坚持到底才能成功，不能只有 ＿＿＿ 的热情。

6. 失败了也不要紧。_____ 再从头开始。

7. 为了 _____ 股，他把存折里的钱全部都 _____ 出来了。

8. 他 _____ 劝我投资股票，_____ 又说股市风险太高，我不知道怎么办才好。

9. 那个在装修房子的人 _____ 你的老房东吗？

10. 这部电影真是太长了，就算 _____ 4 个小时，_____ 3 个半小时。

11. _____ 拿一个高学历却找不到工作，_____ 读职业学校学一点实用的技能。

12. 过去，中国人习惯 _____ 在固定的单位工作。

13. 一个小学 _____ 毕业的孩子竟然能画出这样美的画，真是太令人惊讶了。

14. 看到电视上关于地震的消息后，老王 _____ 自己多年的存款都捐献给了灾区。

2.3. 用"参加"还是"参与"？

1. 我姐姐已经大学毕业 _____ 工作了。

2. 你们之间的事情我不好 _____。

3. 这个工程有了专家的 _____，进度会加快很多。

4. 经理亲自 _____ 这项工程的计划讨论，说明这项工程非常重要。

5. 学校领导也 _____ 了我们的中国新年晚会。

6. 她在学校时就 _____ 了一个环境保护组织。

2.4. 用所给的词汇句型完成下列对话：

1. A: 昨天跟你妹妹一起来的那位女孩有男朋友了吗？

   B: 不知道。你既然对她有兴趣，_____？（何不……呢）

2. A: 老王炒股赚了很多钱吧？

   B: 是啊。他如今的资产 _____（没有……也有……）

3. A: 你和小王合伙办公司的事情定下来了吗？

   B: 还没有呢。他 ＿＿＿＿＿＿＿＿＿＿＿＿＿＿＿＿＿ （一时…… 一时……）

4. A: 你姐姐三十多了吧？为什么还没结婚呢？

   B: 可能是还没找到她的白马王子吧？

   她说 ＿＿＿＿＿＿＿＿＿＿＿＿＿＿＿＿＿ （与其……还不如……）

5. A: 假期快到了，你怎么还没买机票呢？

   B: 急什么？＿＿＿＿＿＿＿＿＿＿＿＿＿＿＿＿＿＿ （大不了）

3.　语法练习

3.1. 用合适的成语填空：

a. 变化无常	b. 省吃俭用	c. 寸土如金	d. 吃苦耐劳

1. 由于物价快速上涨，平常习惯了随意花钱的人也不得不开始 ＿＿＿＿＿＿ 起来。

2. 农民 ＿＿＿＿＿＿ 辛勤耕作了一年，最大的快乐就是看到地里有个好收成。

3. 上海是一个国际化的大都市，也是个 ＿＿＿＿＿＿ 的地方，平均每平方米的房价高达 15000 元以上。

4. 这个人的性情 ＿＿＿＿＿＿，很难跟他做朋友。

3.2. 用合适的成语改写下面的句子：

1. 她还觉得自己很有道理地说："我没做错事情，为什么要说对不起？"

   ＿＿＿＿＿＿＿＿＿＿＿＿＿＿＿＿＿＿＿＿＿＿＿＿＿＿＿＿＿

2. 这是一个以前从来没有过的好机会，你一定不要错过了！

   ＿＿＿＿＿＿＿＿＿＿＿＿＿＿＿＿＿＿＿＿＿＿＿＿＿＿＿＿＿

3. 看到中国那么<u>繁荣有活力</u>的经济市场，他不禁心动了。

　　_____

4. 大家玩儿得非常高兴，<u>一点都没感觉到</u>已经半夜了。

　　_____

5. 他总以为自己是一个<u>有特权的，不同于一般人的人</u>。

　　_____

6. 小聪聪<u>非常有兴趣地</u>问着各种各样关于动物的问题。

　　_____

7. 昆明这个城市一年四季都像春天一样，"春城"的名字<u>就是这样来的</u>。

　　_____

8. 王立在实验室里工作了十六个小时，已经<u>一点力气也没有了</u>。

　　_____

3.3. 选择合适的成语完成句子：

1. 由于国家巨额投资于西部建设，这几年这个西部边远城市的面貌 _____。

　　a. 自由自在　　　b. 寸土如金　　　c. 日新月异　　　d. 突飞猛进

2. 他最近的成绩 _____。父母师长都非常高兴。

　　a. 日新月异　　　b. 突飞猛进　　　c. 翻天覆地　　　d. 欣欣向荣

3. 恋人们结婚时都希望自己的爱情会 _____。但现实常常不完全这样。

　　a. 天长地久　　　b. 欣欣向荣　　　c. 井井有条　　　d. 兴致勃勃

4. 他们俩都被这个 _____ 的消息惊呆了。

　　a. 翻天覆地　　　b. 兴致勃勃　　　c. 突如其来　　　d. 突飞猛进

5. 自从有了这位能干的助手以后，办公室每天都整理得 _____。

    a. 翻天覆地　　　　b. 有所作为　　　　c. 日新月异　　　　d. 井井有条

6. 改革开放以后，中国的经济发展 _____。

    a. 突如其来　　　　b. 欣欣向荣　　　　c. 兴致勃勃　　　　d. 寸土如金

7. 老朋友见面，他俩谈得 _____，几乎连吃饭都忘了。

    a. 欣欣向荣　　　　b. 天长地久　　　　c. 兴致勃勃　　　　d. 不知不觉

8. 这个城市发生了 _____ 的变化，连从小在这儿长大的我都认不出它来了。

    a. 翻天覆地　　　　b. 寸土如金　　　　c. 突飞猛进　　　　d. 井井有条

9. 买房的人越来越多，于是房地产开发公司如 _____ 般纷纷涌现出来。

    a. 寸土如金　　　　b. 千军万马　　　　c. 应运而生　　　　d. 雨后春笋

10. 谁不希望自己的孩子长大以后 _____ 呢？

    a. 理直气壮　　　　b. 有所作为　　　　c. 突飞猛进　　　　d.天之骄子

3.4. 请改正下面成语的使用错误：

1. 80 后这一代人都喜欢自由自在生活方式。

    _____

2. 每次看到进来一个客人她就会紧张的脸红心跳。

    _____

3. 人们对住房条件的要求越来越高，房地产开发公司就应运而生在这种情况下。

    _____

4. 以前中国人结婚的主要目的就是传宗接代他们的家庭。

    _____

5. 谁不想找一个有所作为人做自己的伴侣呢?

_____

6. 这些学生都被父母惯坏了，老师也无可奈何他们。

_____

7. 听说这次音乐会由著名歌手演出，大家都兴致勃勃来了。

_____

4. 综合练习

4.1. 选词填空

a. 于	b. 沮丧	c. 盈利	d. 筹资	e. 心动
f. 员工	g. 之内	h. 尚未	i. 业务	j. 探亲
k. 房东	l. 行情	m. 股份	n. 规模	o. 合伙
p. 投资	q. 直线	r. 吃苦耐劳	s. 与此同时	t. 欣欣向荣

台商投资故事

　　林先生 1952 年出生 _____ 台北市，18 岁中学毕业以后，就在两个姐姐 _____ 开办的服装公司工作，_____ 地做了十多年以后，取得了不少经验，也赚了不少钱。

　　1987 年底，台湾政府开始允许台湾人赴大陆 _____，台商纷纷以探亲名义赴大陆寻找投资机会。林先生在一次去大陆旅行时，看到那里 _____ 的经济发展带来的商机，不禁 _____，于是决定要去大陆 _____ 创业。

1990 年，他终于来到大陆，先后在广州、苏州等地开了服装店，从事服装贸易。_____，他也到别的地方考察服装业 _____，最后决定在深圳发展服装生产业。 1994 年，他跟几个台湾朋友共同 _____ 30 万美元，在深圳租到一个厂房，成立了长富服装公司，他们的公司以生产出口服装为主，开始几年业务 _____ 上升，_____ 不少。但 1998 年，长富服装公司跟出租厂房的 _____ 产生了矛盾，服装公司被迫停产。在停产期间，公司亏损 (loss) 严重。他的几个合伙人纷纷退出，把资金撤 (withdraw) 了出来。这一切使林先生感到很 _____。他甚至曾经考虑回台湾去，但最后还是决定留在大陆，一切从头开始。他用自己所有的钱把公司的全部 _____ 买了下来，独自经营。

1999 年，他多方面筹集资金，再投入 30 万美元买新机器，恢复生产，经过多次努力后，公司起死回生 (revived)，_____ 由最初的 100 多人发展到 400 多人，订单不断增加，年出口从几万美元增加到 400 多万美元。2004 年，公司根据 _____ 需要，又在广东增办了十多个加工点。生产 _____ 不断扩大，租用的厂房不再能适应公司发展的需要，林先生最终决定在深圳、广州两地扩大投资，建造自己的厂房。

短短 10 年 _____，林先生把一个小小的工厂发展成了一个中型企业。他现在的难处是，太太与孩子 _____ 搬来大陆，为了家庭和业务需要，他得在台北、深圳、广州三个地方来回跑，每年要花很多时间在旅途上。

4.2. 按照上面这篇文章的意思，下面的说法对不对？(T/F)

1. 1987 年底，台湾政府还不允许台湾人赴大陆投资。

2. 林先生决定去大陆投资的原因是当时大陆的经济形势比较好。

3. 林先生最初是在上海和广州设立服装公司。

4. 1994 年，林先生从服装贸易转行到服装生产业。

5. 林先生的第一个服装生产公司是跟几个台湾朋友合伙办的。

6. 林先生的长富服装公司头几年亏损太严重，导致合伙人退出。

7. 林先生最终决定建造自己的厂房是因为租用厂房太贵了。

8. 林先生的家人仍然居住在台湾。

9. 林先生很喜欢旅行，所以每年在台北、深圳和广州来回跑。

4.3. 英译汉

1. The stock market is doing so well. Why don't we buy some stocks as an investment too? (何不)

    _____

2. His friends say that he is too prudent, but he actually lacks confidence. （谨慎）

    _____

3. Twenty years ago, Chinese people were not used to the concept of investment. But now almost everyone is buying stocks. (习惯于)

    _____

4. She feels that rather than marrying a person whom she doesn't love, she would be better off living a free and easy life by herself. (与其……不如……)

    _____

    _____

5. You don't need to return that book to me. Just take it as your birthday gift. (当)

    _____

6. My grandma is a woman inured to hardship. Throughout her life, she never complained about the difficulty of living. (吃苦耐劳)

    _____

    _____

7. New York's real estate is extremely expensive. A small apartment in midtown will sell for up to a million dollars.（寸土如金）

_____

_____

8. The weather in the mountain area changes constantly. You should bring another jacket.（变化无常）

_____

9. This money was saved by my parents through pinching and scraping. I can't use it for investing in the stock market.（省吃俭用）

_____

_____

5. 阅读练习

阅读短文（一）
她的新选择

　　1995 年，小李 35 岁。她和丈夫带着孩子从农村来到了城市。小李是个很能干的人，一到城市就在一个国营饭店里找到了一份清洁工 (*cleaner*) 的工作，每个月工资 200 元，比在农村干农活好多了。而且饭店工作不太忙，下班后除了照顾孩子以外还有些空闲时间。小李太需要时间了。她一向羡慕读书人、文化人；从小，她就希望长大后能上大学、当作家。现在，她决定自学一段时间，报考业余大学，实现自己的理想。

　　可是，一年以后，她交给饭店领导一份辞职 (resign) 报告，说要离开饭店去当个体户。饭店领导觉得很惊讶，因为大家都知道小李一直很喜欢这个工作，而且也做得很好。领导希望她留下来，甚至要把她的工资提高到 300 元一个月。但是她说："我现在最大的问题就是穷。我就是挣 300 一个月也还是太少了。要是我自己开一个小饭馆儿，也许可以挣得多一些。现在政府鼓励个体创业，我为什么不去试试呢？"

　　就在她的新饭馆儿开张的前一天，她收到了业余大学的入学通知书。她笑着对丈夫说："一辈子都想当文化人，学学写小说。现在机会来了，又要挣钱去了。"

　　十几年过去了，小李的存款已经超过 100 万了。一家的生活也富裕起来了，孩子也大学毕业参加工作了。现在她还是喜欢读书，还关心文学。不过，当"读书人，文化人"已经是一个过去的梦了。

5.1. 按照上面这篇文章的意思，下面的说法对不对？ (T/F)

_____ 1. 小李刚到城市的时候，没有文化，也没有能力。

_____ 2. 小李很快就在城里找到了工作。

_____ 3. 小李从小就想当文化人。

_____ 4. 小李并不喜欢在国营饭店的工作，因为没有时间照顾孩子。

_____ 5. 如果饭店领导给小李加了工资，小李就不会辞职。

_____ 6. 小李离开饭店，不是因为工作不稳定，而是因为想挣更多的钱。

_____ 7. 当时政府的政策对小李的决定影响很大。

_____ 8. 为了创业，小李没有去上业余大学。

_____ 9. "富裕"就是有很多钱、生活很好的意思。

_____ 10. 小李现在做梦都想写小说，当文化人。

5.2. 讨论题：小李为了挣钱放弃了自己的理想，你觉得她作的这个选择对不对？

<h2 style="text-align:center">阅读短文（二）
我的股民老婆</h2>

那天，老婆回来，一脸的兴奋："老公，你知道今天小王炒股赚了多少钱吗？"不等我回答，她已经说了："光今天一天就赚了 4000 多块！都快顶你一个月的工资了！"为了让我同意她投资炒股，老婆已经在我耳边唠叨 (nag) 了几个月了。我一直在看报纸，没回话。看我不理 (take notice, manage) 她，她又说："你听过这句话吧？你不理财，财不理你！"见我仍在低头看报，她终于急了："你要不理财，我就不理你！"

为了家庭的安定 (stability) 团结，我勉强同意她做股民。看到我点头，她开心地冲上来给了我一个拥抱 (hug) ——拥抱之后，我家的银行存款就少了两万。

自从学会看股市行情，知道"红涨绿降"的规律之后，她对颜色的喜好起了很大变化。以前总说红色太难看，现在却说红色是幸福的颜色。喜欢上红色的同时，她也开始排斥 (reject) 一切绿色事物。例如，原来她最爱吃绿豆汤，现在，改吃红豆汤了；又例如，我家的绿色窗帘，不知道什么时候被她悄悄地换成了粉红 (pink) 色；更奇怪的是，开车出去，她希望的不再是"一路绿灯"，而是希望"一路红灯"了！

一个月后，股市大跌，老婆一个月来的盈利，一转眼就全没有了。看着她沮丧的样子，我赶快教育她："股市有风险，投资须谨慎！"可她仍然说："牛市还没有结束呢！"结果股市连续跌了两个月，老婆绝望了："再跌我就跳楼去！"我忍不住说："看你现在什么样子？整个儿一条死鱼似的！"谁知几天后股市全面反弹，我下班回到家，老婆冲上来又给了我一个大拥抱："老公！我现在不是死鱼，是生猛 (alive) 海鲜了！"

5.3. 根据短文内容，选择最佳答案回答问题：

1. 在短文中，"股民"指的是 _____。
   a. 投资赚钱的人
   b. 在股市投资的人
   c. 股市行情分析专家
   d. 喜欢红色的人

2. 老婆开始炒股时，第一次投资是多少钱？
   a. 两万块。
   b. 四千多块。
   c. 一万块。
   d. 不知道，短文中没提到。

3. 老婆原来最爱吃绿豆汤，现在为什么改吃红豆汤了？
   a. 因为红豆汤更有利于健康。
   b. 因为她一直最爱红色。
   c. 因为在中国股市中，绿色代表下跌，红色代表上涨。
   d. 因为炒股的人都喜欢红豆汤。

4. 最后一段中，我下班回到家时，老婆为什么给了我一个大拥抱？
   a. 因为那天是我们的结婚纪念日。
   b. 因为我给老婆买了生猛海鲜。
   c. 因为股市终于开始上涨了。
   d. 因为股市已经连续上涨了两个月。

5. 以下哪项最好地说明了短文的主题？
   a. 红色是幸福的颜色。
   b. 股市有风险，投资须谨慎。
   c. 你不理财，财不理你。
   d. 中国普通老百姓的炒股热情。

6. 口语练习：讨论题

1. 你知道哪些投资的方法？

2. 在你的国家什么投资比较有稳定性？

3. 什么样的投资风险最大？

4. 如果你只有一块钱，你会把它用在什么投资上？为什么？

5. 最近你听到了什么关于投资的新闻？

6. 一个谨慎的投资者跟一个冒险的投资者有什么不同？他们中谁比较能成功？

7. 有人很幸运地在投资中发了大财，甚至有人因中彩票 (Lotto) 奖而一夜之间变成了百万
   或亿万富翁。你想这种人发财后会做什么？他们会面临什么样的问题？

8. 可能大多数人都希望发财，但也有人宁可做穷人。说说做穷人有什么好处？
   （用"与其……不如……"）

7. 写作练习 (600-700 字)

作文题：敢冒风险的投资人

Write a narrative of a famous person's investment story (either a success or a failure). You can
organize paragraphs in chronological order, including important dates, times, and events.

Required vocabulary and expressions:

1. Use at least 10 of the following new vocabulary words and phrases:

升值	倍增	全面	合伙	心动	参与
谨慎	观察	行情	体会	沮丧	绝望
富裕	惊讶	装修	保险	利息	成本
收益	出售	盈利	尚未	省吃俭用	吃苦耐劳
寸土如金	变化无常				

2. Use at least 4 of the following expressions:

与其……不如……	……为此，……	……，大不了……
何不……呢？	一时……一时……	没有……也有……

都市消费面面观

课文提要

This lesson offers a "bird's-eye view" of urban consumption. In the late 1970s when China had just started its policies of reform and opening up, a person was considered rich with an annual income of 10,000 yuan (US $1,200). This standard has become outdated; such people are now too common to stand out, especially in cities and towns. China's rapid economic growth during the past decades has multiplied personal wealth and household income. Conspicuous wealth is displayed in people's life - housing, food, fashion, tourism, higher education and faster communication, although there is still the issue of the income gap. Many people (especially in big cities) now enjoy larger living space with better decoration, furniture and domestic appliances. Their diet has become more nutritious, and their modern, varied, colorful clothing is a sharp contrast to the monotone image of blue and gray suits that typified Chinese dress in earlier years. More importantly, people in China now enjoy more holidays than ever and have an increased amount of time available for entertainment and relaxation.

阅读前讨论：

1. 你所在的城市的消费市场有什么特点？
2. 现代人的饮食习惯有什么改变？
3. 你对流行服饰有什么看法？
4. 你在休息日通常选择什么休闲娱乐活动？为什么？
5. 人们的消费行为与国家的经济发展有什么关系？请举例说明。

自学生词

Match each new word in the left column with its English translation in the right column by guessing the word's meaning from the characters that it is composed of.

	生词	繁体	序号	英文
( )	选购	選購	1.	custom make
( )	歌舞厅	廳	2.	song and dance hall
( )	健身房		3.	frequent caller
( )	定做		4.	gym
( )	加快		5.	tourist industry, tourism
( )	速冻	凍	6.	choose and buy
( )	旅游业	遊業	7.	day tour
( )	都市		8.	accelerate, speed up
( )	方便面	麵	9.	quick-freeze
( )	常客		10.	dining table
( )	餐桌		11.	instant noodles
( )	服饰	飾	12.	big city, metropolis
( )	一日游	遊	13.	dress and personal adornment

生词

	简体	繁体	拼音	词性	英文	HSK 等级
1.	饮食	飲	yǐnshí	*n.*	diet, food and drink	丁
2.	全麦	麥	quánmài	*n.*	whole wheat	乙
3.	玉米		yùmǐ	*n.*	corn	乙
4.	豆子		dòuzi	*n.*	pea, bean	丙
5.	反映		fǎnyìng	*v.*	reflect, report	乙
6.	萝卜	蘿	luóbo	*n.*	radish, turnip	乙
7.	辣椒		làjiāo	*n.*	hot pepper, chili pepper	丙
8.	紫		zǐ	*adj.*	purple	乙
9.	茄子		qiézǐ	*n.*	eggplant	丁
10.	黄瓜		huángguā	*n.*	cucumber	乙
11.	例外		lìwài	*n.*	exception	丁
12.	节奏	節	jiézòu	*n.*	rhythm	丁
13.	服装	裝	fúzhuāng	*n.*	clothes, clothing	丁
14.	飘	飄	piāo	*v.*	float in the air, flutter	乙
15.	裙子		qúnzǐ	*n.*	skirt	乙
16.	个性	個	gèxìng	*n.*	individual character, individuality	丙
17.	得体	體	détǐ	*adj.*	appropriate, proper	
18.	打扮		dǎban	*v.*	dress up, deck out	乙
19.	入时	時	rùshí	*adj.*	fashionable	
20.	避免		bìmiǎn	*v.*	avoid	乙
21.	选定	選	xuǎndìng	*v.*	select, designate	丁
22.	的确	確	díquè	*adv.*	indeed, really	乙
23.	外表		wàibiǎo	*n.*	outward appearance	丁
24.	穿着	著	chuānzhuó	*n.*	dress, apparel	
25.	单调	單調	dāndiào	*adj.*	monotonous, dull	乙
26.	埋		mái	*v.*	cover, bury	乙
27.	得以		déyǐ	*v.*	can, may	丁

简体	繁体	拼音	词性	英文	HSK 等级
28. 释放	釋	shìfàng	*v.*	release, set free	丁
29. 时尚	時	shíshàng	*n.*	vogue, trend, fashion, fad	
30. 品牌		pǐnpái	*n.*	brand name	
31. 敏感		mǐngǎn	*adj.*	sensitive	丁
32. 融入		róngrù	*v.*	blend in	丁
33. 主流		zhǔliú	*n.*	mainstream	丁
34. 旅游		lǚyóu	*v.*	travel, tour	丙
35. 此后	後	cǐhòu	*conj.*	afterwards	丁
36. 隔		gé	*v.*	alternate, be after an interval of (time)	乙
37. 之外		zhīwài	*adv.*	apart from, in addition	丙
38. 逛街		guàngjiē	*v.o.*	stroll along the street, go (window) shopping	丙
39. 游览	覽	yóulǎn	*v.*	tour, go sightseeing	乙
40. 麻将	將	májiàng	*n.*	mahjong	
41. 开展	開	kāizhǎn	*v.*	develop, launch	乙
42. 促销	銷	cùxiāo	*v.*	urge, cause, spur on	丙
43. 带动	帶動	dàidòng	*v.*	lead, bring along	丙
44. 项目	項	xiàngmù	*n.*	item, project	乙
45. 游		yóu	*v.*	travel, tour; swim	丙

成语和惯用语

成语/惯用语	繁体	单字解释	意思
走亲访友 zǒu qīn fǎng yǒu	親 訪	走 : visit, call on 亲 : relatives 访 : visit 友 : friends	visit relatives and friends 例：春节期间走亲访友是中国人自古以来的习俗。 Visiting relatives and friends during the Spring Festival has been a tradition since antiquity.
亲朋好友 qīn péng hǎo yǒu	親	亲 : family, relative 朋 : friend 好 : good 友 : friend	relatives and friends 例：离圣诞节还有一个月，人们就开始为亲朋好友准备礼物。 There is still a month until Christmas and people are already starting to prepare gifts for relatives and friends.
取而代之 qǔ ér dài zhī		取 : remove; take 而 : conjunction 代 : replace 之 : it	remove and replace 例：曾经流行一时的传呼机很快就被先进的手机取而代之了。 The once-popular pager was soon replaced by the modern cell phone.
丰富多彩 fēng fù duō cǎi	豐	丰 : abundant, full 富 : rich; plentiful 多 : many 彩 : color	rich and colorful 例：丰富多彩的课堂游戏使孩子们提高了学习兴趣。
随之出现 suí zhī chū xiàn	隨 現	随 : along with, follow 之 : it, him, her, etc. 出现 : appear;	appear along with it 例：一只母虎走出树林，不久，两只小老虎也随之出现。 A female tiger wandered out of the woods, and soon, two cubs appeared after her.

课文

■ 第一读：掌握课文大意

快速阅读课文，看下面三个选择中哪一个最能说明本课主要意思：
　　1. 中国人越来越重视吃和穿
　　2. 中国人的休闲娱乐活动在不断改进
　　3. 中国人的消费活动的变化和趋势

都市消费面面观

　　中国的消费市场越来越丰富多彩，如今的都市消费有哪些新特点呢？请看下面生活的几个方面：

　　一、吃"好"、吃"鲜"、吃"快"

　　过去，中国人对饮食的要求是能吃饱，现在的要求是要吃好，要有营养。近年来，全麦、玉米、豆子等又变得热门起来，这反映了老百姓对饮食营养的重视。

　　追求"鲜"是近年来中国人餐桌上的另一个特色。过去，受季节的影响，中国北方居民往往要靠土豆、萝卜和大白菜度过整个冬天；现在呢？每个城市每天都有大量新鲜蔬菜出现在市场上，红辣椒、紫茄子、黄瓜、青菜……要什么有什么。即使冬天也不例外，人们每天都能吃到新鲜的蔬菜。

　　随着生活节奏的加快，中国人日常的饮食也变得越来越简单了。原来居民花很长时间做饭的现象有了很大的改变，速冻饺子、方便面、包子、盒饭……这些中国式快餐已成为许多居民家中餐桌上的"常客"，而且，随着生活水平的不断提高，出去吃饭已经很平常了。与此同时，中国孩子们对"洋快餐"也越来越感兴趣，儿童们走进"洋"快餐店，既是因为喜欢西式食品，也是因为想得到一份有趣的小礼物。

二、穿出不同

在北京的王府井百货大楼，当记者问一位正在选购服装的小姐"现在什么服装最流行"时，她说："想穿什么，什么就是流行"。这就是现在的年轻人对服装的追求。前些年满街飘起红裙子或黄裙子的现象已不见了，取而代之的是既有个性又得体的服装。一位打扮入时的女士说："如果发现街上有人穿得跟我一样，第二天我一定会让自己换一种打扮。为了避免这种情况，我现在常常定做服装，而不太去商店买衣服了。穿着自己选定的有特色的衣服，感觉特别好。"

的确，这些年来，中国人的外表发生了很大的变化。七十年代初，一位意大利记者在参观中国首都北京后写道："北京是一个灰色的城市，人们穿着既单调又统一……"80年代初国门打开后，中国人深埋几十年的爱美之心，开始在服饰上得以释放。现在，每个人可以根据自己不同的性格、职业、爱好，选择最适合自己的服装穿在身上。特别是现在大多数中国年轻一代都会上网，并通过网络了解欧美同龄人的喜好和兴趣，他们对时尚品牌充满了热情和敏感，希望融入全球主流。"全球性"和"时尚性"是这些年轻人的追求。

三、休闲旅游

1994年3月以前，中国人每周只有一个休息日：星期日。此后，有一段时间实行隔周双休：这一周休息一天，下一周休息两天。从1995年5月开始，中国人终于可以每周休息两天了。实行"双休制"后，人们都感觉到，在工作和家务之外，有了更多属于自己的自由时间。一个新的热门话题：休闲，也随之出现。

据调查：一般城市人外出休闲的选择是：逛街购物、走亲访友、游览参观、去歌舞厅、去健身房和看电影。在家休闲的人主要是看电视、听音乐和打麻将。商店也利用双休日这个好机会，开展各种促销活动，吸引顾客购物消费。

双休日不仅促进了商业的发展，还带动了旅游业的迅速发展。如今，周末休闲旅游已经成为热门的旅游项目。旅游的人们多数参加旅游公司组织的一日游或两日游，而且常常是一家人亲朋好友一块儿去，既方便又热闹。近年来有车族越来越多，自驾游方式已经成为假期旅游一种新时尚，正受到越来越多年轻人的喜爱。

随着消费市场的发展，中国人的生活水平也在不断地提高。

■ **第二读：细节和理解**

A. 根据课文内容回答下列问题：

1. 文章从哪些方面来分析都市消费的新特点？

2. 现代中国人对饮食有些什么要求？

3. 为什么中国人的日常饮食越来越简单？

4. 文章中提到的那位女士为什么选择定做服装？

5. 中国人的服装观念和过去相比有什么不同？

6. 中国人的休息日制度经历了哪些变化？

7. "双休制"的实行对人们的生活有什么影响？

8. 都市人的休闲选择一般有哪些？

9. 推行"双休制"有什么好处？

B. 根据课文推论：(Making Inferences)

Choose the best inference from the three possible choices for each sentence, and underline the clue(s) that helped you choose.

1. 近年来，高粱、玉米、豆子等又变得热门起来，这反映了老百姓对食品营养的重视。
   a. 高粱、玉米和豆子以前没有营养，现在有营养了。
   b. 高粱、玉米和豆子虽然有营养，可是老百姓不喜欢吃。
   c. 高粱、玉米和豆子以前不受重视，现在受重视了。因为他们很有营养。

2. 过去，受季节的影响，中国北方居民往往要靠土豆、萝卜和白菜过整个冬天。
   a. 中国的北方人冬天喜欢吃土豆、萝卜和白菜。
   b. 中国北方冬天除了土豆、萝卜和白菜以外没有别的菜。
   c. 中国北方不管什么季节都只有土豆、萝卜和白菜。

3. 过去，中国人对饮食的要求是能吃饱，现在的要求是要吃好，要有营养。

    a. 现在中国人只要求吃好，不要求吃饱。

    b. 现在中国人的生活质量提高，吃饱已经不是问题。

    c. 过去中国人都觉得饮食的营养价值不重要。

4. 当记者问一位正在选购服装的小姐"现在什么服装最流行"时，她说："想穿什么，什么就是流行"。

    a. 这位小姐不了解服装的流行趋势。

    b. 这位小姐觉得自己穿的衣服最流行。

    c. 这位小姐觉得流行没有标准，有个性的服装就是流行。

5. 如今，周末休闲旅游已经成为热门的旅游项目。

    a. 以前人们不喜欢周末出去旅游。

    b. 现在人们比以前更喜欢旅游。

    c. 以前人们没有时间在周末出去旅游。

■ 批判性阅读技能：区分事实与观点 • Critical Reading Skills: Distinguishing Fact and Opinion

Being able to distinguish fact from opinion in readings and spoken language is a critical language learning skill. A fact is information that can be verified and backed up with evidence, while an opinion is based on a belief or view and may not rely on verifiable evidence. When you read academic texts or listen to lectures, you should always consider whether the writer or speaker is telling you a fact, or trying to persuade you with an opinion. If you can do this, you can make clearer judgments about the information you receive.

Writers often mix fact and opinion, so it is not always easy to tell whether something is based on verifiable information or someone's particular viewpoint. For this reason, it is important to read with a questioning mind. Just because someone says something is true, it doesn't mean it is true. Here is a short part of the text in Chapter 18. Look at how the article starts out by using facts, then moves on to expressing an opinion (the underlined part):

过去，中国人对饮食的要求是能吃饱，现在的要求是要吃好，要有营养。近年来，全麦、玉米、豆子等又变得热门起来，<u>这反映了老百姓对饮食营养的重视</u>。

Examine the following sentences taken from the Reading text of this chapter. Mark the statements as F (fact) or O (opinion). Compare your answers with classmates.

_____ 1. 中国的消费市场越来越丰富多彩。

_____ 2. 过去，受季节影响，中国北方居民往往靠土豆萝卜白菜度过整个冬天。

_____ 3. 1994 年 3 月以前，中国人每周只有一个休息日：星期日。

_____ 4. 此后，有一段时间实行隔周双休：这一周休息一天，下一周休息两天。

_____ 5. 从 1995 年 5 月开始，中国人终于可以每周休息两天了。

_____ 6. 80 年代初国门打开后，中国人深埋几十年的爱美之心，开始在服饰上得以释放。

_____ 7. 想穿什么，什么就是流行。

_____ 8. 七十年代初，一位意大利记者在参观中国首都北京后写道："北京是一个灰色的城市，人们穿着既单调又统一⋯⋯"

_____ 9. 随着消费市场的发展，中国人的生活水平也在不断地提高。

词汇与句型

1. 丰富多彩 • rich and varied, flourishing and colorful

1. 中国的消费市场越来越丰富多彩。
   China's consumer market is becoming more and more flourishing and colorful.

2. 中国历史悠久、丰富多彩的饮食文化吸引了众多外国游客。
   China's rich and varied culinary culture with a long history attracted numerous tourists from abroad.

3. 生活是丰富多彩的，只要你有一双善于发现的眼睛。
   Life is full of variety, as long as you have eyes for discovery.

2. 例外 exception • （无一例外 with no exception）

1. 如今，城市居民每天都能吃到新鲜的蔬菜，即使冬天也不例外。
   Nowadays, urban residents are able to eat fresh vegetables every day, even in winter.

2. 所有的受访者在这个问题上都不肯讲真话，你却是个例外。
   All the other interviewees were not willing to tell the truth on this question, yet you are an exception.

3. 董事会无一例外地否决了这项提案。
   The board of directors vetoed this proposal unanimously.

3. 取而代之 • replace sb./sth., take it over

1. 老前锋 (*[sports] forward*) 受伤了，教练只能让替补球员取而代之。
   The original forward was injured; the coach had to replace him with a substitute player.

2. 他对老李被选为下一任经理非常不满，一心想取而代之。
   He had a grudge against Old Li, who was selected to be the next manager. He had always wanted to take his place.

3. 胶卷相机已经过时，取而代之的是方便、高效的数码相机。
   Film cameras are already outdated. Replacing them are the convenient and efficient digital cameras.

4. 打扮入时 （穿着入时/衣着入时）• nattily attired, stylishly dressed

1. 车在宾馆门口停住了，走出来一位打扮入时的女士。
   The car pulled up at the entrance of the hotel; a stylishly dressed lady walked out.

2. 她是一位时装设计师，所以穿着不但很入时，而且很有自己的特色。
   She is a fashion designer, so what she wears is not only trendy, but also of her own style.

3. 参加这次记者招待会，你衣着不一定要入时，但一定要得体。
   To attend this press conference, you don't have to be dressed fashionably, but you should be dressed appropriately.

5. 得体 • befitting one's position or suited to the occasion, appropriate

1. 穿牛仔裤参加这样正式的晚会可能不太得体。
   It may be inappropriate to go to such a formal party in jeans.

2. 学语言不但要学词汇，懂语法，而且要知道怎样得体地运用语言。
   Learning a language is not only acquiring vocabulary and grammar. One has to know how to use the language in the proper way.

3. 这个年轻人在聚会上的大方得体的表现吸引了她。
   This young man's suave behavior at the party attracted her.

6. 的确 • really, indeed

1. 快餐店的竞争的确一天比一天激烈了，我们收到的订单没有以前多了。
   The competition between fast-food restaurants really became more intense day by day; we aren't receiving as many orders as before.

2. 有人告诉我小王是个很细心的人，和她工作一段时间后，我发现的确是这样。
   Somebody once told me that Xiao Wang was a very attentive person. After working with her for a while, I can see that she really is.

3. 的确，环保措施实行以来，我市的环境质量得到了一定程度的改善。
   Indeed, since the measures of environmental protection were carried out, the environmental quality of our city has been improved to some extent.

7. 适合 • fit, suit

1. 每个人根据自己不同的性格、职业、爱好，选择最适合自己的服装穿在身上。
   People choose their most suitable clothing according to their different personalities, careers and interests.

2. 这本书浅显而生动，适合儿童阅读。
   This book is easy and lively, suitable for children.

3. 这种场合不适合穿休闲服。(or（穿）休闲服不适合这种场合。)
   It is not appropriate to wear casual clothes for such an occasion.
   or: Casual clothing is not suitable/appropriate for such an occasion.

适合 vs. 合适

适合 and 合适 are similar in their meaning. However, 适合 is a verb that can take objects, while 合适 is an adjective and cannot take an object. For example:

4. 这种场合不适合穿休闲服装。(not 合适)

5. 这种场合穿休闲服装不太合适。(not 适合)

8. 得以 • be able to, can (or may)...

得以 is one of those classical expressions that are still in use in modern formal writing. In classical Chinese, 得 means 能 while 以 is a function word, connecting 得 to the verbal phrase that follows it, the same as the 以 in 可以. 得以 means "(someone) is finally able to do something after a long time or great effort," so it is usually used with adverbs such as 才, 终于 or 总算.

1. 离开老家二十多年，他今天总算得以重回家乡。
   After more than twenty years, he was finally able to go back to his hometown today.

2. 同学们毕业十年了，今天终于得以相聚。
   The class has finally been able to reunite ten years after graduation.

3. 由于老师的指导，他的论文才得以顺利通过。
   Thanks to the teacher's advice, his dissertation was able to pass smoothly.

9. 释放 • release, set free

1. 明年他就将刑满 (xíngmǎn, *have completed one's sentence*) 释放了。
   He will be released next year upon the completion of his term of imprisonment.

2. 关键是知道怎样把你自己由所有的限制中释放出来。
   The key is to know how to free yourself from all the restrictions.

3. 反应堆 (fǎnyìngduī, *reactor*) 在运行过程中会释放大量的热。
   The running of the reactor will release tremendous heat.

10. 促进 • facilitate, promote, boost, accelerate

1. 经济体制改革，必然促进经济发展，提高人民生活水平。
   Reform of the economic system will definitely boost economic development and thus improve people's living standards.

2. 这些去中国学中文的外国学生也促进了中外文化的交流。
   These foreign students going to study Chinese in China also promoted cultural exchange between China and foreign countries.

3. 竞争机制的建立，对提高工作效率起到了很好的促进作用。
   The establishment of competitive mechanisms facilitated the improvement of working efficiency.

语法

1. 之 as a classical third person pronoun

In Lesson 10, Volume 1, we learned that 之 can be used as a classical function word similar to the modern Chinese particle 的 (e.g., 一家之主，长城之外). In this lesson, we are going to learn the other function of 之: it can also serve as a third person pronoun, "it, her, him, or them." The antecedent for 之 must be established in previous discourse. Note that this pronoun 之 can only be used as an object of a verb or preposition, never as a subject.

实行"双休制"后，人们都感觉到，在工作和家务之外，有了更多属于自己的自由时间。一个新的热门话题：休闲，也随之出现。

After the implementation of the "two-day weekend" system, people feel that they are having more free time of their own, apart from work and household duties. A new hot topic, enjoying leisure, then emerged with this (new situation).

随之 means "along with it, in the wake of it" and can be used with different verbs to indicate that "something happens with it."

随之出现 appear/emerge with it	随之增长 increase with it
随之消失 disappear with it	随之下降 decrease with it
随之产生 result with it	随之而来 come with it
随之结束 end with it	随之而去 go with it

The following are some idiomatic phrases with 之 as a third person pronoun:

1. 学而时习之   study and constantly practice it (Confucius)

2. 取而代之   replace it (lit., to take it and replace it)

3. 为之感动   be moved by it (被它感动)

2. 设问句 ● Rhetorical questions with answers

A question is rhetorical if it is asked merely for effect with no answer expected. The purpose of this figure of speech is not to secure a response, but to assert or deny a point implicitly because the answer is obvious. Sometimes the writer or speaker may ask a rhetorical question and immediately provide the answer. In this case, the rhetorical questions are used to call the readers' or listeners' attention to the question and encourage them to think about the issues raised.

1. 过去，受季节的影响，中国北方居民往往要靠土豆、萝卜和大白菜过整个冬天；现在呢？每个城市每天都有大量新鲜蔬菜出现在市场上。
   In the past, due to the seasonal effect, residents of northern China usually relied on potatoes, turnips and cabbage to survive the winter. But what's it like now? Every city has so many fresh vegetables in the market every day.

2. 过生日去哪儿吃饭庆祝？不少孩子选择麦当劳。
   Where to hold birthday celebrations? Many children choose McDonald's.

3. 如今的都市消费有哪些新特点呢？请看下面生活的几个方面：
   What are the new features of urban people's consumption? Please read about the following aspects of their life:

3. 词汇的音节对称 ● Rhythmic parallelism in word formation and collocation

Perhaps due to the conventional preference for symmetrical structure in Chinese culture, rhythmic parallelism seems to be an essential requirement in Chinese word formation and collocation. The principle is to match the rhythm of the constituent elements: monosyllabic words usually match up with monosyllables and disyllables with disyllables. The resulting words are either two-character words or four-character words. That is the reason why most Chinese words are two characters (about 75%) and most idioms are four characters. For example, 杯 cannot be used by itself as a word. It has to take 子 to make a disyllabic word 杯子. But when it's combined with 茶 to form "a teacup," it has to drop 子 to form 茶杯; it is never 茶杯子. Look at the following words:

杯子 (cup)	→茶杯 (teacup)	(*茶杯子)
衣服 (clothes)	→衣架 (clothes hanger)	(*衣服架)
身体 (body)	→体重 (body weight)	(*身体重)
明星 (star)	→影星/电影明星 (movie star)	(* 电影星 or *影明星)

书面语体的音节对称 Rhythmic parallelism in written Chinese

It is worth noting that disyllabic words are even more prominent in the written language. Many multi-character expressions in the spoken language can be replaced by disyllabic written words. For example:

Spoken	买东西	找工作	从今以后	窗户外头	桌子旁边儿	一天比一天
Written	购物	求职	今后	窗外	桌旁	日益

Interestingly, some one-character words in spoken language (especially basic verbs) will become disyllabic in written language to add "formality" to the expressions. Examine the following examples:

Spoken	帮	买	看	读	要	能	好	河	树
Written	帮助	购买	观看	阅读	需要	能够	美好	河流	树木

In written discourse, disyllabic words tend to be used with other disyllabic words. You have been practicing the "word collocation exercise" in every chapter of this book, so this principle should not be unfamiliar to you now. For example:

Spoken	开会	买书	读报	种树	有权利
Written	举行会议	购买书籍	阅读报纸	种植树木	拥有权利
Incorrect	*举行会	*购买书	*阅读报	*种植树	*拥有权

练习

1. 语音

Write pinyin for the following underlined Chinese characters. Pay special attention to their different pronunciations in different contexts.

都是（ ）	得体（ ）	穿着（ ）	长处（ ）
都市（ ）	觉得（ ）	着急（ ）	处理（ ）
的确（ ）	麻将（ ）	单调（ ）	喜好（ ）
真的（ ）	将来（ ）	调整（ ）	好像（ ）

2. 词汇句型

2.1. Match the following words on the left with the words appropriately associated with them on the right.

Group One		**Group Two**	
(Verb + Object) (Formal)		(Verb + Noun) (Informal)	
1. 追求 ＿＿＿	节奏	1. 走 ＿＿＿	物
2. 重视 ＿＿＿	生日	2. 访 ＿＿＿	网
3. 加快 ＿＿＿	时尚	3. 打 ＿＿＿	亲戚
4. 庆祝 ＿＿＿	服装	4. 逛 ＿＿＿	麻将
5. 选购 ＿＿＿	名胜	5. 购 ＿＿＿	友
6. 游览 ＿＿＿	营养	6. 上 ＿＿＿	街

2.2. 近义词辨析："适合"还是"合适"？

1. 这件衣服我穿大小正＿＿＿＿＿。

2. 请你帮他挑一件＿＿＿＿＿他穿的衣服。

3. 你的性格＿＿＿＿＿当老师。

4. 我们要选一个代表参加演讲比赛，你认为谁＿＿＿＿＿？

5. 如果有＿＿＿＿＿的机会，我想去中国工作。

6. 这种电影不＿＿＿＿＿小孩子看。

7. 这么做恐怕不太＿＿＿＿＿吧?

8. 这种工作只＿＿＿＿＿年轻人做。

9. 温哥华 (Vancouver) 连年被联合国评为最＿＿＿＿＿人类居住的城市之一。

2.3. 选词填空

a. 敏感	b. 得体	c. 避免	d. 得以	e. 选购
f. 取而代之	g. 丰富多彩	h. 融入	i. 带动	j. 外表
k. 释放	l. 单调	m. 个性	n. 例外	o. 与此同时
p. 主流				

1. 暑假期间，学校举办了一系列 _____ 的课外活动。

2. 我上个月天天加班，只有国庆节那天 _____。

3. 多亏有他相助，这项试验才 _____ 成功。

4. 一次雷电所 _____ 出来的能量 (energy) 大约有多少？

5. 现在，电话、VCR 都已经不流行了，_____ 的是手机、DVD。

6. 他巧妙地避开了记者提出的这个 _____ 问题。

7. 他的工作很 _____，每天做一样的事情，很没意思，所以他辞职了。

8. 网络经济的发展 _____ 了这个国家国民经济的发展。

9. 小张很会打扮，她常常是穿得既有个性又很 _____。

10. 人与人之间需要互相交流，这样才能 _____ 误解的产生。

11. 我们当然要努力学习，_____ 也要注意锻炼身体。

12. 她长得很漂亮，可是没有鲜明的 _____。

13. 谈恋爱不能只看对方的 _____，而应该注重他/她的内心。

14. 下个星期她有一个面试，所以周末想去商场 _____ 一套正式的服装。

15. 很多华人家长将子女视为 _____ 社会的希望。

2.4. 选用合适的词汇完成下面短文

| a. 游览 | b. 管理 | c. 达到 | d. 兴起 | e. 入时 | f. 流行 |
| g. 都市 | h. 双休 | i. 逛街 | j. 丰富多彩 | k. 购物 | l. 旅游 |

随着 _____ 日旅游热的 _____，北京、天津这两个大 _____ 的市民从来没有像去年那样频繁地 (*frequently*) "交往" 过。在天津第一大商场，_____ 的商品吸引了很多北京人。商场的 _____ 人员说，有时候商场的北京游客一天能 _____ 一万人。北京人去天津的主要目的是 _____ 购物。在天津大商场的服装厅，一位打扮 _____ 的北京姑娘正在把新买的皮衣往 _____ 袋里装。她告诉记者，这种皮衣今年很 _____，她花了4400多元，可是在北京5000元都买不到。天津人到北京去则不同，主要是去 _____。他们早晨到北京，直接去要 _____ 的景点，当天晚上就可以回家。

3. 语法练习

3.1. 用"随之……"短语完成句子：

| a. 随之结束 | b. 随之而去 | c. 随之产生 | d. 随之增长 |
| e. 随之下降 | f. 随之而来 |

1. 独生子女政策在一定程度上控制了中国的人口增长。但 _____ 的人口老龄化与新生儿性别失调的问题又成了新的挑战。

2. 住房建设逐年加快，人均住房面积也 _____。

3. 四年的大学生活就要结束了，_____ 的将是就业的巨大压力。

4. 和平条约签订后，战争 _____。

5. 由于能源价格越来越低，石油公司利润也 _____。

6. 他的公司垮了，钱没了，婚姻也 _____。

3.2. 区别书面语与口语词汇：

Decide which of the following pairs of words are spoken or written. Write them down in the corresponding categories:

爸爸/父亲、官儿/官员、差异/不同、选/选择、找/觅、抵/到、还是/依然、没有/无、除了这个以外/此外、否则/要是不这样、

口语	书面语

3.3. 选用合适的书面语或口语词汇填空。注意音节的对称：

1. 经济发达地区有义务 _____ 不发达地区。　　（a. 帮　b. 帮助）

2. 你 _____ 我看看，这里面有没有错字儿。　　（a. 帮　b. 帮助）

3. 天气 _____ 热起来了。　　（a. 日益　b. 一天比一天）

4. 来华参观访问的外宾 _____ 增多。　　（a. 日益　b. 一天比一天）

5. 以前北京居民人 _____ 住房面积只有 7 平方米。　　（a. 均　b. 平均）

6. 这个地方百姓的收入高于全国 _____ 水平。　　（a. 均 b. 平均）

7. 妈妈说："要听话啊，_____ 不带你出去玩。"　　（a. 不然　b. 否则）

8. 我们一定要保护好环境，_____ 后果会相当严重。　　（a. 不然　b. 否则）

9. 随着农村经济发展，农民生活日益 _____。　　（a. 富　b. 富裕）

10. 中国现在面临的挑战之一是贫 _____ 差距的问题。　　（a. 富　b. 富裕）

3.4. 用口语形式改写下列书面语句子：

例：考试之事，今晚是否可以决定？

→ 考试的事情，今天晚上是不是可以决定下来？

1. 各科考试均已通过。

→ _____

2. 抵京后，请来电话，以免家人挂念。

→ _____

3. 中秋节将至，商家争相推出促销活动。

→ _____

4. 会议仍在进行，协议尚未达成。

→ _____

5. 机票尚未购定，下周恐难成行。

→ _____

6. 论文已如期写完。下月即将毕业。

→ _____

7. 通过网络了解欧美同龄人的喜好和兴趣。

→ _____

8. 中国人深埋几十年的爱美之心，开始在服饰上得以释放。

→ _____

9. 此后，有一段时间实行隔周双休。

→ _____

10. 有的人用较少的预付款买下尚未建好的新房，等房价上升后再出售盈利。

→ _____

4. 综合练习

4.1. 选词填空

a. 节奏	b. 个性	c. 融入	d. 入时	e. 品牌
f. 日新月异	g. 随之出现	h. 丰富多彩	i. 情调	j. 饮食
k. 休闲	l. 都市	m. 时尚	n. 取而代之	
o. 亲朋好友	p. 毫无疑问			

酒吧和咖啡屋

随着中国经济 _____ 的发展，中国人的消费需求普遍提高。现在 _____ 外出用餐或聚会时，除了考虑 _____ 的口味以外，还开始讲究优雅 (yōuyǎ, elegant) 的环境和时尚的享受。于是，各种装修 _____、情调轻松、富有 _____ 的休闲餐饮模式也 _____。品尝各种口味的美食名酒、体验风情各异的餐饮文化成了一种新的时尚潮流。

20 世纪 90 年代初期，北京的三里屯 (Sānlǐtún)[1] 一带逐渐形成了"酒吧一条街"。每天晚上，一群群的商务人士、白领人员、艺术工作者、大学生和在北京的外国人纷纷来到这条开满酒吧的小街。此后，三里屯的酒吧老大地位又被西城区的"后海[2] 酒吧街" _____。后海酒吧街是一道将老北京的传统民俗与西方的酒吧文化融合在一起的奇异风景。跟三里屯酒吧的快 _____ 与喧闹相比，后海的酒吧更追求优雅的环境和含蓄的文化 _____。后海的夜晚，灯红酒绿，湖光荡漾 (dàngyàng, glistening waves)，成为京城白领、老外们休闲的最佳选择。而在上海、广州、西安，以及西藏、云南、广西等著名的旅游胜地，_____ 的地方民族文化与西方文化融合的各色酒吧也已相当普遍。酒吧为当代中国人的 _____ 生活增添了时代特色。调查显示，超过 90% 的四十岁以下的白领人士去过酒吧。

---

[1] 三里屯 is a famous bar street located in the embassy district in eastern Beijing.
[2] 后海 is a lake located in the Xicheng District of Beijing. The Houhai Café and Bar Street is a mixture of ancient Beijing and modern Western culture. It is full of trendy bars and unique pubs.

在酒吧文化兴起的同时，咖啡也正在迅速 _____ 这个有着几千年茶文化的国家。从 1999 年 1 月第一家星巴克咖啡店登陆北京至今，短短十几年间，在中国各大 _____ 已经发展了 500 多家星巴克咖啡店。一杯香浓的咖啡，舒适的环境，轻松的音乐，还有网络相伴，这是大多数到过星巴克的中国人感受到的一种气氛、一种文化。星巴克咖啡的目标是为中国的中产阶层提供一个风格清新的 _____ 社交场所。在这里，人们可以关注别人，也同时被人关注。在一家中美合资公司工作的罗先生就是这类人。其实他更喜欢茶的味道，所以他在家里喝茶，而在公共场所喝咖啡。罗先生在买星巴克咖啡的同时，也买到了现在在中国非常需要的一种东西：一种 _____、一种生活方式。在中国小资[3] 当中流行着这样一句话："我不在办公室，就在星巴克，我不在星巴克，就在去星巴克的路上。" _____，喝星巴克咖啡，已经成了小资 的代名词，代表一种有品位 (taste) 的时尚文化。

按照上面这篇文章的意思，下面的说法对不对？ (T/F)

_____ 1. 当代中国人外出用餐时主要考虑饭店的环境，饮食的口味并不重要。

_____ 2. 三里屯一带曾经是北京的酒吧中心。

_____ 3. 三里屯的酒吧没有后海的酒吧喧闹。

_____ 4. 北京的白领和老外现在更喜欢去后海的酒吧。

_____ 5. 在中国的大城市，咖啡店越来越普遍。

_____ 6. 对很多中国人来说，星巴克是时尚文化的象征。

_____ 7. 中国的星巴克不提供电脑上网服务。

---

[3]小资 is short for 小资产阶级, petite bourgeoisie, people who are well educated, have economic strength and pursue a life of quality, sentiment and style.

_____ 8. 罗先生觉得喝咖啡更时尚，所以他更喜欢咖啡。

_____ 9. 现代中国的小资阶层非常重视生活情调。

4.2. 英译汉

1. My younger brother is preparing for the university entrance examination and has a pile of homework to do every day, even with no exception on Sundays. （例外）

   _____

   _____

2. In the past, young people's marriages were decided by parents. What's it like now? They can have the freedom to choose boyfriends or girlfriends for themselves without the influence of external pressures.

   _____

   _____

3. Making investments in the stock market and real estate has gradually become popular among young people.

   _____

4. As computers are playing a more and more important role in our lives, many people believe that the traditional post office will soon be replaced by e-mail. （由于、取而代之）

   _____

   _____

5. Lily accompanied her friend to the modeling contest and was persuaded into entering herself for the competition too. How did it turn out? Her friend didn't get in, but Lily won second prize. （设问句）

   _____

   _____

   _____

5. 阅读练习

阅读一：从"票"到"卡"— 中国百姓消费变化

从上世纪 50 年代中到 90 年代初近 40 年时间里，中国人钱包里放的是各种各样的<u>票</u> (*ration coupons*)：粮票、油票、布票、煤票、糖票、豆腐票、肥皂票等等。它们对老百姓来说，比钱还重要。因为，当时居民每人每月只发半斤油票，用油票才能到粮油店买半斤油做一个月的菜，多买一两也不可能。到饭店吃饭不但要付钱，还得按吃饭多少给粮票。只有钱没粮票是吃不到饭的。

这个时代被称为"票证时代"。人们买粮食要有粮票，买布买衣服要有布票，买肉要有肉票，连买豆腐也要凭豆腐票……衣食住行、柴米油盐全部列入"计划"，<u>凭</u> (*by*) 票证供应。食品类除了各种粮、油、肉票外，还有蛋票、糖票、豆制品票及蔬菜票等。服装日用品类有布票、鞋票、毛巾、肥皂、甚至火柴票等。至于"贵重"物品，如自行车票、手表票等，那都是发到工作单位上，普通人很多年都轮不到一张票。那时的中国人，生活在一大堆各种各样的票证里，每项购物都被计划数字控制，有人开玩笑说，那是真正的"<u>数字化</u> (*numbered, digital*) 生存"。

现在商场里商品丰富多彩，老百姓可随意选购，购物的各种票证也因此失去了价值。取而代之的，是各种信用卡和银行卡。"一卡在手，购物不愁"已经成为现实。去购物只需将卡轻轻一刷，消费就完成了。如今，在大型商场和酒店，银行卡的<u>刷卡</u> (*shuākǎ, swipe card, pay by card*) 率远远超过了现金支付。科技现代化突飞猛进，更使刷卡消费扩展到生活的其他方面。人们已经习惯刷卡交水费、电费、煤气费、手机电话费等等。除了银行卡，信用卡以外，退休工资卡、医疗保险卡、<u>公交</u> (*public transportation*) 卡、商场的<u>会员</u> (*membership*) 卡、健身房的 VIP 卡等等也如雨后春笋般纷纷出现。这些五花八门的"卡"成了市民的新朋友，给人们的生活增添了几分<u>轻松</u>、便利和快乐。

从出门要带大量的票证和现金，到现在"一卡走天下"的便利生活。"卡时代"的来临见证 (witness) 了过去几十年中国人消费观念和消费方式的翻天覆地的变化。

5.1. 根据短文内容，选择最佳答案回答问题

1. 为什么说"票"对老百姓来说，比钱还重要？
   a. 因为票很值钱。
   b. 因为票可以用来买东西，钱不可以。
   c. 因为如果没有票，很多东西有钱也买不到。
   d. 因为票很珍贵，很多年都轮不到一张。

2. 关于"票证时代"，以下哪种说法是<u>不正确</u>的？
   a. 老百姓的衣食住行都需要票。
   b. 如果没有粮票，就不能在饭店吃饭。
   c. 买一只手表可能要等很多年。
   d. 买家用电器不需要票。

3. 为什么中国会有"票证时代"？
   a. 因为政府想了解人民的消费情况。
   b. 因为可以方便政府控制人口数量。
   c. 因为当时中国经济落后，物质资源缺乏。
   d. 因为当时科技不发达，各种卡还没有出现。

4. 中国的票证时代是什么时候结束的？
   a. 50 年代中。
   b. 90 年代初。
   c. 40 年代中。
   d. 80 年代初。

5. 为什么有人说票证时代是真正的"数字化生存"？
   a. 因为票证上有很多数字。
   b. 因为人们有很多票证。
   c. 因为那时人们用的数字化电器很先进。
   d. 因为那时买很多东西都要受到数量控制。

6. 以下哪一项<u>不是</u>"卡时代"的特征？
   a. 很多商场和酒店都可以用卡消费。
   b. 粮票、油票等改进成了粮卡、油卡。
   c. 人们可以用银行卡支付水费、电费、煤气费。
   d. 坐公共汽车时可以使用公交卡。

7. 从"票"到"卡"说明了中国百姓消费方面的什么变化？
   a. 现在物资供应越来越丰富了。
   b. 科学技术越来越现代化了。
   c. 人们的生活越来越舒适便利了。
   d. 以上都是。

阅读二：独生子女消费行为 ——"月光族"

　　大都市里的独生子女一代在消费方面有"月光族"之称，意思是每个月都会把自己的钱用光。当然，月光族并不代表中国所有年轻人的消费行为。但至少可以代表一部分年轻人的生活方式。有时候，他们不仅用光自己的钱，甚至还要向父母或祖父母伸手。"月光族"又被称为"血拼族"。"血拼"是英文 shopping 的<u>谐音</u> (xiéyīn, homophonous) 翻译，在中文中，大量花钱被形象地比喻为"出血"，而"拼"则是"拼命，不顾一切"的意思，"血拼"这个词形象地说明了这种人不顾一切大量花钱的不成熟、不<u>理性</u> (reasonable, rational) 的消费。他们在领到薪水之后，往往会与好友一起大量购物，虽然他们已拥有足够多的衣服、饰品、皮包、电器等，但面对自己喜爱的商品时，往往还会"血拼"一场。与市场发展比较成熟的欧美发达国家相比，中国高消费群体的年龄层至少要年轻 5 岁。许多拥有名牌服饰的年轻人，其实并没有很高的收入，但他们会用几个月的薪水去买一身 Chanel 服装，或者省下饭钱来买一只 LV 皮包。

　　与上一代相比，他们的消费习惯有明显的差异：他们的时尚感和消费欲望更高；他们更喜欢花钱，而不是存钱。他们没有经历过物资<u>贫乏</u> (poor, lack)，家庭收入低下的生活，其成长过程正好是中国经济和个人生活水平不断上升的过程，因此，他们在消费中对价格不敏感（虽然他们对名牌商品<u>打折</u> (discount)、降价的消息很敏感），而更在意质量、个性、品牌和舒适程度。与父辈相比，这一代人有着强烈的"享受生活"的意识。上一代人看重的是"资产 (*property*) 型消费"—— 大到住房，小到冰箱、彩电等；而独生子女则强调的是"感官 (*sensory*) 型消费"—— 买CD、mp3、上网、互动游戏、旅游、聚会、出国……

不过，由于社会竞争日益激烈，非国有单位工作者增多，相对其父母辈，独生子女就业与生活中不确定因素更多。独生子女的血拼消费，常常预支 (*advance against*) 了家庭的潜在消费能力，而他们日后将面临上有老下有小的巨大压力。随着如今房价、教育、医疗费用直线上升，月光族们可能不得不抑制 (*restrain*) 一下自己的血拼欲望，为将来的"不时之需 (*unexpected needs*)"做一点准备。

5.2. 根据短文内容，选择最佳答案回答问题

1. 以下哪一项<u>不是</u>"月光族"的特征？
   a. 收入很高
   b. 喜欢消费
   c. 独生子女
   d. 追求名牌

2. 月光族喜欢血拼的原因是：
   a. 他们没有足够的衣服、鞋子或其他生活用品。
   b. 他们的父母支持他们消费。
   c. 他们追求享受，只要自己喜欢的，就无所谓价钱。
   d. 他们有太多钱。

3. 月光族的消费习惯和上一代相比有什么差别？
   a. 他们更喜欢存钱。
   b. 比起价格，他们更在意商品的质量和品牌。
   c. 他们更看重"资产型消费"。
   d. 他们对钱更为敏感。

4. 从这篇短文你可以看出作者的什么观点？
   a. 作者很欣赏月光族的消费行为。
   b. 作者很羡慕月光族的消费能力。
   c. 作者觉得月光族的消费行为很正常。
   d. 作者不赞成月光族的血拼消费行为。

5. 这篇短文的主要意思是：

    a. 独生子女大多都是月光族。

    b. 月光族的消费行为很不成熟。

    c. 月光族需要抑制消费，为将来做准备。

    d. 中国的月光族现象及其产生原因和潜在问题。

5.3. 按照上面这篇文章的意思，下面的说法对不对？(T/F)

    _____ 1. 中国的独生子女都是月光族。

    _____ 2. 有些独生子女还会向父母和祖父母要钱。

    _____ 3. "血拼"就是不顾一切大量花钱买东西的意思。

    _____ 4. 月光族们"血拼"时不太考虑东西贵还是便宜。

    _____ 5. 血拼族喜欢买打折的名牌商品。

    _____ 6. 血拼族都很有钱。

    _____ 7. 独生子女的工作比上一辈的稳定。

    _____ 8. 为了减少将来的压力，月光族们应该更理智地消费。

6. 口语练习：讨论题

1. 如果你近期去过中国，能不能谈谈你对中国消费市场的印象？

2. 中国人由以前的花长时间做饭到现在流行的快餐、盒饭，你觉得哪一种饮食模式更好？为什么？

3. 洋快餐（麦当劳，肯德鸡）现在在中国特别受孩子欢迎。你觉得这种情况有什么好处？有什么坏处？

4. 在你们国家，什么样的服装是流行的服装？穿着流行对什么人来说比较重要？为什么？

5. 谈一谈中国人的消费和你们国人的消费有什么异同。

6. 你对中国年轻人追求时尚名牌的消费方式有什么看法？

7. 你的休闲生活主要是做什么？跟中国人的休闲活动有什么相同或差异？

8. 为什么星巴克能在中国这个有几千年茶文化的国家发展得这么快？

9. 根据当代中国人的消费特点，如果你要到中国去投资，你觉得在哪方面投资比较有希望成功？

7. 写作练习：（任选一题，600-700 字）

1. 美国圣诞节的血拚族

2. 快餐对现代人生活的利与弊

3. 我最喜爱的休闲活动

4. 我们跟父母辈的不同之处

Required vocabulary and expressions:

1. Use at least 10 of the following new vocabulary words and phrases:

消费	饮食	节奏	个性	得体	入时	避免
选定	项目	外表	穿着	单调	得以	释放
时尚	品牌	敏感	融入	主流	此后	之外
开展	促销	带动	走亲访友	亲朋好友	取而代之	
丰富多彩						

2. Use at least 4 of the following expressions:

既是……也是……	即使……也不例外……	随着……	……，这反映了……
只……而不……	既……又……	的确……	取而代之的是……

癌症村

课文提要

During the three decades since Deng Xiaoping set China on a course toward market-style growth, rapid industrialization and urbanization have lifted hundreds of millions of Chinese out of poverty and made the country the world's largest producer of consumer goods. But there is little question that growth has come at the expense of the country's air, land and water. Intending to catch the immediate attention of the reader, the author starts this essay with a heart-rending story on the dire conditions of a village in the region of the Huai River (淮河). In his own words, a villager tells about the pain and suffering of the people in the village who are gradually dying of cancer caused by water pollution. He sorrowfully remembers the place when it was beautiful and tranquil. The story leads to a discussion of the various aspects of the environmental problems in China.

Besides its contents, this essay is also interesting in the way it is written. The language is formal, often using concise literary words, but interwoven with vernacular speech and folksy "doggerel satire" to reflect the intense emotion of the people suffering from pollution. In addition, the essay is rich in four-character poetic phrases intended to evoke mental images in the readers' mind and engage them more closely with the reading.

阅读前讨论：

1. 看了课文题目，你能不能猜出来什么是"癌症村"？
2. 人类在什么情况下会污染环境？
3. 你所居住的城市有什么环境问题？
4. 谁最应该对环境污染负责？
5. 你知道哪些跟"环境保护"有关的词汇？

自学生词

Match each new word in the left column with its English translation in the right column by guessing the word's meaning from the characters that it is composed of.

	生词	繁体	序号	英文
( )	疾病		1.	experience many times
( )	戏水	戲	2.	be interrelated
( )	记忆	記憶	3.	work
( )	死亡		4.	play in water
( )	干活	幹	5.	running water, tap water
( )	自来水	來	6.	go up to heaven, i.e., die
( )	高发	高發	7.	high occurring
( )	升天	昇	8.	remember; memory
( )	排放		9.	fast
( )	历经	歷經	10.	hydrology
( )	遍及		11.	disease, sickness
( )	快速		12.	extend (everywhere)
( )	高速		13.	discharge
( )	相关	關	14.	high-speed
( )	水文		15.	paper
( )	纸张	紙張	16.	death

生词

	生词	繁体	拼音	词性	英文	HSK 等级
1.	癌症	癌	áizhèng	*n.*	cancer	丙
2.	村		cūn	*n.*	village	丙
3.	割		gē	*v.*	cut with a knife	乙
4.	患		huàn	*v.*	contract (an illness)	丙
5.	幽灵	靈	yōulíng	*n.*	ghost, spirit, phantom	
6.	时刻	時	shíkè	*adv.*	constantly, always	丙
7.	威胁	脅	wēixié	*v.*	threaten	丙
8.	相继	繼	xiāngjì	*adv.*	one after another	丁
9.	去世		qùshì	*v.o.*	die, pass away	丁
10.	塘		táng	*n.*	pool, pond	丁
11.	清澈		qīngchè	*adj.*	crystal-clear	
12.	透明		tòumíng	*adj.*	transparent	丙
13.	鸭子	鴨	yāzi	*n.*	duck	丙
14.	追逐		zhuīzhú	*v.*	pursue, chase	
15.	臭		chòu	*adj.*	stinky, smelly	乙
16.	县	縣	xiàn	*n.*	county	乙
17.	污染	汙	wūrǎn	*v.*	pollute, contaminate	乙
18.	物		wù	*n.*	thing, matter, substance	丁
19.	致		zhì	*v.*	cause, incur, invite	丙
20.	流域		liúyù	*n.*	river basin, valley	丙
21.	普查		pǔchá	*n.*	census, general investigation	丁
22.	结论	結論	jiélùn	*n.*	conclusion	乙
23.	密切		mìqiè	*adj.*	close, intimate	乙
24.	民谣	謠	mínyáo	*n.*	folk rhyme, popular verse	
25.	首		shǒu	*m*	measure word for poems and songs	乙
26.	升迁	昇遷	shēngqiān	*v.*	be promoted	
27.	针对	針對	zhēnduì	*v.*	be directed against	乙
28.	皮革		pígé	*n.*	leather	丁
29.	治理		zhìlǐ	*v.*	control, manage	丁
30.	启动	啓動	qǐdòng	*v.*	start, initiate, launch	丁
31.	扩散	擴	kuòsàn	*v.*	spread	丁

	生词	繁体	拼音	词性	英文	HSK 等级
32.	致富		zhìfù	*v.o.*	become rich	丁
33.	矿山	礦	kuàngshān	*n.*	mine	丁
34.	忽视	視	hūshì	*v.*	ignore, neglect	丙
35.	农场	農場	nóngchǎng	*n.*	farm, ranch	丙
36.	代价	價	dàijià	*n.*	price, cost	丙
37.	能源		néngyuán	*n.*	energy sources	乙
38.	耗费	費	hàofèi	*n.*	waste, consume	丁
39.	破坏	壞	pòhuài	*v.*	destroy, damage	乙
40.	效益		xiàoyì	*n.*	effectiveness, benefit	丁
41.	官员	員	guānyuán	*n.*	official	丁
42.	部		bù	*n.*	minister, department	乙
43.	频繁	頻	pínfán	*adv.*	frequently	丁
44.	反思		fǎnsī	*v.*	self-examination, introspection	丁
45.	单纯	單純	dānchún	*adj.*	pure, simple	丙
46.	持续	續	chíxù	*v.*	sustain, continue	丁
47.	严峻	嚴	yánjùn	*adj.*	severe	丁
48.	淮河		Huái Hé	*prop. n.*	Huai River (a main river of East China which runs through three provinces: Henan, Anhui, and Jiangsu.)	

成语和惯用语

成语/惯用语	繁体	单字解释	意思
绿树成荫 lǜ shù chéng yīn	綠 樹 蔭	绿：green 树：tree 成：result, become 荫：shade	canopy of green trees 例：街道两侧，绿树成荫。 On both sides of the street, there is a canopy of flourishing trees.
触目惊心 chù mù jīng xīn	觸 驚	触：touch 目：eye 惊：startle, shock 心：heart	startling, shocking (scene) 例：去年的一场飓风留下了这触目惊心的凄凉景象。 Last year's hurricane left us with this startling and desolate sight.
鱼米之乡 yú mǐ zhī xiāng	魚 鄉	鱼：fish 米：rice 之：particle "的" 乡：land, place	fertile land of rice and fish 例：在中国，长江中下游一直被称为"鱼米之乡"。 In China, the middle and lower reaches of the Yangzi Rriver are always called the fertile region of rice and fish.
无能为力 wú néng wéi lì	無 爲	无：without 能：ability 为：do, act, handle 力：power, influence	cannot do anything, helpless, powerless 例：很抱歉，对于你的事，我实在无能为力。 I'm sorry, but there is really nothing I can do to help you.

■ 第一读：掌握课文大意

快速阅读课文，看下面三个选择中哪一个最能说明本课主要意思：
1. "癌症村"的历史和现状
2. 王子清的家庭状况
3. 中国的环境污染问题

"癌症村"

王子清已记不清村里死了多少人了。"每死一个人，我的心就像刀割一样。"从上世纪90年代以来，村里的人就开始纷纷得病。每年村里因患癌症而死去的少则五六人，多时达20多人。由于得癌症的病人多，他们村被当地人称作"癌症村"。

王子清一家便是这个不幸村庄中的不幸家族。2004年6月，短短一个月内，王子清便失去了3位亲人：他哥哥、弟弟、叔叔都因癌症而相继去世。这些年，村里王姓130人中，便有35人死于癌症。死者最年长的不到70岁，最年轻的只有30岁。"人活得都没有希望了，"王子清说，"村里的人总担心，下一个死的会不会是自己。"死亡像一个可怕的幽灵，时刻在威胁着这个村子。

王子清家正对着一个大水塘，村里人吃的用的都是这塘水，村南两公里外就是淮河。在王子清的记忆中，从前淮河和水塘里的水都曾经清澈透明，河塘边绿树成荫，白色的鸭子在河塘内追逐戏水。村里的人去地里干活时，从来不带水。渴了，随便从河塘中捧一口水就喝。"可甜了，比现在的自来水都好喝。"王子清说。

可是，从80年代末开始，淮河边建起了一些工厂，淮河水开始变坏变臭。据县水文站提供的一份资料显示，1990年、1994年和2000年，淮河水中共查出90种污染物，其中致癌物高达67种。河水污染了土地和地下水，也污染了空气。2005年，国家疾病控制中心曾对淮河流域癌症高发地区进行全面普查，最终结论是：一、淮河流域地区为癌症高发区；二、癌症高发与受污染的淮河水密切相关。以前，曾有"走千走万，不如淮河两岸"的民谣；而如今，这个自古以来的鱼米之乡，却变成了"癌症村"频发地区。

难怪当地居民中流传着这样一首民谣："你们得利，我们得病；你们升迁，我们升天。"这首民谣针对的就是那些建在淮河流域的高污染的纸张、皮革和塑料制造企业。这些企业的工业污水基本上都排放到淮河中，污水一流就是几十年，迟迟得不到治理。虽然早在 1994 年国家就启动了治理淮河的工程，历经二十几年，投资 600 亿，但至今尚未实现"水体还清"的目标。

上世纪 90 年代，"癌症村"只在个别地方出现，如今却扩散到全国 20 个省。在快速致富的过程中，工厂和矿山忽视了环境保护，将有毒的化学品和污水排放到河流湖泊中，使中国各地的水污染达到了触目惊心的程度。面对那些只重视短期经济效益和就业机会的企业领导和政府官员时，连国家环保部门也一度感到无能为力。

中国国家环境保护部副部长潘岳表示，过去几十年中国经济的高速发展是以牺牲环境为代价的。中国创造同等经济价值的能源耗费量是世界其他地区平均水平的三倍。对环境的严重破坏，已经给中国造成了灾难性的后果。3 亿多农村人口喝不到干净的水，三分之一的城市居民呼吸不到清洁空气。高耗能、高污染、高消费的经济发展模式使中国成为了世界耗水第一、污水排放量第一的国家。

近年来频繁发生的环境污染事件，使人们越来越意识到这种可怕的不断增长的环境代价。中国社会各界已经开始反思多年来单纯追求经济增长的发展模式。"绿色 GDP"、"可持续发展"的概念已经被越来越多的人所关注和接受。潘岳说，"中国的环境保护形势依然严峻，可以说，环境状况已经进入了'冬天'，但由于社会各界的广泛重视，环境保护工作已经进入了'春天'。"[1]

■ 第二读：细节和理解

A. 根据课文内容回答下列问题：

1. 王子清的村子为什么被称为"癌症村"？

2. 村子里的大水塘有些什么变化？

3. 河水变坏的原因是什么？

---

[1]潘岳接受上海《第一财经日报》记者访问时发言。原载"第一财经日报"2006 年 1 月 10 日

4. "癌症村"里的居民为什么会得病？

5. 民谣"你们得利，我们得病；你们升迁，我们升天"中的"你们"指的是谁？"升天"是什么意思？

6. 国家对于污水问题采取了什么措施？有没有成效？

7. "癌症村"的扩散现象说明了什么问题？

8. 为什么环境保护官员也感到无能为力？

9. 中国污染问题得不到解决的根本原因是什么？

10. 中国环境保护的"春天"是什么意思？

B. 根据课文推论：

Choose the best inference from the three possible choices for each sentence, and underline the clue(s) that helped you choose.

1. 王子清已记不清村里死了多少人了。
   a. 是因为王子清记性不好。
   b. 是因为王子清不知道村里的具体死亡人数。
   c. 是因为死去的人太多了。

2. "走千走万，不如淮河两岸"
   a. 淮河有千万公里长
   b. 许多地方都不如淮河两岸的风景美丽
   c. 要看淮河两岸的风景，需要走很多路

3. 上世纪 90 年代，"癌症村"只在个别地方出现，如今却波及全国 20 个省。
   a. 上世纪 90 年代，"癌症村"并不存在。
   b. 上世纪 90 年代，中国环境污染问题没有现在严重。
   c. 上世纪 90 年代，中国环境污染问题比现在严重。

4. 中国的环境保护形势依然严峻，可以说，环境状况已经进入了"冬天"，但由于社会各界的广泛重视，环境保护工作已经进入了"春天"。

　　a. 虽然环境状况非常差，但是人们已经开始意识到保护环境的重要性。

　　b. 中国环境状况非常严峻，可是春天快来了，环境问题将随之改善。

　　c. 中国环境状况非常差，是由于社会各界的广泛重视。

■ 阅读技巧

1. 语篇分析 • Reading Processing – Grouping Information for Comprehension

Grouping together information on the same subject makes your reading easier and comprehension better. In general, one paragraph is about one topic. But this is not always the case. This lesson has eight paragraphs but only five topics:

1. the gradual deaths of 王子清's family and the people of his village

2. the history of the environmental issues of the Huai River region

3. the local people's feelings about the dire conditions of their environment

4. the reasons for environmental degradation

5. the rising awareness of environmental issues in China

Practice: Below are eight statements summarizing each paragraph, out of order.

1. Write the number corresponding to the paragraph each statement summarizes.

（　　）王子清的家乡以前的情况。

（　　）企业领导和政府官员只重视短期经济效益是环境污染的原因。

（　　）"癌症村"已扩散到全国 20 个省，环境污染越来越严重。

（　　）王子清和他死去的家人 —"癌症村"里的一个不幸家族。

（　　）人们已经开始意识到环境问题的严重性。

（　　）老百姓对被污染的环境非常不满，但是国家治理淮河的工程却没有什么成效。

（　　）"癌症村"的产生是由于淮河边工厂的废水污染了淮河水。

（　　）淮河边上的"癌症村"。

2. Group the paragraphs by the five categories of subject matter stated above.

1. _____   2. _____   3. _____   4. _____   5. _____

2. 比喻：形象的语言 • Metaphor – Creating Imagery

Practice: Read the following sentences and make pictures in your mind about the sentences. Translate the following sentences into English in a way that best expresses your mental images.

1. 死亡像一个可怕的幽灵，时刻在威胁着这个村子。

　　_____

2. 这个自古以来的鱼米之乡，却变成了中国"癌症村"最集中的地区。

　　_____

3. 每死一个人，我的心就像刀割一样。

　　_____

4. 中国的环境保护形势依然严峻，可以说，环境状况已经进入了"冬天"，但由于社会各界的广泛重视，环境保护工作已经进入了"春天"。

　　_____

　　_____

词汇与句型

1. 记不清/记得清 • cannot/can remember clearly

1. 他一生得了很多音乐奖，多得连他自己也记不清了。
   He won so many music awards throughout his life that even he himself couldn't remember them all.

2. 十几年没见面，我还记得清他当年是什么样子。
   I haven't seen him for more than ten years; still, I remember clearly how he looked then.

3. 我记不清河水污染是从什么时候开始的。
   I can't remember clearly when the river pollution started.

2. 少则……多时达…… ● range from... to...; at least... and sometimes as many as...

1. 每年村里因患癌症而死的，少则五六人，多时达 20 多人。
   Of the number of people who died because of cancer every year, the minimum number was 5 or 6, and the largest number reached more than 20.

2. 这个高中每年有很多学生考上重点大学，少则七八十，多时达一百。
   Every year, many students from this high school get into key universities: at least seventy to eighty; sometimes as many as one hundred.

3. 他是一位勤奋而高效的作家，每天少则能写五千字，多时达一万字。
   He is a diligent and productive writer. He can write at least 5,000 words everyday, and sometimes as many as 10,000 words.

3. 相继 ● in succession, one after another

1. 这个村子的人们相继患上癌症。
   People in this village got cancer one after another.

2. "癌症村"相继出现在全国 20 几个省。
   The "cancer villages" appeared one after another in more than twenty provinces throughout the country.

3. 他的三个妹妹在两年内相继结婚。
   His three younger sisters got married one after another within two years.

4. 时刻 ● 1. (adv.) constantly, always 2. (n.) time, moment

1. 死亡像一个可怕的幽灵，时刻在威胁着这个村子。
   Death is constantly threatening this little village, like a terrifying ghost.

2. 恐怖分子 (*terrorist*) 的活动一刻也没有停止过，我们要时刻防备。
   We should always guard against terrorists, for they would never stop their actions.

3. 这名船长在最后的危急时刻仍然留在船上。
   The captain remained in the boat until the last fatal moment.

4. 在关键时刻，他失去了勇气。
   At the last minute, his courage failed him.

5. 致 • cause, incur, induce, lead to (usually bad result)

1. 污染的河水里含有致癌的物质。
   The polluted river contains the elements which cause cancer.

2. 至今为止，癌症仍是一种致命疾病。
   So far, cancer is still a kind of disease which causes death.

3. 他昨天晚上被送去急诊，医生们现在还没找到致病原因。
   He was sent to the emergency room last night. The doctors haven't found out what caused the disease.

6. 高 • high (degree, extent)

1. 加州属于地震高发地区。
   California belongs to the areas of high incidence of earthquakes.

2. 股票是一种高风险投资。
   Playing the stock market is a kind of high-risk investment.

3. 这是一座高污染的工业城市。
   This is a highly polluted industrial city.

7. 早在 • as early as...

1. 早在五十年前，他就提出"可持续发展"的概念。
   As far back as fifty years ago, he proposed the concept of "sustainable development".

2. 他的家族早在 20 世纪 30 年代就开始做出口生意。
   His family started an export business as far back as the 1930s.

3. 这所学校早在 100 年前就建立了。
   This school was founded as early as 100 years ago.

8. 历经 • experience many times, live through

1. 他的家人历经许多危险，终于来到美国。
   His family lived through many dangers and finally got to America.

2. 历经三十年的写作，他终于完成了那部长篇小说。
   After thirty years of writing, he finally finished his novel.

3. 他在创业过程中历经种种困难，变得越来越成熟。
He experienced various kinds of difficulty in establishing his own business, and he became more and more mature during this process.

9. 至今 ● up to now, to this day, so far

1. 他在一个月内失去了三位亲人，至今悲伤不已。
He lost three relatives within one month; he is still grieving to this day.

2. 我的家乡污染很少，人们至今仍然喝河水。
There is very little pollution in my hometown. To this day, people still drink river water.

3. 花木兰 (*Mulan*) 这个古代女英雄故事至今仍受人们喜爱。
The ancient heroic story "Mulan" is still popular among people to this day.

10. 触目惊心 ● startling, a ghastly sight

1. 近年来，北京的离婚率达到触目惊心的程度。
In recent years, the divorce rate in Beijing has reached a startling point.

2. 我一打开报纸，就看到那个触目惊心的标题。
I saw the startling headline as soon as I opened the newspaper.

3. 战争造成的破坏让人触目惊心。
People were startled by the ghastly sight of damage caused by the war.

11. 无能为力 ● cannot do anything about it

1. 当地居民对湖水污染无能为力。
The local residents cannot do anything about the lake pollution.

2. 无论他怎么说，女儿都不听，他觉得他实在是无能为力了。
His daughter wouldn't listen to him, no matter how he tried. He felt completely helpless.

3. 对不起，虽然我很想帮助你，可我对这件事确实是无能为力。
Sorry, although I would love to help you, I really can't do anything about this matter.

语法

1. 书面语特殊句型 • Special sentence patterns in formal/written Chinese

Although most sentence patterns can be used in both spoken and written Chinese, there are some sentence patterns that are used exclusively in the written Chinese style. Most of them are from classical Chinese. The following examples illustrate their distinctive usages and their spoken versions. One important point to keep in mind is that when written style is converted to spoken style, the adjustments will involve not only vocabulary change, but also sentence structure alterations.

1. **Adj./V 于……** (Adj./V at/in/with...) (Review of grammar point 于 in Lessons 8 and 14)

   他善于绘画。
   （口语：他在绘画方面很有才能。）

   最近她一直忙于饭店业务。
   （口语：最近她在饭店的生意很忙。）

   投资人要敢于冒险。
   （口语：作投资的人要不怕冒险。）

   网上购物便于人们进行价格比较。
   （口语：在网上买东西可以让人们比较方便地比较价格。）

2. **将……V 于/V 为……** （把……V 在/V 作……）

   他将多年存款全部投资于股票市场。
   （口语：他把很多年来存下的钱全都拿来买股票了。）

   公司应将此资金用于扩大再生产。
   （口语：公司应该把这笔资金用在扩大再生产方面。）

   很多华人家长将子女视为融入主流社会的希望。
   （口语：很多华人父母把孩子看做融入主流社会的希望。）

3. 为……而 V (do something for a certain purpose)

他特为此事而来。

（口语：为了这件事情，他特地来到这里。）

他们无比感谢警方为此而作出的种种努力。

（口语：他们非常感谢警察为了这个案子做出的各种努力。）

4. 与其 A，不如 B (rather than A, it's better to B, not so much A as B)

与其羡慕别人，不如自己努力。

（口语：不要只羡慕别人，还是自己多努力吧。）

老板的话与其说是鼓励，不如说是责备。

（口语：你不要以为老板说的话是鼓励（你），那实际上是一种批评。）

5. A 无异于 B (A is no different from B, A = B) (Review of 无异于 in Lesson 14)

这样大量饮酒无异于慢性自杀。

（口语：喝这么多的酒实际上就是慢性自杀。）

法律已有此条，如果再作规定，无异于画蛇添足。

（口语：法律上已经有了这一条，要是再作一条类似的规定，那就是画蛇添足了。）

6. 以 A 为 B (take/regard A as B) (Review of 以……为…… in Lesson 10)

过去 30 年中国经济的高速发展是以牺牲环境为代价的。

（口语：过去 30 年中国经济发展得那么快，是用污染环境换来的。）

医疗卫生工作应该以预防 (prevention) 为主。

（口语：医疗卫生工作应该把预防生病作为主要任务。）

7. 因……而…… (action because of/due to...)

他哥哥、弟弟、叔叔都因癌症而相继去世。

（口语：他的哥哥、弟弟和叔叔都因为得了癌症，先后去世了。）

本公司明年预算因今年盈利不多而被削减。

（口语：我们公司因为今年赚钱太少，所以明年的预算被削减/减少了。）

2. 民谣

民谣, also known as 顺口溜 ("doggerel satire" or "slippery jingles" in English), are rhythmic and rhyming popular sayings full of clever wordplay that are passed around in society. They are often of unknown authorship. Sometimes they are characteristic of children's game rhymes or nursery rhymes. But mostly they appear as a powerful form for comedy and satire, expressing public emotions and opinions in Chinese society.

Even in ancient times, powerless people at the bottom of society used 民谣 to express veiled criticism, sarcasm or anger in reaction to the dominance of officials. 民谣 have gained popularity today again in the Chinese vernacular with their sharp critical irony and ridicule against some problematic social, cultural and political phenomena, with corruption being the most common target of their biting wit.

民谣 used to get passed around by word of mouth, but now in the Internet age, they are quickly spread through blogs and text messages. Their language is usually humorous, folksy and vivid. In order to appreciate them, you need knowledge of the (local) culture and the ability to fill in what is missing from the (veiled) expressions.

In this lesson, the old 民谣 "走千走万，不如淮河两岸" praises the region of the Huai River before pollution as the best land, better than any other places even if you go or search for thousands of miles (here 走千走万 means 走一千里，走一万里 or 无论走多远，无论走到哪里).

A similar old 民谣 about another place, the poor province of 贵州, went like this: 天无三日晴，地无三尺平，人无三分银。(*There were no three continued sunny days or three square feet of smooth surface; and people had less than three ounces of silver in their pocket.*[2])

The second 民谣 in this lesson is a more contemporary piece, a bitter expression of plain folks against the ambiguous "你们", which might refer to the leaders of the big factories or the officials of the local government. 你们得利，我们得病；你们升迁，我们升天。The sharp contrast between the fate of "你们" and "我们" reflects alarming social inequities.

---

[2]贵州, a mountainous plateau located in southwest China, was regarded as a very poor place with bad weather, terrible geographic conditions and a poor standard of living. But now 贵州 has become a famous tourist attraction due to its beautiful natural forests and waterfalls, and the colorful cultures of 49 different ethnic minorities.

Below is another Internet-circulated 民谣 about corrupt officials:

身体越来越胖，心胸越来越窄。
头衔越来越多，学问越来越浅。
讲话越来越长，真话越来越少。
职位越来越高，威信越来越低。
年纪越来越老，情人越来越小。

A rough translation of the above 民谣:

The body grows fatter and fatter, the mind narrower and narrower.

The titles accumulate more and more, the knowledge shallower and shallower.

The speeches longer and longer, the truth less and less.

The position higher and higher, the popular trust lower and lower.

The age grows older and older, the mistresses younger and younger.

练习

1. 语音

Write pinyin for the following underlined Chinese characters. Pay special attention to their different pronunciations in different contexts:

水体还清 （　　）	密切 （　　）	年长 （　　）	干活 （　　）
还是　　（　　）	切开 （　　）	长期 （　　）	干净 （　　）
无能为力 （　　）	集中 （　　）	种类 （　　）	相关 （　　）
为此　　（　　）	中奖 （　　）	种树 （　　）	照相 （　　）

2. 词汇句型

2.1. Match the following words on the left with the words appropriately associated with them on the right.

Group One (Verb + Object)				Group Two (Adj. + Noun)		
1. 实现	_____	代价		1. 短期	_____	结论
2. 付出	_____	能源		2. 清澈的	_____	普查
3. 启动	_____	环境		3. 最终	_____	关系
4. 耗费	_____	后果		4. 严重	_____	湖水
5. 造成	_____	目标		5. 全面	_____	后果
6. 污染	_____	工程		6. 密切	_____	效益

2.2. 选词填空

a. 致癌	b. 致病	c. 致富

1. 有些日常用品如药品、塑料制品中的 _____ 物，已经引起人们的关注。

2. 这些国家都是靠石油能源 _____ 的。

3. 现代社会因烟酒过度而 _____ 的人仍然不少。

d. 致癌物	e. 易燃物	f. 交换物	g. 飞行物

4. 请不要携带 _____ 上车。

5. 在以金钱为 _____ 的商品世界里，许多美好的感情都变得没有价值了。

6. 有人说他们亲眼看到过不明 _____ (UFO)，你相信吗?

7. 这里的河水被工厂废水污染，含有多种 _____。

a. 治理	b. 威胁	c. 污染	d. 效益	e. 代价	f. 密切
g. 相继	h. 时刻	i. 相关	j. 针对	k. 破坏	l. 保护
m. 环保	n. 启动	o. 扩散	p. 忽视		

8. 最近公司职员们 _____ 辞职，公司领导人正 _____ 关注此事，并将 _____ 此事开会讨论。

9. 这些企业总想以最小的 _____ 换取最大的 _____，所以 _____ 了对环境的 _____。结果是森林被 _____、河流被 _____，人们的身体健康受到严重的 _____。

10. 老人的肺癌 _____ 了，在他生命的最后 _____，他把所有存款捐给了 _____ 组织。

11. 新 _____ 的黄河河水 _____ 工程与当地农民的利益密切 _____。

2.3. 短文填空 (Not all words will be used.)

| 1. 重要 | 2. 解决 | 3. 污染 | 4. 环境 | 5. 而 | 6. 结果 |
| 7. 增长 | 8. 认为 | 9. 造成 | 10. 主要 | | |

近几年来，北京的汽车数量迅速 _____，汽车尾气 (*tail gas*) 排放量猛增，_____ 了空气污染。研究 _____ 表明，北京空气中的污染 65% 来自汽车尾气污染。专家 _____，以前，城市污染大多是来自工业污染。_____ 现在，因交通造成的空气 _____ 已经超过传统的工业污染，成为城市污染的 _____ 来源。因此，控制汽车污染对 _____ 空气污染问题非常 _____。

3. 语法练习

3.1. 用口语形式改说/改写下列书面语句子：

1. Adj./V 于……

   a. 回收废品有利于减少环境污染。

   _____

b. 以前很多人习惯于在国有企业吃大锅饭。

_____

c. 这些年，村里王姓 130 人中，便有 35 人死于癌症。

_____

2. 将……V 于/V 为……

　　a. 该县政府是否已将所有捐款用于救灾？

_____

　　b. 政府官员应将百姓利益置于个人利益之上。

_____

　　c. 2005 年，韩国将汉城改名为首尔。

_____

3. 为……而 V

　　a. 任何企业都不能为谋取暂时的利益而污染环境。

_____

　　b. 工会为争取更好的工作条件而组织工人罢工。

_____

4. 与其 A，不如 B（A 不如 B）

　　a. 与其整天在家闲着，不如找个工作。

_____

　　b. 她迟早会知道真相的。与其长期瞒着她，还不如将实话告诉她。

_____

5. A 无异于 B（A 跟 B 没有什么不一样，A=B）

　　a. 有了这本字典，无异于身旁多了一位良师益友。

_____

b. 跟他谈电脑，无异于对牛弹琴。

_____

6. 以 A 为 B

a. 政府官员的工作应以人民利益为重。

_____

b. 普通话是"以北京语音为标准音，以北方话为基础方言"的现代汉民族共同语。

_____

7. 因……而……

a. 每年村里因患癌症而死去的少则五六人，多时达 20 多人。

_____

b. 文革后因感情不和而导致离婚者日益增多。

_____

8. 至今，不已

他在一个月内失去了三位亲人，至今悲伤不已。

_____

9. 早在，历经，至今，尚未

虽然早在 1994 年国家就启动了治理淮河的工程，历经二十几年，投资 600 亿，但至今尚未能实现"水体还清"的目标。

_____

_____

3.2. Use "因……而……" or "以……为……" to translate the following sentences. Pay attention to the written style of the whole sentences.

1. Many fish died from the river pollution.

   _____

2. We shouldn't develop the economy at the expense of people's health.

   _____

3. Children's behavior may change because of the environment in which they grow up.

   _____

4. In the past, people in northern China had to depend on turnips and cabbages as their main vegetables in the winter.

   _____

   _____

3.3. 民谣: Translate the following 民谣 into English (you can use the information in the parentheses to help you).

1. About "whole nation doing business":

   十亿人民九亿商，还有一亿要开张。

   _____

2. About economic reform and making a fortune (this 民谣 was popular in the 1980s):

   东西南北中，发财到广东。(广东 is the forerunner of China's economic reform.)

   _____

3. About water pollution:

   50 年代淘米洗菜，60 年代浇地灌溉，70 年代水质变坏，80 年代鱼虾绝代。(淘米 wash rice; 浇地 water fields; 灌溉 irrigate; 绝代 extinct)

   _____

   _____

4. 没钱人跟有钱人

民谣	Translation
没钱人养猪， 有钱人养狗。 没钱人在家里吃野菜， 有钱人在酒店吃野菜。 没钱人在马路上骑自行车， 有钱人在客厅里骑自行车。 没钱人想结婚， 有钱人想离婚。 没钱人假装有钱， 有钱人假装没钱。	

4. 综合练习

4.1. 选词填空

a. 能源　　b. 过程　　c. 威胁　　d. 排放　　e. 破坏　　f. 疾病
g. 代价　　h. 应运而生　　i. 污染　　j. 浪费　　k. 耗费　　l. 森林
m. 持续　　n. 快速　　o. 触目惊心　　p. 必不可少

一次性筷子的危害

　　筷子是中国人的主要餐具，是中国饮食文化的重要体现。近年来，古老的传统遇到现代社会"快速、方便、卫生"的价值观，一次性木筷 ＿＿＿＿。但很多人不知道的是，中国人在这项餐具上所付的 ＿＿＿＿ 实在让人 ＿＿＿＿。

　　在中国的很多餐馆里，一次性筷子早已成了 ＿＿＿＿ 的餐具。随着经济 ＿＿＿＿ 发展，国内流动人口增加，中国从上世纪八十年代开始推广使用一次性筷子，以提高公共用餐卫生水平，预防 ＿＿＿＿ 传染。

据统计，中国每年消耗和出口一次性木筷 800 亿双。每年为生产一次性筷子要 ＿＿＿＿＿＿ 木材 166 万立方米，需要砍伐大约 2500 万棵大树，减少 ＿＿＿＿＿＿ 面积 200 万立方米。

中国森林<u>覆盖率</u> (coverage) 仅为 18.21%，居世界第 130 位。其中还存在森林质量不高、树种单一、树龄低等问题。中国长期以来由于经济 ＿＿＿＿＿＿ 发展的需要已对森林造成了严重的破坏。但如果为了十三亿人每日用餐的需要而失去那么多的森林，这种不必要的 ＿＿＿＿＿＿ 确实让人痛心。

其实，在市场上两块钱就能买到一百双的一次性筷子消耗的远远不止宝贵的森林。因为大多数筷子的生产都需要经过漂白的 ＿＿＿＿＿＿，漂白后，还需要大量的水蒸煮或冲洗。因此，一次性筷子的生产不仅浪费大量的水电 ＿＿＿＿＿＿，其漂白后 ＿＿＿＿＿＿ 的污水更会对环境造成 ＿＿＿＿＿＿，对人们身体健康造成 ＿＿＿＿＿＿。

4.2. 按照上面这篇文章的意思，下面的说法对不对？ (T/F)

＿＿＿＿＿＿ 1. 在中国，大多数的餐馆都使用一次性木筷。

＿＿＿＿＿＿ 2. 使用一次性木筷主要是为了预防传染性疾病。

＿＿＿＿＿＿ 3. 制造一次性木筷要耗费大量木材。

＿＿＿＿＿＿ 4. 中国的森林覆盖率虽然低，森林的质量却很高。

＿＿＿＿＿＿ 5. 中国森林遭到破坏的主要原因是一次性筷子的普及。

＿＿＿＿＿＿ 6. 一次性筷子价格十分便宜。

＿＿＿＿＿＿ 7. 一次性筷子的生产过程还造成其他方面的环境污染。

＿＿＿＿＿＿ 8. 使用一次性筷子的利大于弊。

4.3. 英译汉

1. You will <u>witness</u>（见证）one of the greatest moments in history.

＿＿＿＿＿＿＿＿＿＿＿＿＿＿＿＿＿＿＿＿＿＿＿＿＿＿＿＿＿

2. Government officials should always bear the welfare of the masses in mind.（将……置于……）

＿＿＿＿＿＿＿＿＿＿＿＿＿＿＿＿＿＿＿＿＿＿＿＿＿＿＿＿＿

3. The real estate prices in this city are really expensive. A two-bedroom apartment costs at least 500,000 yuan, and sometimes as much as 800,000 yuan.（少则……多时达……）

_____

_____

4. In my memory, my hometown had a little river of crystal clear water with canopies of green trees on both sides.（绿树成荫）

_____

_____

5. The water of the Huai River was polluted due to the waste water discharged by the factories on the riverside.（因……而……）

_____

_____

6. Those who want to establish their own business should take him as an example: be cautious in investment but also unafraid of taking risks when the opportunity comes.（以……为……）

_____

_____

7. Since the launch of environmental protection, this city gradually became a place of green trees which provided pleasant shade.

_____

_____

8. They started their band（乐队）as long ago as 1970. After undergoing many difficulties, the band is now gaining worldwide popularity.（早在，历经）

_____

_____

9. A newspaper photographer happened to be on the spot and took some pictures of the startling accident site.（触目惊心）

_____

_____

5. 阅读练习

<h3 style="text-align:center">短文一：<u>沙尘暴</u> (dust storm)</h3>

近年来，中国北方越来越成为沙尘暴高发地区。有时一个月能发生几次。大风一起，大街小巷尘土飞扬，风沙吹得人睁不开眼睛白天好像黄昏一样。特别具有<u>讽刺</u> (irony) 意味的是，今年 3 月 31 号，北京举行"绿色中国 — 环保公益日"之时，却偏偏遇到沙尘天气。中国环保总局副局长站在满天飞舞的黄沙中说："触目惊心的环境问题已经成为威胁经济、影响社会的大问题。"他强调，要积极推动公众参与环境保护，因为解决中国严重环境问题的最终<u>动力</u> (driving force) 来自公众。

北京居民张小姐说，沙尘暴太可怕了。遇到沙尘暴，她总是请假躲在家里。张小姐认为，环保问题的关键在<u>上层</u> (upper level)，"最终动力来自公众"，只是不负责任的说法。她说："上层不制定保护环境的政策法令，公众恐怕没那么大的热情，也没那么大的力量。现在企业都讲究经济效益，你让他停产搞环保，他会愿意吗？"

香港评论人刘先生认为："中国在发展经济的时候，只追求 GDP 的增长，却忽视了对环境的保护。除了中国政府以外，整个中国社会也非常<u>短视</u> (short-sighted)，不考虑长久的利益，因为在环保上的投入在短期内是看不到效益的。"

刘先生表示，"目前中国政府能做的就是加大环保部门的权力，因为环保工作会跟地方政府重经济发展的政策有利益冲突，在这种情况下，如果环保部门的权力很小，对监督地方政府就无能为力。另外，中国政府也应该加大在环保方面的投资。而且还要在学校里进行环保生态教育，因为环保是一个全国的问题，长期的问题，必须整个社会从上到下都去关注。"

1. 根据短文内容，选择最佳答案回答问题：

1. 今年 3 月 31 日，_____。
   a. 是环保公益日
   b. 北京遇到沙尘暴天气
   c. 中国环保总局副局长发表关于环保问题的讲话
   d. 以上都对

2. 中国环保总局副局长认为，解决环保问题的根本在于 _____。
   a. 上层
   b. 公众
   c. 企业
   d. 教育

3. 北京居民张小姐认为，解决环保问题的根本在于 _____。
   a. 上层
   b. 公众
   c. 企业
   d. 教育

4. 香港评论人刘先生认为，造成环保问题的根本原因在于 _____。
   a. 中国在追求短期经济效益时，忽视了长久利益和环境保护
   b. 中国政府没有制定明确的保护环境的政策法令
   c. 中国民众对于保护环境的关注和热情不够
   d. 以上都对

5. 香港评论人刘先生认为，解决环保问题的措施包括 _____。
   a. 中国政府应该加大环保部门的权力
   b. 中国政府应该加大在环保方面的投资
   c. 中国政府应该在学校里进行环保教育
   d. 以上都对

6. 下面哪项最好地说明了短文的主题？
   a. 各界人士对北京沙尘暴及环保问题的看法。
   b. 解决中国严重环境问题的最终动力来自公众。
   c. "最终动力来自公众"只是不负责任的说法。
   d. 在环保上的投资在短期内是看不到效益的。

短文二：藏羚羊 (*Tibetan antelope*) 的命运

在神秘 (*mysterious*)的西藏高原，在那片空气极度稀薄 (*thin*)、气温极度寒冷的大地上，生存着一种美丽的生灵 (*creature*)，在雪地上飞一般地成群奔跑，它们就是藏羚羊。20 世纪初，在西藏大约生活着 100 万只以上的藏羚羊。一个世纪过去了，西藏已经没有了以前那种到处是藏羚羊的景象。到 20 世纪末时，藏羚羊的数量已经不到 75,000 只。

是什么原因使藏羚羊的数量迅速减少呢？美国的一位科学家从 1985 年到 1997 年对西藏的野生动物作了深入的调查和研究，发现了藏羚羊数量越来越少的原因。据说，藏羚羊在晚上最怕灯光，它们白天奔跑如飞，但只要在黑暗中看见刺眼的灯光，就会惊呆，站在原地一动不动。很多偷猎者 (*poachers*) 就在晚上打开车灯，从汽车上向藏羚羊开枪 (*shoot*)。一次打死一二百是很平常的事。

一张藏羚羊皮可以卖到人民币 500 元以上。藏羚羊皮上的羊绒 (*cashmere*) 又轻又软，被称为"羊绒之王"。用这种羊绒做成的披肩 (*cape*) 既保暖又漂亮，在欧美市场上最高可以卖到一万美元。但是，披肩的真正价值远远不止这个价钱，因为我们付出的是青藏高原上平均每天 50 只藏羚羊丧生 (*lose life*) 的代价。除了羊皮以外，藏羚羊头还被做成羊头标本 (*specimen*) 卖给游客，而藏羚羊角更是藏药中不可缺少的药材。

人们为了暂时的经济利益，大量枪杀藏羚羊。由此可见，正是人类的贪婪 (*greed*) 才造成了藏羚羊数目迅速减少。如果我们现在还不赶快保护藏羚羊，那么在不远的将来，我们的子孙后代就只能在博物馆和历史书上看到藏羚羊了。

按照上面这篇文章的意思，下面的说法对不对？（T/F）

_____ 1. 20 世纪初西藏有很多藏羚羊。

_____ 2. 每年有大约一万多只藏羚羊死去。

_____ 3. 偷猎者们都是晚上去捕杀藏羚羊。

_____ 4. 藏羚羊只有羊皮有用。

_____ 5. 人们捕杀藏羚羊主要是为了得到羊绒。

_____ 6. 一条披肩要用 50 只藏羚羊的羊绒才能织成。

_____ 7. 人类的贪婪是藏羚羊数目减少的真正原因。

_____ 8. 如果不赶快采取措施，以后的孩子将看不到活着的藏羚羊了。

_____ 9. 这篇文章的主要意思是我们应该赶快保护藏羚羊。

6. 口语练习：

1. 一位工厂厂长因该工厂污染环境（当地河流）而被老百姓告上法庭。法官判决如果他愿意参加一个环境保护学习班，就可以免去六个月的有期徒刑。你觉得这个法官判得怎样？要是你是法官，你会怎么判？

2. 如果因为工厂污染环境而停产，那些工厂的工人就要失业。是人们的就业重要还是保护环境重要？

3. 你有没有用过一次性筷子？对于一次性筷子破坏森林的问题，你觉得应该用什么办法解决？

4. 由于发展中国家的环境保护法不够完善，有些发达国家把他们的化工和制造业转移到发展中国家来，这样就不会对他们自己的国家的环境造成破坏。这种做法你觉得怎样？

5. 我们日常生活中有没有污染环境的行为？请举例说明。

6. 保护环境到底是谁的责任？我们每个人都能做些什么？

7. 下列国家据说是对环境保护做得最好的国家：你同意吗？为什么？

芬兰 (Finland)

德国 (Germany)

加拿大 (Canada)

日本 (Japan)

英国 (UK)

西班牙 (Spain)

韩国 (Korea)

美国 (USA)

俄国 (Russia)

印度 (India)

尼日利亚 (Nigeria)

墨西哥 (Mexico)

委内瑞拉 (Venezuela)

8. 你的国家对环境保护得怎么样？请举例说明。

9. 完成下列句子：
要是我看见有人在街上扔垃圾，我就会……
要是我知道我工作的工厂在偷偷地污染环境，我就会……
要是我是中国环保总局局长，我就会……
要是政府要在我们家附近建一个垃圾回收站，我就会……
要是我上学或工作的地方离我家太远，我就会……

7. 写作练习（650-750 字）

1. 有人觉得人类的行为破坏了地球的环境，也有人说人类的行为让地球成为一个更适合于人类居住的地方。你的观点是什么？请用具体的例子支持你的观点。

2. 人类正在一步一步地占有更多的土地，而很多动物却因为失去生存的地方而灭绝。有人觉得人类生产和居住对土地的需要比动物的需要更重要。你同不同意这种观点？为什么？请给出具体的理由和例子来说明你的观点。

Required vocabulary and expressions:

1. Use at least 10 of the following new vocabulary words and phrases:

疾病	记忆	高发	排放	历经	遍及	快速
高速	相关	清澈	透明	流域	普查	结论
密切	针对	治理	启动	扩散	致富	忽视
代价	能源	污染	耗费	破坏	效益	官员
触目惊心	无能为力	绿树成荫				

2. Use at least 4 of the following expressions:

少则……，多时达……　　　　A 与 B 密切相关　　　　因……而……

由于……　　　　　　　　　　……时，从来不……　　　据……显示，……

……，其中……　　　　　　　从……以来……　　　　　以前……；而如今……

早在……，历经……，至今……　　以……为……

互联网改变中国

课文提要

On September 14th, 1987, the first email written in China was created in Beijing with the contents "Across the Great Wall, we can reach every corner in the world" (越过长城，走向世界). Later it was sent via the Internet to other countries for the first time in China's history. That event marked the beginning of China's online communication with the global Internet community. In the decades since then, the Internet in China has experienced exponential growth. According to the China Internet Network Information Center (CNNIC), China had 338 million Internet users, more than any other country, by mid-2009.

The Internet has transformed the daily lives of many people in China. Chinese "netizens" are able to use the Internet to communicate with others, find entertainment, engage in commercial activities, obtain government services, and access a wide variety of cultural, social and academic information. The proliferation of mobile phones, e-mail, instant messaging and bulletin boards is becoming an important platform for citizens to raise their voices, something that is new to them in the history of China.

阅读前讨论：

1. 根据课文题目，你可不可以猜猜看互联网是如何改变中国的？
2. 你认为互联网在中国的普及有什么好处和弊端？
3. 互联网在你的生活中有什么作用和影响？你能不能想象没有互联网的生活？
4. 你知道哪些跟"互联网"有关的词？

自学生词

Match new words in the left column with the English translation in the right column, by guessing the words' meanings from characters that compose them.

	生词	繁体	序号	英文
( )	菜农	農	1.	overseas
( )	海外		2.	destination
( )	排名		4.	underestimate
( )	惊人	驚	6.	peddle goods, hawk one's wares
( )	生意		7.	ranking
( )	引发	發	8.	business
( )	平台	臺	9.	astonishing, amazing
( )	叫卖	賣	10.	online shopping
( )	有害		11.	temporarily reside
( )	暂住	暫	12.	platform
( )	低估		13.	vegetable grower
( )	目的地		14.	harmful
( )	网购	網購	15.	trigger

生词

	生词	繁体	拼音	词性	英文	HSK 等级
1.	大众	眾	dàzhòng	*n.*	general public	丙
2.	文明		wénmíng	*n.*	civilization	乙
3.	思维	維	sīwéi	*n.*	thought, thinking	丙
4.	范围	範圍	fànwéi	*n.*	scope, range	乙
5.	集散		jísàn	*v.*	(of goods) to collect and distribute	
6.	依赖	賴	yīlài	*v.*	rely on, depend on	丁
7.	推进	進	tuījìn	*v.*	promote, push on	丙
8.	改进	進	gǎijìn	*v.*	improve	乙
9.	扛		káng	*v.*	carry on one's shoulders	乙
10.	集市		jíshì	*n.*	fair, market	丁
11.	悠闲	閑	yōuxián	*adj.*	leisurely	
12.	获取	獲	huòqǔ	*v.*	obtain	丁
13.	种子	種	zhǒngzǐ	*n.*	seed	乙
14.	植物		zhíwù	*n.*	plant	乙
15.	销路	銷	xiāolù	*n.*	sales channels	丁
16.	手段		shǒuduàn	*n.*	means, method, approach	乙
17.	搜索		sōusuǒ	*v*	search	丁
18.	娱乐	樂	yúlè	*n.*	entertainment	丙
19.	媒介		méijiè	*n.*	medium	丁
20.	预定	預	yùdìng	*v.*	book, reserve	丁
21.	酒店		jiǔdiàn	*n.*	hotel	丙
22.	同伴		tóngbàn	*n.*	companion	丙
23.	舆论	輿論	yúlùn	*n.*	public opinion	丁
24.	拘留		jūliú	*v.*	detain	丁
25.	移民		yímín	*n.*	migrant, immigrant	丁
26.	收容		shōuróng	*v.*	take in, internment	
27.	警察		jǐngchá	*n.*	police	乙

	生词	繁体	拼音	词性	英文	HSK 等级
28.	殴打	毆	ōudǎ	*v.*	beat up	丁
29.	激起		jīqǐ	*v(c)*	arouse, stir up	丁
30.	强烈	強	qiángliè	*adj.*	strong, intense	乙
31.	抗议	議	kàngyì	*v.*	protest, demonstrate	丙
32.	威力		wēilì	*n.*	power, force	丁
33.	国务院	國務	Guówùyuàn	*p.n.*	State Council (the highest government administrative authority of China)	丙
34.	废除	廢	fèichú	*v.*	abolish, do away with	丙
35.	遣送		qiǎnsòng	*v.*	send back, repatriate	
36.	普及		pǔjí	*v.*	popularize	丙
37.	产业	產業	chǎnyè	*n.*	industry	丁
38.	变革	變	biàngé	*n.*	transform, reform	丙
39.	攻击	擊	gōngjī	*v.*	attack, assault	丙
40.	犯罪		fànzuì	*v.o.*	commit a crime	丙
41.	色情		sèqíng	*n.*	pornography	
42.	暴力		bàolì	*n.*	violence	丙
43.	泛滥	濫	fànlàn	*v.*	overflow	丙
44.	瘾		yǐn	*n.*	addiction	
45.	负面	負	fùmiàn	*adj.*	negative, bad	

成语和惯用语

成语/惯用语	繁体	单字解释	意思和例句
酷暑严冬 kù shǔ yán dōng	嚴	酷 : brutal 暑 : summer 严 : harsh, severe 冬 : winter	brutal summer and severe winter, extreme weather 例：不论酷暑严冬，在工地上每天都能看到他的身影。 You will find him on the work site every day, no matter if it's hot summer or severe winter.
成千上万 chéng qiān shàng wàn	萬	成 : make 千 : thousand 上 : reach 万 : ten thousands	by the thousands and tens of thousands 例：成千上万的学生聚集在广场上。 Tens of thousands of students gathered on the public square.

电脑网络特殊词汇
SPECIAL COMPUTER AND INTERNET VOCABULARY

	生词	繁体	拼音	词性	英文	HSK 等级
1.	互联网	聯網	Hùliánwǎng	*p.n.*	Internet	
2.	电子	電	diànzǐ	*n./adj.*	electron, electronic	丙
3.	搜索		sōusuǒ	*v.*	search	丁
4.	引擎		yǐnqíng	*n.*	engine	
5.	邮件	郵	yóujiàn	*n.*	mail	
6.	游戏	戲	yóuxì	*n.*	game	丙
7.	论坛	論壇	lùntán	*n.*	forum	
8.	页面	頁	yèmiàn	*n.*	webpage	
9.	屏幕		píngmù	*n.*	(TV or movie) screen	
10.	鼠标	標	shǔbiāo	*n.*	(computer) mouse	

■ 第一读：掌握课文大意

快速阅读课文，看下面三个选择中哪一个最能说明本课主要意思：
1. 中国网民利用互联网赚钱
2. 互联网对中国社会各方面的影响
3. 中国互联网的发展史

互联网改变中国

中国对大众开放互联网服务是从 1995 年开始的。根据中国互联网网络信息中心 (CNNIC) 的统计报告，14 年以后，网民总人数已达到 338 亿，排名世界第一。网民增长数量惊人，平均每秒钟增加两个网民。对有着 5000 年文明史的中国，14 年是一段很短的时间，但就在这短短的 14 年中，互联网已进入到中国社会的各方面。网络正在迅速地改变中国传统的经济模式，中国人的日常生活和思维方式，以及中国的文化和政治。

在经济方面，互联网推动了新的经营模式和消费模式。搜索引擎已经成为网民使用互联网最重要的工具。互联网逐渐成为中国最大的市场信息集散和交易平台，它与传统产业的结合也已经成为经济新的推动力。在新的经营模式下，中小企业的商业联系范围不断扩大，大型进出口企业更是依赖互联网来直接与海外建立生意关系。就连相当落后的农村地区也开始用互联网来推进业务。不少农民学会了使用互联网的技术，改进了他们的经营方式。例如，河北省某县的菜农，以前卖菜大多是肩扛手提。不论酷暑严冬，都得早早起床到集市上叫卖。现在他们可以悠闲地坐在蔬菜交易大厅的屏幕前，轻点鼠标，就可以在网上把菜卖个好价钱。据河北省农业厅调查，农民通过网络学习技术，获取种子、植物，销售信息，为产品找到了更多销路。这些手段使农民每年的收入大大增加。

人们也通过网络寻找工作信息。现在一些大学的网站上有专门为毕业生设计的页面，不断更新各单位的招聘信息，浏览量相当大。根据一项调查，2004 年人民大学就业的本科毕业生中，通过网络找到工作的占 13%；硕士以上毕业生通过网络求职成功的占 23%。

中国人的消费方式也由于互联网的发展，而有了很大的改变。越来越多的人喜欢上了既方便又便宜的网购方式。他们可以搜索各种网上商店，用最理想的价格，购买他们所需要的商品。网站也已成为人们旅游出门的新媒介。人们不但可以在旅游网站上获取目的地的信息，也可以购买机票、车票、船票，预定酒店，加入旅行团等，更可以通过旅游网站的论坛，找到兴趣相同的旅行同伴，一同去旅游。

对青少年来说，互联网已经是他们生活中很重要的一部分。根据互联网网络信息中心统计报告，当前中国网民的年龄多半在30岁以下，这年轻的一代，有半数以上经常在网络上玩电子游戏、跟朋友聊天、听音乐、看电影，或在网上交流，用电子邮件交新朋友等。

在政治方面，互联网为公众提供了一个前所未有的开放的舆论平台，使老百姓们有机会参与政治。2003年3月17日，大学毕业生孙志刚，从外地到广州去找工作，但他因为没有暂住证而被拘留在移民收容中心，3月20日被警察殴打致死。这个消息在网络上激起了强烈反应，成千上万的抗议信，出现在全国各大网站上。互联网的舆论威力最终促使国务院决定废除这一实行了多年的收容遣送制度。

互联网的发展和普及，引发了前所未有的信息革命和产业革命，也引发了深刻的社会变革。但另一方面，网络攻击、网络犯罪、色情暴力信息泛滥、青少年上网成瘾等问题，对社会也产生了不可低估的负面影响。

■ 第二读：细节和理解

A. 根据课文内容回答下列问题：

1. 互联网对中国社会的哪些方面有影响？

2. 互联网对经济发展有什么影响？

3. 农民是如何使用互联网技术的？

4. 大学生又是如何使用互联网的？

5. 在互联网普及的今天，中国人的消费方式有什么改变？

6. 年轻一代对互联网的使用有什么特点？

7. 互联网对中国的政治有什么积极作用？

8. 国务院为什么最终决定废除收容遣送制度？

9. 互联网有什么负面影响？

B. 根据课文推论：

Choose the best inference from the three possible choices for each sentence, and <u>underline</u> the clue(s) that helped you choose.

1. 不论酷暑严冬，都得早早起床到集市上叫卖。
   a. 河北的夏天特别热，冬天特别冷。
   b. 只有冬天和夏天才需要很早起床去集市。
   c. 无论天气多坏，都需要很早起床去集市。

2. "就连相当落后地区的农村也开始用互联网来推进业务。"这说明：
   a. 农村的互联网已经相当普及。
   b. 互联网在中国普及很广。
   c. 农村的互联网业务相当落后。

3. 在政治方面，互联网为公众提供了一个前所未有的开放的舆论平台，使老百姓们有机会参与政治。
   a. 中国老百姓在使用互联网以前没有舆论平台。
   b. 中国老百姓在使用互联网以前没有这样开放的舆论平台。
   c. 中国老百姓在使用互联网以前没有这样开放的政治舆论平台。

■ 阅读技巧总结

Now that you have reached the final lesson of the book, the time is right to review the methods you have learned for reading a text. Rather than decoding a text word for word, or sentence to sentence, you will understand a text more quickly and accurately by reading it strategically. Here, we sum up the reading skills from previous lessons (mainly for expository texts, which make up the majority of readings of this book) in a broad outline. You can use this as a reference in your reading outside the two volumes of *Reading Into a New China.*

I. Comprehending Narrative Texts

Narrative texts are most often organized by general structure, such as setting, characterization, theme, key episode, and resolution of a problem that motivated the character to take action. A narrative text can also incorporate both psychological and physical causality to explain the sequence of actions and events, and offer a moral of the story.

II. Comprehending Expository Texts

A. Basic Composition of an Expository Text

An expository text should include three components: 1. the thesis or the main point of the discussion, 2. the grounds of argument, meaning the background, motivation and/or reasons for writing the text, 3. a conclusion that summarizes or reiterates the main point of the text.

B. Overarching Logical Structure of an Expository Text

Generally speaking, two kinds of reasoning can be used to compose an expository text, the deductive method or the inductive method. In the deductive reasoning method, the author raises the overall topic first, then provides details, and then reiterates the main point. This style is easy to follow because it is similar to the most common style of expository essays you may have read in English.

The inductive reasoning method, essentially the opposite of the deductive method, can be more difficult to comprehend because the development of the thesis is not linear. It starts from observations of individual cases, separate facts, or various angles of a topic, and then makes judgments about them near the end. Various aspects and viewpoints can be brought to bear on a subject if the author thinks they would enrich understanding.

In addition, in order to grasp the attention of the reader, some texts begin with an element that does not appear directly relevant to the piece as a whole. The text may begin with apparently irrelevant lines of a poem, famous sayings or even a summary of a chapter from a popular novel. The significance of this introductory epigraph (called 引论) is often highly literary and culture-bound. While it would evoke admiration from a Chinese reader for the author's literary talent and subtlety, it could create a problem for a student who does not have the background knowledge to understand it. Since this section does not have a direct impact on the understanding of the essay as a whole, if you don't understand it, you may skip it and continue your reading of the text. (Of course, understanding the 引论 does add to your understanding of the essay, but it is not absolutely essential.)

The above discussion allows that, for expository essays, the overall organization differs from one to another. For that reason alone, you should first identify the overall structure of the piece you are going to read so that you can plan how you are going to process the reading.

C. Reading Process for an Expository Text

1. Identify the key issues

First, before a full reading, skim the text quickly, without looking up unfamiliar words, to see what the key issues are. Previewing the text before beginning to read enables you to establish your own expectations about what information you will find in the text, and gives you a framework to help make sense of the information. Several features in the text are helpful: the title, the source, subtitles, headings, photographs, drawings, charts, and tables. Working with the title of a text is one way of establishing expectations about the content of a text.

2. Identify the overarching structure of the text

Determine if the text is written in deductive style or inductive style. This is an important step. It will save you a lot of time and energy if you find where the main point of the text is located, and see how information is arranged according to the right structure. This is how you do it:

    a. Read the first paragraph.

    b. Read the first sentence of each paragraph after the introduction and before the conclusion to see what ideas are mentioned in them.

    c. Read the concluding paragraph, if present, carefully.

    d. Scan parts of the text for specific information.

3. Full reading for complete comprehension

Having completed the first two steps and secured in your mind the knowledge of the key issues and the overarching structure, you are now ready to read the text in its entirety with full attention. You now want to find out how the author organizes his or her ideas in the text in order to provide proof, evidence or reasons for the thesis. To achieve this, you need to read carefully, paragraph by paragraph. You can use the following procedures as a reference to check as your reading progresses.

    a. Find the topic sentence for each paragraph (review Lesson 3 for topic sentences).

    b. Determine what rhetorical pattern is used to support or elaborate on the topic sentence.

    c. Pay attention to the connectives in the paragraph. (review Lesson 9 for connectives). These serve two functions. First, they connect clauses and sentences to form logical relationships. Second, they signal the organization of the paragraph.

    d. Steps a–c are the steps that you should undertake when reading a paragraph. There are also other details to take care of, such as comprehending long sentences, making inferences, understanding metaphorical and figurative language, understanding four-character set phrases, etc.

The following table lists several organizational/rhetorical patterns that authors frequently use to develop their paragraphs. Authors may use various combinations of these patterns.

RHETORICAL PATTERN	CORRESPONDING TEXT STRUCTURE
description	define and describe X and the features of X
temporal sequence	trace the development of X, give the steps in X, describe the progress of X
explanation	explain X, explain the cause(s), explain the effect(s)
make a prediction about X	predict what will happen to X, hypothesize about the cause of X
comparison-contrast	compare and contrast X and Y, list the similarities and differences between X and Y
definition-examples	define and give examples of X, classification
problem-solution	explain the development of a problem and the solution(s) to the problem
draw a conclusion	summarize the significance of X, make a judgment about X

4. Post-reading review

After you've read the text, you can use the scanning technique to check your understanding of the text.

　　a. Choose a specific piece of information in the text.

　　b. Determine what the key words are for that piece of information.

　　c. Scan through the text for those words.

　　d. When you find each word, read the sentences around it to see whether they provide the information you are seeking.

　　e. If they do, you can stop reading. If they do not, continue scanning. You can do several of these checks for the entire text.

词汇与句型

1. 肩扛手提 • hold on shoulders and lift in hands

1. 河北省某县的菜农，以前卖菜大多是肩扛手提。现在呢？他们可以悠闲地坐在蔬菜交易大厅的屏幕前，轻点鼠标，就可以在网上把菜卖个好价钱。
   The truck farmers from a town in Hebei Province used to transport and sell vegetables all by hand. What's it like now? They can leisurely sit in front of the screen on the vegetable trading floor, lightly clicking mice, and they will be able to sell vegetables at a good price on the Internet.

2. 朋友们肩扛手提，帮我把行李搬进了新家。
   Holding the luggage on their shoulders and in their hands, my friends helped me move my belongings into the new place.

3. 以前教学楼里没有电梯，运输教材只能靠肩扛手提。
   There was no elevator in the educational building before; books and teaching materials would only be transported by shoulders and hands.

2. 酷暑严冬 • extremely hot summer and bitterly cold winter

This phrase is often used to refer to extremely difficult external conditions.

1. 无论酷暑严冬，菜农们都得早早起床去集市买菜。
   No matter the season or the weather, the truck farmers have to get up really early to sell their vegetables in the market.

2. 和加拿大的大多数城市不同，温哥华的气候温和，没有酷暑严冬。
   Unlike most Canadian cities, Vancouver's climate is fairly mild; there are neither extremely hot summers nor bitterly cold winters.

3. 她每天跑步 5 公里，即使是酷暑严冬也不例外。
   She runs 5 kilometers every day, with no exceptions, even in extremely hot summer or bitterly cold winter.

3. 参与 • participate, take part in

1. 在政治方面，互联网为公众提供了一个前所未有的开放的舆论平台，使老百姓们有可能参与政治。
   In terms of politics, the Internet provided an unprecedented open platform for public opinions, which has enabled ordinary people to participate in politics.

2. 社会各界都积极参与到救灾赈灾活动当中。
People and organizations from all walks of life have taken an active part in the post-disaster rehabilitation.

3. 虽然没能进入前三名，这次比赛对我来说仍然是次很开心的经历，重在参与嘛。
Though I didn't get to the top three, this competition was still a delightful experience to me. The most important thing is participation, isn't it?

4. 致……（致死/致残/致伤/致命/致富）• cause..., incur..., result in...

致死 (cause death, kill)

1. 据消息说，该男子是被暴徒殴打致死的。
It is reported that this man was beaten to death by thugs.

致残 (disable, maim)

2. 她虽然在车祸中幸存下来，但却终生致残，再也不能行走。
She survived the car accident, but was maimed for life and will never be able to walk again.

致伤 (injure)

3. 著名影星周雨也出席了首映式，这是她去年滑雪致伤后的首次公开露面。
The famous movie star Zhou Yu also attended the premiere. This is the first public appearance she made since her skiing injury last year.

致命 (mortal, deadly, fatal)

4. 这对于国家经济来说是次致命的打击。
This is a crushing blow to the economy of the country.

5. 懒惰是他致命的弱点，他常常因此丢掉工作。
Laziness is his Achilles' heel, due to which he has often lost his job.

6. 他靠辛勤劳动而致富。
He has obtained his wealth by hard work.

5. 激起 • arouse, trigger, evoke

1. 潮水冲到礁石，激起了高高的浪花。
The tide washed over the reef and sent up high breakers.

2. 市长在洪灾期间出国度假，激起市民强烈不满和谴责。
The fact that the mayor went abroad on vacation during the flood disaster aroused strong complaints and censure among the citizens.

3. 一篇报纸的报道激起了我对整个事件的好奇。
A newspaper report evoked my curiosity about the whole incident.

6. 成千上万 • thousands of

千、万 both mean big numbers. When they are used in idiomatic expressions, they metaphorically express a large quantity.

1. 港口停泊着成百上千艘船。
Hundreds of boats are anchored at the port.

2. 近年来，农村出现大量剩余劳力，成千上万的农民涌入大城市寻找工作机会。
In recent years, large amount of surplus labor emerged in rural areas; thousands of rural residents swarmed into big cities for employment.

3. 海上的焰火表演吸引了成千上万的当地居民和外地游客。
The fireworks display at the sea attracted thousands of local residents and foreign tourists.

7. 不可低估 • should not underestimate, cannot be underestimated

1. 这项工程看起来复杂而艰巨，我们不可低估它将带来的挑战。
This project looks quite complicated and exacting; we should not underestimate the challenges it will bring.

2. 在经济体制改革的过程中，私有企业的作用不可低估。
In the reform of the economic system, the role of private enterprises should not be underestimated.

3. 网络的普及给人们的生活带来了前所未有的便捷，与此同时，随之而来的网络问题也对社会造成了不可低估的负面影响。
The popularity of the Internet has made people's lives unprecedentedly convenient and efficient; at the same time, problems that came along with it also have a negative impact on society that should not be underestimated.

语法

1. Numbers in Chinese idioms

Numbers are widely used to form idioms and slang in Chinese. They make the language more vivid and expressive. However, there are very few numbers in the idioms that still retain their original meanings. A few examples:

一箭双雕: One arrow kills two eagles. (Kill two birds with one stone.)

一举两得: One action serves two purposes.

一见钟情: fall in love at first sight

Since most numbers in idioms have lost their surface meanings, it is necessary to know their extended meanings and cultural connotations for a better understanding. Below we introduce some basic functions of numbers in idioms:

1.1. Numbers 百、千、万 in idioms usually mean "many, a lot, all, every."

1. 千方百计: thousands of methods and hundreds of ways, by every possible way

   医护人员千方百计抢救病人。
   The hospital staff did everything in their power to save the patient.

2. 千军万马: thousands of soldiers and horses—a powerful army; a mighty force

   有人说中国学生考大学就像"千军万马过独木桥"。
   Some people say that Chinese students trying to get into university is like a massive army trying to pass the river on a single-log bridge.

3. 千变万化: thousands of changes, ever-changing

   她喜欢躺在草地上欣赏天上千变万化的云彩。
   She likes to lie in the grass, enjoying the ever-changing cloud formations in the sky.

4. 千家万户: many households or families; every family

   现在市面上的冷冻食品特别丰富，给千家万户带来了方便。
   There are abundant frozen foods in the market nowadays, which brings convenience to thousands of families.

5. 成千上万: thousands and millions, thousands upon thousands

过去短短几十年里，成千上万的私人企业如雨后春笋般涌现出来。
During the short time of the past few decades, thousands upon thousands of private businesses sprung up like spring bamboo shoots.

6. 千辛万苦: go through countless hardships; all kinds of hardships

她父母为了孩子的前途，经历了千辛万苦，才移民到了美国。
For the future of their children, her parents went through all kinds of hardships to immigrate to America.

7. 千言万语: many words, a lot to say/tell

她心里有千言万语，可一句也说不出来。
Her heart was filled with unspoken words, but she failed to utter a single one.

1.2. Numbers 七、八 in idioms usually mean "mess, disorder"

1. 七上八下: be agitated, be perturbed

这两天我心里总是七上八下的。
I'm at sixes and sevens these days.

2. 乱七八糟: be in wild disorder; be at sixes and sevens; in a mess

她的屋子乱七八糟的，衣服丢在地板上，书凌乱地放在桌子上。
Her room was so messy, clothes on the floor, books scattered around the table.

3. 七手八脚: with a lot of people lending a hand; great hurry and bustle

大伙儿七手八脚把他抬了出来。
Everybody lent a hand to carry him out.

4. 七嘴八舌: saying/discussing with everybody talking at once without order

人们都围了上去，七嘴八舌，他不知听谁的好。
People crowded round him, all talking at once, so that he didn't know who to listen to.

1.3. Numbers 三、四 in idioms usually have negative connotations:

1. 不三不四: neither fish, flesh nor fowl; nondescript; frivolous; suspicious (characters); dubious

他交了很多不三不四的朋友。
He has relations with a lot of dubious characters.

2. 丢三落四: miss this and that; forget this and that; forgetful; scatterbrained

他老是这么丢三落四的。你看，又忘了带书了。
He's so scatterbrained. Look, he's forgotten to bring his book again.

3. 颠三倒四: incoherent; disorderly; all in confusion; turn everything upside down

为什么他今天说话这么颠三倒四的?
Why is he talking so incoherently today?

练习

1. 语音

Write pinyin for the following underlined Chinese characters. Pay special attention to their different pronunciations in different contexts.

目<u>的</u>地 ( ) 　　　 <u>种</u>子 ( ) 　　　 娱<u>乐</u> ( ) 　　　 <u>更</u>新 ( )

<u>的</u>确　( ) 　　　 <u>种</u>植 ( ) 　　　 音<u>乐</u> ( ) 　　　 <u>更</u>多 ( )

2. 词汇句型

2.1. Match the following words on the left with the words appropriately associated with them on the right.

Group One (Verb + Object)		**Group Two** (Adj. + Noun)	
1. 拘留 _____	信息	1. 负面 _____	反应
2. 推进 _____	制度	2. 有害 _____	数量
3. 获取 _____	政治	3. 强烈 _____	价格
4. 浏览 _____	移民	4. 落后 _____	影响

Group One
(Verb + Object)
_____

5. 参与 _____ 业务

6. 废止 _____ 页面

Group Two
(Adj. + Noun)
_____

5. 惊人 _____ 地区

6. 理想 _____ 信息

2.2. 选词填空

a. 悠闲	b. 废止	c. 变革	d. 惊人	e. 强烈	f. 引发
g. 泛滥	h. 有害	i. 犯罪	j. 排名	k. 抗议	l. 获取
m. 激起	n. 低估	o. 舆论	p. 媒介	q. 攻击	r. 致
s. 酷暑严冬	t. 成千上万				

1. 在古代，每当洪水 (flood) _____ 之时，便有 _____ 的人失去生命。

2. 在网络上 _____ 别人算不算 _____?

3. 由地震 _____ 的海啸 (tsunami) 对这个岛国造成了 _____ 的破坏。

4. 空气是声音传播的 _____。

5. 燃烧塑料时会产生 _____ 气体，影响人们的身体健康。

6. 中国正在经历巨大的社会 _____。开放的 _____ 对政府是一种监督，是压力，也是动力，所以我们决不能 _____ 网络批评的力量。

7. 许多年前被 _____ 使用的钱币，现在却变成了价值很高的收藏品。

8. 都市人每天工作繁忙，压力很大，很多人开始向往乡村的 _____ 生活。

9. 想要在一场篮球赛中 _____ 胜，关键在于队员之间的合作。

10. 广告的目的就是要 _____ 消费者的购买欲望。

11. 昆明的气候四季如春，没有明显的 _____，所以很适合人居住。

12. 互联网的开通，使人们不用出门买报纸，就可以从网上 _____ 每天的新闻。

13. 他目前是世界 _____ 第五的高尔夫球选手。

14. 游行的群众聚集在市政府门口，_____ 种族歧视 (discrimination)。

3. 语法练习

3.1. 用最合适的"带数字的成语"填空：

1. 见我不高兴，他又是给我倒茶，又是给我讲笑话，_____ 地逗我开心。

   a. 千言万语   b. 七上八下   c. 七嘴八舌   d. 千方百计

2. 中国人各地的方言 (*dialect*) _____，如果没有普通话，很难互相沟通。

   a. 千差万别   b. 颠三倒四   c. 千言万语   d. 乱七八糟

3. 不到二十年的时间，网络已经进入了 _____。

   a. 千家万户   b. 千方百计   c. 七上八下   d. 乱七八糟

4. _____ 也说不尽我对你们的感激之情。

   a. 千家万户   b. 千方百计   c. 千言万语   d. 乱七八糟

5. 他心里 _____ 的，不知怎么办才好。

   a. 丢三落四   b. 七上八下   c. 颠三倒四   d. 千言万语

6. 是谁把我桌子上的东西弄得 _____ 的？我的书都找不到了。

   a. 千差万别   b. 颠三倒四   c. 千言万语   d. 乱七八糟

7. 他们 _____ 地说个不停，我根本没有机会说话。

   a. 七嘴八舌   b. 千差万别   c. 七上八下   d. 千言万语

8. 他父母不准他跟那些 _____ 的人交朋友。

   a. 七上八下   b. 颠三倒四   c. 丢三落四   d. 不三不四

9. 他家孩子做事儿总是 _____，上学不是忘了带作业，就是忘了带书本。

   a. 七上八下   b. 颠三倒四   c. 丢三落四   d. 不三不四

10. 他糊涂得很，说话做事常常 _____ 的。

    a. 七上八下   b. 颠三倒四   c. 丢三落四   d. 不三不四

4. 综合练习

4.1. 短文填空

a. 暴力	b. 舆论	c. 负面	d. 游戏	e. 泛滥	f. 有害
g. 强烈	h. 激起	i. 信息	j. 废止	k. 浏览	l. 犯罪
m. 上网	n. 软件	o. 低估	p. 范围	q. 尚未	r. 不良
s. 互联网	t. 无能为力	u. 上网成	v. 取而代之		

"绿坝" 风波

风波初起：

2009 年 5 月 19 日，中国工业和信息化部 (*Ministry of Industry and Information Technology*) 发布通知，要求 7 月 1 日以后在中国国内销售的电脑必须预先安装 (*pre-install*) "绿坝 (*Green Dam*)" 上网软件。这套由政府花 4000 多万人民币买进，免费提供用户使用的 _____，可以过滤 (*filter*) 不良网站，控制上网时间、查看上网记录等，方便父母了解子女的 _____ 情况。通知说这一措施主要是为了创建绿色健康的网络环境，避免网瘾对青少年的危害，防止青少年受互联网中不良信息的影响。然而这个软件和政府大规模的推行软件预装措施 _____ 了民众和媒体的 _____ 反应。有人支持，更有人反对。

支持者的意见：

这套由政府部门推出的绿色上网过滤软件，其目的是很好的。虽然 _____ 极大地增加了消费者获得信息的广度和速度，但色情、暴力等不良信息的 _____ 也带来了各种社会问题，其中最严重的就是对未成年人的危害。青少年思想 _____ 成熟，分析力不够强，而好奇心特别强，很容易受网上 _____ 信息的影响。现在中国因迷恋 (*infatuated with*) 网络 _____ 而上瘾的青少年已高达 1300 多万。而且，网络中的 _____ 信息影响已成为中国青少年 _____ 的首要原因。中国的家长一直都对孩子 _____ 的问题 _____。绿坝软件能够保护孩子们健康上网，当然是一件好事。

虽然有人说，安装一个软件不可能完全抵制网络的 _____ 影响，孩子只会对不可知的东西更加感兴趣。其实，即使这个软件不能起到百分之百的作用，我们也不能因为它不能完全解决问题就不采取任何措施。当然我们同时还应该加强学校的教育和家长的引导，培养孩子的分析能力和自我控制能力，构建孩子们心理上的"绿坝"。

反对者的意见：

网络上的不良信息对青少年的危害是不可 _____ 的。通过上网过滤软件来保护电脑使用者，特别是青少年的安全，是全世界很多国家的普遍做法。但过滤软件的使用者、使用范围和使用方式，各国做法有很大不同。由于言论自由和信息透明等价值对于社会<u>正义</u>(*justice*) 的重要性，对互联网的管理也需要特别谨慎，寻找合理有效的方法。

绿坝软件被工信部花<u>纳税人</u> (*taxpayer*) 的钱，统一安装到新出产的电脑上进行销售，不仅<u>侵犯</u> (*violate, infringe*) 消费者的选择权利，更严重的是侵犯公民自由 _____ 网上信息而不受限制的权利。

政府对网络色情、_____ 等有害信息的<u>监督</u> (*supervise*) 管理，应当区分公共范围和私人范围。对网吧、公共场所（学校、图书馆等）、办公场所等的上网电脑应加强监督和控制，<u>打击</u> (*crack down*) 非法网站；但是否在家庭电脑中安装过滤软件，应该由用户个人决定。政府可以推荐，但不应<u>强制</u> (*force*) 预装指定的软件。家长可以自主选择软件，也可以根据需要自己决定控制/限制未成年子女接触的信息 _____。

总之，即使是为了保护未成年人，政府不能代替成年的公民来决定什么是有害或无害的 _____。政府可以通过各种措施引导和协助家长负起责任，而不是 _____，成为无所不能的"大家长"。

风波平息

由中国最大的门户网站新浪进行的一项调查显示，超过 80% 被调查者反对预装绿坝。互联网的 _____ 威力最终促使工信部决定 _____ 预装绿坝的要求。2009 年 8 月 13 日，工信部宣布："中国不会强制要求在个人电脑及其他消费产品上大规模安装绿坝互联网过滤软件。"

4.2. 按照上面这篇文章的意思，下面的说法对不对？ (T/F)

_____ 1.   2009 年 7 月 1 日以后在中国国内销售的电脑都必须安装绿坝软件。

_____ 2.   绿坝软件可以帮助父母保护子女免受网络的负面影响。

_____ 3.   政府推行绿坝软件的行为得到了社会各界的支持。

_____ 4.   比起绿坝软件，我们更应该加强培养孩子的自我控制能力。

_____ 5.   工信部购买绿坝软件花的是政府的钱。

_____ 6.   绿坝软件侵犯了公民自由上网的权利。

_____ 7.   只要对老百姓有益，政府就应该强制安装指定的软件。

_____ 8.   新浪的调查显示大多数人反对预装绿坝。

_____ 9.   世界上用过滤软件来保护电脑使用者的安全的国家很少。

_____ 10.   政府应该关心民众，成为无所不能的大家长。

4.3. 根据短文内容，选择最佳答案回答问题：

1. 绿坝反对者不满意政府预装软件的原因是：
    a. 决定是否使用过滤软件的人应该是公民自己，不是政府。
    b. 政府强制安装绿坝软件的方式不对。
    c. 家庭环境是不应该属于政府控制的私人范围。
    d. 以上都对。

2. 以下哪一项不代表绿坝支持者的意见？
    a. 青少年自制能力差，需要使用网络过滤软件。
    b. 网络上的负面信息会对未成年人带来危害。
    c. 如果安装绿坝，就可以全面保护青少年。
    d. 构建孩子心理上的"绿坝"更加重要。

3. 这篇短文的主题是什么？

    a. 安装绿坝的好处和坏处

    b. 网络对青少年的负面影响

    c. 政府不应该干涉公民上网的自由

    d. 中国政府推行绿坝工程的经过和结果

4.4. 英译汉

For many people today, it's difficult to imagine life without a cellular phone. Once the preserve of the rich, they have now become an indispensable part of modern day life.

The technology for cellular phones was patented in 1975, but it wasn't until 1982 that the first commercial cell phone network was established in the United States. Since that time, the cellular phone has changed from a bulky machine to something that can fit into the palm of your hand.

The functions available in modern-day cell phones are increasing rapidly. E-mail access is now standard. Cellular phone cameras, which were once little more than a gimmick, now rival stand-alone digital cameras in terms of quality. With "Third Generation" telephones, broadband access offers the possibility of video phones, television and full Internet access.

All this comes at a cost, however. Many people bemoan a society where people seem glued to their phone, but oblivious to all that is going on around them.

5. 阅读练习

短文一：手机与中国人的日常生活

在中国，手机已经成为人们生活中不可缺少的一部分。清晨手机是闹钟；在上班的路上，手机成为收音机或 MP3；开会的时候，手机是录音机；外出旅行时，手机是照相机；回到单位，手机又成了 U 盘 (USB)。手机网络服务可以让用户寻找各地新闻、天气预报、股票行情或体育赛事。手机短信更是中国人特别喜爱的通讯方式。

2007 年 7 月 7 日那一天，中国人手机上流传着一条短信，"今天是一百年来才遇到的 070707，祝收到短信的，欢天喜地；阅读的，工作顺利；储存 (save) 的，万事如意；转发 (forward) 的，年轻美丽；回复 (reply) 的，爱情甜蜜；删除 (delete) 的，天天捡到人民币"。这条祝福短信简单地说出了用手机的人每日的习惯动作。对很多人来说，没有手机的生活是不可想象的。

其实，手机进入大众生活，只是十几年前的事情。80 年代后期的中国，很多人连固定电话都没有。装个电话要申请、要排队、还要有"后门"。90 年代初，人们从香港的电影、电视上，知道了那种大砖头 (brick) 式的移动电话叫"大哥大"。90 年代中期，比较小的"手机"代替了砖头般的"大哥大"，但用手机那时还只是少数有钱人的特权。一直到了 90 年代后期，手机才开始进入平常百姓家。根据中国信息产业部 (Ministry) 的统计，到 2007 年 12 月底，大陆手机用户超过 5.4 亿户，普及率达到 41.63%。

人们现在越来越从固定生活走向移动生活，而手机使我们可以随时随地和世界联系。手机不只是一部简简单单的小设备，它能改变整个文化。有人认为，如果说汽车文化是六十年代美国文化的标志 (sign, mark)，那么手机文化将是二十一世纪中国文化的象征。

5.1. 根据短文内容，选择最佳答案回答问题：

1. 短文中提到的手机用途包括 _____。
   a) 闹钟、游戏机、照相机、MP3 等
   b) 录像机、录音机、闹钟、U 盘等
   c) MP3、照相机、U 盘、计算器等
   d) 闹钟、收音机、MP3、照相机、U 盘等

2. 根据短文，以下哪种是中国人特别喜欢的通讯方式？
   a) 大哥大。
   b) 电脑网络。
   c) 手机短信。
   d) 固定电话。

3. 手机什么时候开始进入大众生活？
   a) 80 年代后期。
   b) 90 年代初期。
   c) 90 年代中期。
   d) 90 年代后期。

4. 短文中的"大哥大"指的是 _____。
   a) 哥哥
   b) 砖头
   c) 有钱人的手机
   d) 早期的移动电话

5. 六十年代的美国文化与二十一世纪的中国文化分别以 _____ 为标志。
   a) 股票和网络
   b) 汽车和手机
   c) 电影和电脑
   d) 电视和手机

6. 以下哪项最好地说明了短文的主题？
   a) 手机在中国人生活中的作用。
   b) 中国大陆手机的普及率。
   c) 手机已不是少数有钱人的象征。
   d) 中国的手机文化。

5.2. 按照这篇文章的意思，下面的说法对不对？（T/F）

_____ 用手机的人习惯动作包括储存、转发、回复、删除、更新。

_____ 手机网络服务可以让用户查看股票行情。

_____ 在 80 年代后期，安装固定电话需要有关系。

_____ 九十年代后期，41.6% 的中国人拥有手机。

_____ 手机使生活变得方便，人们可以随时随地与外界联系。

阅读二：网络语言

互联网拉近了人与人之间的距离，使人们沟通起来更加方便。上世纪 90 年代末，中国的大众开始知道了什么是电子邮件、什么是聊天室、什么是论坛。网民们在网上写作的时候，为了方便、幽默起见，改造了汉语和英语的一些词汇，并把文字和图片、数字、符号（symbol）等结合在一起，创造了符号型、数字型、谐音型等带有明显的互联网时代特征的网络语言。

符号型网络语言：以简单符号表示某种表情或文字。如

O.O	表示"惊讶"
^_^	表示"高兴"
:-(	表示"不高兴"
<@-@>	表示"醉了"
（）	表示"脸红"

数字型网络语言：一般是利用数字的谐音，例如

9494	= 就是，就是
7456	= 气死我了
555~~~~	= 呜呜呜（哭声）
886	= 拜拜了，再见
246	= 饿死了
1314520	= 一生一世我爱你

谐音型网络语言：用英文的谐音翻译

<u>粉丝</u>	= fans
<u>伊妹儿</u>	= e-mail
<u>荡</u>	= download（下载）
<u>黑客</u>	= hacker

字母型：以单纯字母的发音代替原有的汉字或英文，例如

MM	= 妹妹
GG	= 哥哥
GF	= 女朋友
BF	= 男朋友
cu	= see you

混合型：把文字、符号、数字、英文和中文等混合在一起，例如

3q	= thank you
3x	= thanks

■ 古字新用型：用已经失去生命力的古汉字表示新的意思。

这一类型中最典型的就是古汉字"囧"。这是一个大多数人可能都不认识的古字，现在却在网络世界大为流行。这个字读 jiǒng，本来的意思是"光明"。可是，流行于网络的"囧"字有了新的意思。由于它看起来像一个在哭的人脸，它便成为表达沮丧、悲伤和无奈心情的一个符号。比如说，"这次考试还差一分就及格了！真囧……"这样的表达在 90 后的网民交流中已很平常。

■ 网络语言的特点：创新的符号语言

网络语言的两个主要特质是<u>生动</u> (vivid) 性和创新性。网络语言一般都比较生动有趣而又富有创意，特别是<u>象形</u> (pictographic) 的符号化表达则是网络语言的一大特点。另一方面，网络用语力求创新、创意，追求与主流表达习惯的差异，用不同一般的表达方式体现出'<u>酷</u>'(cool) 和时尚。

面对越来越多的新生词汇，很多人担心汉语的纯洁性将会因此受影响，并认为网络语言是对传统语言的破坏。但也有人认为，语言的多样化是语言生活的需要，网络语言可以说是时代的语言。随着互联网日新月异的发展，网络语言将以鲜活的多样化特点日益显示出强大的影响力。

5.3. 按照上面这篇文章的意思，下面的说法对不对？(T/F)

_____ 1. 网络语言最早出现在上世纪 90 年代末。

_____ 2. 网络语言是互联网时代的产物。

_____ 3. 网络语言主要由文字和符号组成。

_____ 4. 流行于网络的"囧"字的意思是"光明"。

_____ 5. 在有网络语言以前，很多人都不认识"囧"字。

_____ 6. 网络 50 语言很生动因为它常常用象形的符号。

_____ 7. 网络用语追求主流表达习惯，因为那样很'酷'和时尚。

_____ 8. 有人认为网络语言不够纯洁。

_____ 9. 有人认为网络语言是时代发展的需要。

_____ 10. 互联网的发展可能使网络语言更有影响力。

6. 口语练习

6.1. 讨论题

1. 网络在现代人的生活中起了什么作用？

2. 互联网有什么好处？有什么不好的地方？

3. 电邮、手机对人们的交流方式有什么影响？

4. 手机的那些功能对你特别重要？你手机上的那些功能你并不需要？

5. 有人说网络是一个工具，人们可以用它来做好事或者做坏事，你同意吗？请举例说明。

6. 现代社会的科学技术正在创造一种新的人类：他们愿意与机器打交道而不愿与人打交道，他们宁可活在一个<u>虚拟</u> (virtual) 的世界而不愿意有一个实实在在的家庭。你觉得这话对不对？请举例说明。

6.2. 同意还是不同意

To what extent do you agree with the following statements? Circle the answers, then share your responses with several classmates.
(1-strongly disagree　　2-disagree　　3-neutral　　4-agree　　5-strongly agree)

1. 电脑和网络给人们带来了很多方便。　　　　　1　　2　　3　　4　　5

2. 网络是争取民主的一个有力工具。　　　　　1　　2　　3　　4　　5

3. 将来网购会取代商店。　　　　　1　　2　　3　　4　　5

4. 要是没有网络，我的生活质量会要降低很多。　　　1　　2　　3　　4　　5

5. 现代人在电子邮件、网络上花的时间太多了。　　　1　　2　　3　　4　　5

6. 给亲友写信比发电子邮件好。　　　　　1　　2　　3　　4　　5

7. 网上的交流一般都不如真正的信件深刻。　　　1　　2　　3　　4　　5

8. 人们的生活越来越被科技所控制。　　　　　1　　2　　3　　4　　5

7. 写作练习（任选一题，600-700 字）

1. 网络的利和弊

2. 怎样避免网络不良信息对孩子的影响

3. 网络让世界变小了

Required vocabulary and expressions:

1. Use at least 10 of the following new vocabulary words and phrases:

排名	惊人	引发	平台	有害	低估	大众
思维	范围	推进	获取	娱乐媒介	舆论	移民
激起	强烈	抗议	威力	普及	产业	变革
攻击	犯罪泛滥	论坛	游戏	互联网	成千上万

2. Use at least 5 of the following expressions:

| 由于……而…… | 在……下 | 同时…… | ……，更…… |
| 只……而不…… | 既……又…… | 的确…… | 一方面……但另一方面 |

Vocabulary Index

English-Chinese

英文	简体	繁体	拼音	词性	HSK 等级	课数
abolish, do away with	废除	廢	fèichú	v.	丙	20
accelerate, speed up	加快		jiākuài	v.(c)		18
accidental, unexpected	偶然		ǒurán	adj.	丙	15
accompany	陪伴		péibàn	v.		14
actually, exactly, after all	究竟		jiūjìng	adv.	乙	12
add, have a baby	添		tiān	v.	乙	12
addiction	瘾		yǐn	n.		20
admire, envy	羡慕		xiànmù	v.	乙	15
admit, acknowledge	承认	認	chéngrèn	v.	乙	15
afterwards	此后	後	cǐhòu	conj.	丁	18
again and again, repeatedly	再三		zàisān	adv.	丙	15
again; once more	重		chóng	adv.	乙	12
all along, the whole time, constantly	一向		yíxiàng	adv.	丙	16
all one's life, lifetime	一辈子	輩	yíbèizi	n.	丙	13
allow, permit	许可	許	xǔkě	v.	丁	15
alone, by oneself	独自	獨	dúzì	adv.	丙	15
alternate, be after an interval of (time)	隔		gé	v.	乙	18
always, all through the ages	历来	歷來	lìlái	adv.	丁	12
anyway, anyhow, in any case	反正		fǎnzhèng	adv.	乙	13
apart from, in addition	之外		zhīwài	adv.	丙	18
appreciate, increase in value	升值	昇	shēngzhí	v.o.		17
appropriate, proper	得体	體	détǐ	adj.		18
approve of, agree with	赞同	贊	zàntóng	v.	丁	13
approve of, endorse	认可	認	rènkě	v.	丁	15
approve, endorse, agree with	赞成	贊	zànchéng	v.	乙	11
arouse, stir up	激起		jīqǐ	v(c)	丁	20
Asia	亚洲	亞	Yàzhōu	p.n.		15
astonishing, amazing	惊人	驚	jīngrén	Adj.	丙	20

英文	简体	繁体	拼音	词性	HSK 等级	课数
at the worst	大不了		dàbuliǎo	adv.		17
attack, assault	攻击	擊	gōngjī	v.	丙	20
avoid	避免		bìmiǎn	v.	乙	18
awkward, uncomfortable	别扭	彆	bièniu	adj.	丁	11
baby, "little treasure"	宝宝	寶	bǎobǎo	n.	丙	12
background	背景		bèijǐng	n.	丙	14
bad, harmful, unhealthy	不良		bùliáng	attr.	丁	15
balanced	平衡		pínghéng	adj.	丙	16
be directed against	针对	針對	zhēnduì	v.	乙	19
be doubtful, uncertain, perplexed	疑惑		yíhuò	v.	丁	11
be flexible; adapt	变通	變	biàntong	v.		14
be interested, be attracted	心动	動	xīndòng	v.		17
be interrelated	相关	關	xiāngguān	adj,	丁	19
be pleased with oneself	得意		déyì	adj.	丙	13
be unemployed, lose one's job	失业	業	shīyè	v.o.	乙	16
be very fond of, to love dearly	疼爱	愛	téng'ài	v.	乙	14
bear hardships, suffer	吃苦		chīkǔ	v.o.	丙	13
bear market	熊市		xióngshì	n.		17
beat up	殴打	毆	ōudǎ	v.	丁	20
become rich	致富		zhìfù	v.o.	丁	19
belong to	属于	屬於	shǔyú	v.	乙	14
big city, metropolis	都市		dūshì	n.	丁	18
blame	怪		guài	v.	丙	11
blend in	融入		róngrù	v.	丁	18
book, reserve	预定	預	yùdìng	v.	丁	20
brand name	品牌		pǐnpái	n.		18
break	断	斷	duàn	v.	乙	14
breathe deeply, pant	喘气	氣	chuǎnqì	v.o.	丙	13
bring into play, give free rein	发挥	發揮	fāhuī	v.	乙	16
broker, agent, dealer	经纪商	經紀	jīngjìshāng	n.	丁	17
bull market	牛市		niúshì	n.		17
business	生意		shēngyi	n.	乙	20
businessman, merchant	商人		shāngrén	n.	丙	16
busy, bustling	繁忙		fánmáng	adj.	丁	12

英文	简体	繁体	拼音	词性	HSK 等级	课数
call on, pay a visit	看望		kànwàng	*v.*	丁	12
can get along well with	合得来	來	hédelái	*v.p.*		11
can, may	得以		déyǐ	*v.*	丁	18
cancer	癌症	癥	áizhèng	*n.*	丙	19
cannot help (doing sth.)	不禁		bùjīn	*adv.*	丙	11
carpet, rug	地毯		dìtǎn	*n.*	丙	14
carry on one's shoulders	扛		káng	*v.*	乙	20
cause, incur, invite, result in	致		zhì	*v.*	丙	19
census, general investigation	普查		pǔchá	*n.*	丁	19
choose and buy	选购	選購	xuǎngòu	*v.*		18
choose, select	挑		tiāo	*v.*	乙	11
civilization	文明		wénmíng	*n.*	乙	20
clash, conflict	冲突	衝	chōngtū	*n.*	丙	14
clean up, clear up, tidy up	清理		qīnglǐ	*v.*	丁	12
clear-cut, straightforward	干脆	乾	gāncuì	*adj.*	乙	13
clench one's teeth	咬牙		yǎoyá	*v.o.*	乙	13
close, intimate	密切		mìqiè	*adj.*	乙	19
clothes, clothing	服装	裝	fúzhuāng	*n.*	丁	18
club	俱乐部	樂	jùlèbù	*n.*	乙	15
command, direct, conduct	指挥	揮	zhǐhuī	*v.*	乙	11
commit a crime	犯罪		fànzuì	*v.o.*	丙	20
commodity	商品		shāngpǐn	*n.*	乙	16
companion	同伴		tóngbàn	*n.*	丙	20
(computer) mouse	鼠标	標	shǔbiāo	*n.*		20
comply with, yield to	依		yī	*v.*	丁	14
conclusion	结论	結論	jiélùn	*n.*	乙	19
consequence	后果	後	hòuguǒ	*n.*	丙	15
constantly, always	时刻	時	shíkè	*adv.*	丙	19
continue, go on, last	延续	續	yánxù	*v.*	丁	15
contract (an illness)	患		huàn	*v.*	丙	19
control, manage	治理		zhìlǐ	*v.*	丁	19
corn	玉米		yùmǐ	*n.*	乙	18
corrupt, rotten, decadent	腐败	敗	fǔbài	*adj.*	丁	16
costs	成本		chéngběn	*n.*	丙	17

英文	简体	繁体	拼音	词性	HSK 等级	课数
county	县	縣	xiàn	n.	乙	19
cover, bury	埋		mái	v.	乙	18
crystal-clear	清澈		qīngchè	adj.		19
cucumber	黄瓜		huángguā	n.	乙	18
custard, a thick soup	羹		gēng	n.		11
custom make	定做		dìngzuò	v.		18
cut with a knife	割		gē	v.	乙	19
daughter-in-law	媳妇	婦	xífu	n.	丙	11
day tour	一日游	遊	yírìyóu	n.		18
deal, trade, transaction	交易		jiāoyì	n.	丙	16
death	死亡		sǐwáng	n.	丙	19
depend on; rely on	依赖	賴	yīlài	v.	丁	14
despairing, hopeless	绝望	絕	juéwàng	adj.	丁	17
despise, look down on	轻视	輕視	qīngshì	v.	丙	16
destination	目的地		mùdìdì	n.		20
destroy, damage	破坏	壞	pòhuài	v.	乙	19
detain	拘留		jūliú	v.	丁	20
develop, launch	开展	開	kāizhǎn	v.	乙	18
die, pass away	去世		qùshì	v.o.	丁	19
diet, food and drink	饮食	飲	yǐnshí	n.	丁	18
dig, scoop out	掏		tāo	v.	乙	13
dining table	餐桌		cānzhuō	n.		18
dinner; supper	晚餐		wǎncān	n.	丁	12
disaster, catastrophe	灾难	災難	zāinàn	n.	丙	15
discharge	排放		páifàng	v.		19
discouraged, depressed	沮丧	喪	jǔsàng	adj.		17
discuss, negotiate	商谈	談	shāngtán	v.		17
disease, sickness	疾病		jíbìng	n.	丙	19
do all one can, try one's best	尽力	盡	jìnlì	v.o.	丙	15
double-character surname	双姓	雙	shuāngxìng	n.		14
dove, pigeon	鸽	鴿	gē	n.	丙	13
dress, apparel	穿着	著	chuānzhuó	n.		18
dress and personal adornment	服饰	飾	fúshì	n.		18
dress up, deck out	打扮		dǎban	v.	乙	18

英文	简体	繁体	拼音	词性	HSK 等级	课数
duck	鸭子		yāzi	*n.*	丙	19
dumbfounded, stupefied	愣		lèng	*adj.*	丙	11
duplicate, reproduce, clone	复制	複製	fùzhì	*v.*	丙	14
dusk, twilight	黄昏		huánghūn	*n.*	丙	11
effectiveness, benefit	效益		xiàoyì	*n.*	丁	19
efficiency	效率		xiàolǜ	*n.*	乙	16
eggplant	茄子		qiézi	*n.*	丁	18
electron, electronic	电子	電	diànzǐ	*n. /adj*	丙	20
emerge in large numbers	涌现	現	yǒngxiàn	*v.*	丁	16
end up	告终	終	gàozhōng	*v.p.*		14
ending	结尾	結	jiéwěi	*n.*		14
endlessly, incessantly	不已		bùyǐ	*adv.*		15
energy sources	能源		néngyuán	*n.*	乙	19
energy, vigor	精力		jīnglì	*n.*	乙	12
engage in trade, be in business	经商	經	jīngshāng	*v.o.*	丁	16
engine	引擎		yǐnqíng	*n.*		20
enjoy (rights, privileges, etc.)	享有		xiǎngyǒu	*v.*	丁	12
enough, ample, sufficient	足够	夠	zúgòu	*adj.*	丙	14
entertainment	娱乐	樂	yúlè	*n.*	丙	20
exceed one's budget	超支		chāozhī	*v.o.*		13
exception	例外		lìwài	*n.*	丁	18
excessive	过分	過	guòfèn	*adj.*	丙	14
ex-husband	前夫		qiánfū	*n.*		15
expenses, expenditure	支出		zhīchū	*n.*	丁	12
experience many times	历经	歷經	lìjīng	*v.*		19
extend (everywhere)	遍及		biànjí	*v.*		19
external	外在		wàizài	*adj.*		15
extramarital affair	婚外情		hūnwàiqíng	*n.*		15
eyebrow	眉头	頭	méitóu	*n.*	丙	13
factor, element	因素		yīnsù	*n.*	乙	15
fair, market	集市		jíshì	*n.*	丁	20
fairy tale	童话	話	tónghuà	*n.*		14
fall, drop	跌		diē	*v.*	乙	17
family name	姓氏		xìngshì	*n.*		14

英文	简体	繁体	拼音	词性	HSK 等级	课数
farm, ranch	农场	農場	nóngchǎng	n.	丙	19
fashionable	入时	時	rùshí	adj.		18
fast speed	快速		kuàisù	adj	丁	19
feel happy, rejoice	开心	開	kāixīn	adj.	丁	11
financial resources	财力	財	cáilì	n.	丁	14
find, detect, discover	发觉	發覺	fājué	v.	丙	15
firewood	柴		chái	n.	丁	14
fix up (a house), renovate	装修	裝	zhuāngxiū	v.	丙	17
flexible	灵活	靈	línghuó	adj.	乙	16
float in the air, flutter	飘	飄	piāo	v.	乙	18
flourishing, prosperous	繁荣	榮	fánróng	adj.	乙	16
folk rhyme, folklore, popular verse	民谣	謠	mínyáo	n.		16/19
follow up, catch up	跟上		gēnshang	v.		13
for this reason	为此	爲	wéicǐ	prep.		17
force, make an effort, strive	强	強	qiǎng	v.	丙	12
form a partnership	合伙		héhuǒ	v.o.	丁	17
form; make up; compose	组成	組	zǔchéng	v. c	丙	14
forum	论坛	論壇	lùntán	n.		20
foster, raise, bring up	抚养	撫養	fǔyǎng	v.	丁	15
frequent caller	常客		chángkè	n.		18
frequently	频繁	頻	pínfán	adv.	丁	19
full-time position	全职	職	quánzhí	n.	丙	12
fund, capital	资金	資	zījīn	n.	丙	17
game	游戏	遊戲	yóuxì	n.	丙	20
gap, disparity	差距		chājù	n.	丁	16
general public	大众	眾	dàzhòng	n.	丙	20
generous	大方		dàfang	adj.	丙	13
gently, softly, stealthily	悄悄		qiāoqiāo	adv.	乙	16
ghost, spirit, phantom	幽灵	靈	yōulíng	n.		19
go (appear) on the market	上市		shàngshì	v.o.		16
go backwards, regress	倒退		dàotuì	v.	丁	12
go home to see family	探亲	親	tànqīn	v.o.	丁	17
go out (esp. on business)	外出		wàichū	v.	丁	12

英文	简体	繁体	拼音	词性	HSK 等级	课数
go through, experience	经历	經歷	jīnglì	*v.*	乙	15
go up to heaven, i.e., die	升天	昇	shēngtiān	*v.o.*		19
good, excellent	棒		bàng	*adj.*	丙	13
grab, seize	抓		zhuā	*v.*	乙	13
gradually, by degrees	渐渐	漸	jiànjiàn	*adv.*	乙	15
grandchildren's generation	孙辈	孫輩	sūnbèi	*n.*		14
gym	健身房		jiànshēnfáng	*n.*		18
harmful	有害		yǒuhài	*adj.*	丁	20
hastily, hurriedly	连忙	連	liánmáng	*adv.*	乙	11
he, she, it, his, her, its (classical)	其		qí	*pron.*	丙	16
heed advice; be obedient	听话	聽話	tīnghuà	*v.o.*	丁	11
high-speed	高速		gāosù	*adj.*	丙	19
hold in one's arms, hug	搂	摟	lǒu	*v.*	丙	11
hold sth. level	端		duān	*v.*	丙	11
Hong Kong, Macao, and Taiwan	港澳台	臺	Gǎng'àotái	*p.n.*		16
hot pepper, chili pepper	辣椒		làjiāo	*n.*	丙	18
hotel	酒店		jiǔdiàn	*n.*	丙	20
household duties	家务	務	jiāwù	*n.*	丁	11
housewife	家庭主妇	婦	jiātíngzhǔfù	*n.*		12
Huai River	淮河		Huái Hé	*p.n.*		19
husband's father, father-in-law	公公		gōnggong	*n.*	丁	12
husband's mother, mother-in-law	婆婆		pópo	*n.*	丁	12
hydrology	水文		shuǐwén	*n.*		19
ignore, neglect	忽视	視	hūshì	*v.*	丙	19
improve	改进	進	gǎijìn	*v.*	乙	20
in a pair, in pairs	成双成对	雙對	chéngshuāng chéngduì	*i.e.*		15
in a second, in a very short time	一转眼	轉	yīzhuǎnyǎn	*adv.*		14
in advance, beforehand	预	預	yù	*adv.*		17
in the days to come; future	日后	後	rìhòu	*adv.*		14
in this way	这样一来	這樣	zhèyàng yīlái	*i.e.*	丙	11
incessantly	不停		bùtíng	*adv.*	丙	13
indeed, really	的确	確	díquè	*adv.*	乙	18
individual character, individuality	个性	個	gèxìng	*n.*	丙	18

英文	简体	繁体	拼音	词性	HSK 等级	课数
individual, individuality	个体	個體	gètǐ	*n.*	乙	16
industry	产业	產業	chǎnyè	*n.*	丁	20
inherit, carry on	传承	傳	chuánchéng	*v.*		14
instant noodles	方便面		fāngbiàn miàn	*n.*		18
intellectual	知识分子	識	zhīshifènzǐ	*n.*	丙	16
intelligence	智力		zhìlì	*n.*	丁	13
interest	利息		lìxī	*n.*	丁	17
Internet	互联网	聯網	Hùliánwǎng	*p.n.*		20
item, project	项目	項	xiàngmù	*n.*	乙	18
join	加入		jiārù	*v.*	丙	15
karaoke	卡拉 OK		kǎlā–ok	*n.*		15
keep thinking of, miss	惦记	記	diànjì	*v.*	丙	11
key, the most crucial thing	关键	關鍵	guānjiàn	*n.*	乙	13
kiss	亲	親	qīn	*v.*	丙	13
lack, miss	缺失		quēshī	*v.*		15
landlord, landlady	房东	東	fángdōng	*n.*	丁	17
large scale, big size	大型		dàxíng	*adj.*	乙	13
latent, hidden, potential	潜在	潛	qiánzài	*attr.*	丁	15
lead to, bring about	导致	導	dǎozhì	*v.*	丙	15
lead, bring along	带动	帶動	dàidòng	*v.*	丙	18
lead, manage, take charge of	主		zhǔ	*v.*	丁	12
leather	皮革		pígé	*n.*	丁	19
legal, legitimate	合法		héfǎ	*adj.*	丙	15
leisure	休闲	閑	xiūxián	*n.*	丙	12
leisurely	悠闲	閑	yōuxián	*adj.*		20
liberate	解放		jiěfàng	*v.*	乙	12
lightning	闪电	閃電	shǎndiàn	*n.*	丙	15
look after, take care of	看		kān	*v.*	丙	11
look at each other	对看	對	duì kàn	*v.p.*		11
look, see, watch (colloquial)	瞧		qiáo	*v.*	乙	11
mahjong	麻将	將	májiàng	*n.*		18
mail	邮件	郵	yóujiàn	*n.*		20
mainstream	主流		zhǔliú	*n.*	丁	18
maintain, keep, preserve	维持	維	wéichí	*v.*	丙	14

英文	简体	繁体	拼音	词性	HSK 等级	课数
make a noise; give vent	闹	鬧	nào	v.	乙	11
make a profit	盈利		yínglì	v.o.	丁	17
make money, make a profit	赚	賺	zhuàn	v.	丙	12
make one's position known	表态	態	biǎotài	v.o.	乙	11
march (music)	进行曲	進	jìnxíngqǔ	n.		13
masses, common people	民众	眾	mínzhòng	n.	丁	15
maternal grandfather	外祖父		wàizǔfù	n.	丙	14
maternal grandmother	外祖母		wàizǔmǔ	n.	丙	14
matter, substance, material	物质	質	wùzhì	n.	乙	16
means, method, approach	手段		shǒuduàn	n.	乙	20
medium	媒介		méijiè	n.	丁	20
member, members	成员	員	chéngyuán	n.	丙	15
migrant, immigrant	移民		yímín	n.	丁	20
millionaire	百万富翁	萬	bǎiwàn fùwēng	n.		17
mind, mind's eye	心目		xīnmù	n.	丙	16
mine	矿山	礦	kuàngshān	n.	丁	19
Ministry of Civil Affairs	民政部		Mínzhèngbù	p.n.		15
miracle	奇迹	跡	qíjì	n.	丙	16
monotonous, dull	单调	單調	dāndiào	adj.	乙	18
moral integrity, human dignity	人格		réngé	n.	丁	12
movement	运动	運動	yùndòng	n.	甲	12
multiplicate, redouble	倍增		bèizēng	v.		17
nanny, housekeeper	保姆		bǎomǔ	n.	丁	12
national economy	国民经济	國經濟	guómín jīngjì	n.		16
needless to say	不用说	說	búyòngshuō	i.e.		11
negative, bad	负面	負	fùmiàn	adj.		20
no different from, the same as	无异于	無異於	wúyìyú	v.p.		14
no wonder	难怪	難	nánguài	adv.	丙	16
not get along well	不和		bùhé	adj.		15
not yet	尚未		shàngwèi	adv.	丁	17
not, no, non-, un-	非		fēi	adv.	丙	16
now, at the moment	这会儿	這會兒	zhèhuìr	adv.	丙	13
observe carefully, watch	观察	觀	guānchá	v.	乙	17
obtain	获取	獲	huòqǔ	v.	丁	20

英文	简体	繁体	拼音	词性	HSK 等级	课数
occasion, time	度		dù	m.	乙	12
official	官员	員	guānyuán	n.	丁	19
old man, old father	老爷子	爺	lǎoyézi	n.		11
online shopping	网购	網購	wǎnggòu	n.		20
on the way	顺路	順	shùnlù	adv.	丙	11
one after another	相继	繼	xiāngjì	adv.	丁	19
one side, a side	一旁		yìpáng	n.	丙	13
open a business	开张	開張	kāizhāng	v.		16
open one's mouth	咧		liě	v.		13
opportunity	机遇	機	jīyù	n.	丁	16
original price	原价	價	yuánjià	n.		17
out of, stem from, be due to	出于	於	chūyú	v.p.		12
outward appearance	外表		wàibiǎo	n.	丁	18
overall, full-scale	全面		quánmiàn	adj.	乙	17
overflow	泛滥	濫	fànlàn	v.	丙	20
overseas	海外		hǎiwài	n.	丁	20
painstaking care or effort	心血		xīnxuè	n.	丁	13
paper	纸张	紙張	zhǐzhāng	n.	丁	19
pardon; forgive; tolerate	包容		bāoróng	v.	丁	15
partake, participate in	参与	參與	cānyù	v.	丁	17
pay, expend	付出		fùchū	v.	丁	13
pea, bean	豆子		dòuzi	n.	丙	18
peaceful	太平		tàipíng	adj.	丁	11
peddle goods, hawk one's wares	叫卖	賣	jiàomài	v.		20
people of a nation	国民	國	guómín	v.	丁	16
person, personage, public figure	人士		rénshì	n.	丙	15
personnel matters	人事		rénshì	n.	丁	12
persuade, advise	劝说	勸說	quànshuō	v.	乙	15
plant	植物		zhíwù	n.	乙	20
platform	平台	臺	píngtái	n.		20
play in water	戏水	戲	xìshuǐ	v.o.		19
police	警察		jǐngchá	n.	乙	20
pollute, contaminate, pollution	污染		wūrǎn	v./n.	乙	16
ponder, think over	琢磨		zuómo	v.	丁	11

英文	简体	繁体	拼音	词性	HSK 等级	课数
pool, pond	塘		táng	*n.*	丁	19
popularize	普及		pǔjí	*v.*	丙	20
pornography	色情		sèqíng	*n.*		20
possess, have, own	拥有	擁	yōngyǒu	*v.*	丁	15
power, force	威力		wēilì	*n.*	丁	20
prepare, plan	筹	籌	chóu	*v.*		17
pressure; burden	压力	壓	yālì	*n.*	丙	12
high occurring	高发	發	gāofā	*adj.*		19
price	价钱	價錢	jiàqian	*n.*	丙	13
price, cost	代价	價	dàijià	*n.*	丙	19
prices of goods on the market	行情		hángqíng	*n.*		17
prince	王子		wángzǐ	*n.*		14
princess	公主		gōngzhǔ	*n.*		14
prize, award, trophy	奖品	獎	jiǎngpǐn	*n.*	丁	13
procedures, formalities	手续	續	shǒuxù	*n.*	乙	15
profit, gain	收益		shōuyì	*n.*	丁	17
promote, push on	推进	進	tuījìn	*v.*	丙	20
promoted	升迁	昇遷	shēngqiān	*v.*		19
property, estate; capital	资产	資產	zīchǎn	*n.*	丙	15
prospects, promise, future	出息		chūxi	*n.*	丙	13
protest, demonstrate	抗议	議	kàngyì	*v.*	丙	20
prudent, careful, cautious	谨慎	謹	jǐnshèn	*adj.*	丙	17
public opinion	舆论	輿論	yúlùn	*n.*	丁	20
purchase, buy	收购	購	shōugòu	*v.*	丁	16
pure	纯	純	chún	*adj.*	丙	16
pure, simple	单纯	單純	dānchún	*adj.*	丙	19
purple	紫		zǐ	*adj.*	乙	18
pursue, chase	追逐		zhuīzhú	*v.*		19
quarrel or argue vehemently	吵架		chǎojià	*v.o.*	丙	15
question closely	追问	問	zhuīwèn	*v.*	丁	15
quick in responding	来得快	來	lái de kuài	*v.p.*		11
quick-freeze	速冻	凍	sùdòng	*v.*		18
radish, turnip	萝卜	蘿	luóbo	*n.*	乙	18
rank	排名		páimíng	*v.o.*		20

英文	简体	繁体	拼音	词性	HSK 等级	课数
rather than, better than	与其	與	yǔqí	*conj.*	丙	17
rational, reasonable	合理		hélǐ	*adj.*	丁	14
realize	体会	體會	tǐhuì	*v.*	乙	17
reason	理由		lǐyóu	*n.*	乙	12
rebound (of price or stock)	反弹	彈	fǎntán	*v.*	丁	17
receive	领	領	lǐng	*v.*	乙	13
reconstruct, recompose	重组	組	chóngzǔ	*v.*		15
reflect, report	反映		fǎnyìng	*v.*	乙	18
regain, get back	找回		zhǎohuí	*v.p.*		12
regiment (in army)	团	團	tuán	*n.*	乙	11
relatively	相对	對	xiāngduì	*adv.*	丙	14
relax	放松	鬆	fàngsōng	*v.*	丙	12
release, set free	释放	釋	shìfàng	*v.*	丁	18
remarry	再婚		zàihūn	*v.*		15
remember, memory	记忆	記憶	jìyì	*v./n.*	乙	19
remove, relieve, get rid of	解除		jiěchú	*v.*	丁	15
Republic of Korea	韩国	韓國	Hánguó	*p.n.*		15
resign, quit one's job	辞职	辭職	cízhí	*v.o.*	丁	12
responsibility	责任	責	zérèn	*n.*	乙	12
results, gains; harvest	收获	穫	shōuhuò	*n.*	乙	13
return, come back, go back	返回		fǎnhuí	*v.*	丁	12
rhythm	节奏	節	jiézòu	*n.*	丁	18
rich man, man of wealth	富翁		fùwēng	*n.*	丙	17
rich, solid, abundant	雄厚		xiónghòu	*adj.*	丁	14
right, privilege	权利	權	quánlì	*n.*	丙	15
river basin, valley	流域		liúyù	*n.*	丙	19
running water, tap water	自来水	來	zìláishuǐ	*n.*	丙	19
sad, sorrowful	悲伤	傷	bēishāng	*adj.*	丁	15
sales channels	销路	銷	xiāolù	*n.*	丁	20
salt	盐	鹽	yán	*n.*	乙	14
salted vegetables, pickles	咸菜	鹹	xiáncài	*n.*		13
save worry, avoid worry	省心		shěngxīn	*v.o.*		11
save, deposit	存		cún	*v.*	乙	16
save, rescue	挽救		wǎnjiù	*v.*	丙	12

英文	简体	繁体	拼音	词性	HSK 等级	课数
scale, scope, extent	规模	規	guīmó	n.	乙	16
scope, range	范围	範圍	fànwéi	n.	乙	20
screen (TV or movie)	屏幕		píngmù	n.		20
search	搜索		sōusuō	v	丁	20
seed	种子	種	zhǒngzi	n.	乙	20
select, designate	选定	選	xuǎndìng	v.	丁	18
self, oneself, ego	自我		zìwǒ	n.	乙	12
self-esteem	自尊		zìzūn	n.		15
self-examination, introspection	反思		fǎnsī	v.	丁	19
sell	出售		chūshòu	v.	丁	17
sell, market	销售	銷	xiāoshòu	v.	丁	16
send back, repatriate	遣送		qiǎnsòng	v.		20
sense of security	安全感		ānquángǎn	n.		16
sensitive	敏感		mǐn'gǎn	adj.	丁	18
sentiment	情调	調	qíngdiào	n.	乙	15
separate, be at a distance from, at an interval	隔		gé	v.	乙	14
severe	严峻	嚴	yánjùn	adj.	丁	19
shadow	阴影	陰	yīnyǐng	n.	丁	15
shame	羞耻		xiūchǐ	n.	丁	15
share of a company	股		gǔ	m(n)	丙	17
shop assistant	售货员	貨員	shòuhuò yuán	n.		13
shopping center, mall	购物中心	購	gòuwù zhōngxīn	n.		13
shoulder	肩头	頭	jiāntóu	n.	乙	12
sigh	叹	嘆	tàn	v.	丁	11
simplify	简化	簡	jiǎnhuà	v.	丁	15
Singapore	新加坡		Xīnjiāpō	p.n.		15
single parent	单亲	單親	dānqīn	n.		15
skirt	裙子		qúnzi	n.	乙	18
smile	微笑		wēixiào	v.	乙	13
social class	阶级	階級	jiējí	n.	丁	15
soft and warm	软和	軟	ruǎnhuo	adj.	乙	13
song and dance hall	歌舞厅	廳	gēwǔtīng	n.		18
sound of crying, wind, siren	呜	嗚	wū	ono.	丁	11

英文	简体	繁体	拼音	词性	HSK 等级	课数
speculate in stocks	炒股		chǎogǔ	*v.o.*		17
split in two	一分为二	爲	yìfēnwéi'èr	*i.e.*		11
spoil (a child)	溺爱	愛	nì'ài	*v.*		14
spread	扩散	擴	kuòsàn	*v.*	丁	19
stable	稳定	穩	wěndìng	*adj.*	乙	14
start, initiate, launch	启动	啓動	qǐdòng	*v.*		19
State Council	国务院	國務	Guówùyuàn	*p.n.*	丙	20
state-run	国营	國營	guóyíng	*attr.*	丙	16
steaming hot, piping hot	热腾腾	熱騰	rèténgténg	*adj.*		11
stepparents	继父母	繼	jìfùmǔ	*n.*	丁	15
stinky, smelly	臭		chòu	*adj.*	乙	19
stock, stock certificate	股票		gǔpiào	*n.*	丁	16
stock market	股市		gǔshì	*n.*		17
straight line	直线	綫	zhíxiàn	*n.*	丁	17
stroll along the street, go (window) shopping	逛街		guàngjiē	*v.o.*	丙	18
strong, intense	强烈	強	qiángliè	*adj.*	乙	20
strong, robust	壮	壯	zhuàng	*adj.*	丙	13
suburb	市郊		shìjiāo	*n.*	乙	17
succeed	成功		chénggōng	*v.*	乙	15
sudden and violent	暴		bào	*adj.*	丙	17
superfluous, extra, unnecessary	多余	餘	duōyú	*adj.*	丙	16
superiority	优势	優勢	yōushì	*n.*	丙	14
support, provide for	赡养	贍養	shànyǎng	*v.*		14
sure, safe, insurance	保险	險	bǎoxiǎn	*adj/n*	丙	17
surprised, amazed	惊讶	驚訝	jīngyà	*adj.*	丙	17
sustain, continue	持续	續	chíxù	*v.*	丁	19
sweater	毛衣		máoyī	*n.*	乙	13
sweet, happy, comfortable	甜蜜		tiánmì	*adj.*	丙	12
system of organization	体制	體	tǐzhì	*n.*	丁	16
take a fancy to, take a liking to	看上		kànshang	*v. c.*		13
take in, internment	收容		shōuróng	*v.*		20
take turns	轮	輪	lún	*v.*	乙	13
target, quota	指标	標	zhǐbiāo	*n.*	丙	16

英文	简体	繁体	拼音	词性	HSK 等级	课数
tease, play with, tantalize	逗		dòu	*v.*	乙	13
temporary	暂时	暫時	zànshí	*attr.*	乙	12
temporarily reside	暂住	暫	zànzhù	*v.*		20
that year, in those years	当年	當	dāngnián	*n.*	乙	11
raise a family	养家	養	yǎngjiā	*v.o.*		12
thing, matter, substance	物		wù	*n.*	丁	19
thorny, troublesome	棘手		jíshǒu	*adj.*		14
thought, thinking	思维	維	sīwéi	*n.*	丙	20
threaten	威胁	脅	wēixié	*v.*	丙	19
to collect and distribute (of goods)	集散		jísàn	*v.*		20
total, sum total	总数	總數	zǒngshù	*n.*	丁	14
touch, feel	摸		mō	*v.*	乙	13
tour, go sightseeing	游览	遊覽	yóulǎn	*v.*	乙	18
tourist industry, tourism	旅游业	遊業	lǚyóuyè	*n.*	丙	18
toy	玩具		wánjù	*n.*	丁	13
transform, reform	变革	變	biàngé	*n.*	丙	20
transformers (toy, King Kong action figure)	变形金刚	變剛	biànxíng jīngāng	*n.*		13
transparent	透明		tòumíng	*adj.*	丙	19
travel, tour	旅游	遊	lǚyóu	*v.*	丙	18
travel, tour; swim	游	遊	yóu	*v.*	丙	18
treasure; endearment (children)	宝贝	寶貝	bǎobèi	*n.*	丁	11
trend, development, situation	动态	動態	dòngtài	*n.*	丁	16
trigger	引发	發	yǐnfā	*v.*		20
turn one's head	转头	轉頭	zhuǎntóu	*v.o.*		13
type, category	类型	類	lèixíng	*n.*	丙	16
type, style	式		shì	*n.*	丁	15
unavoidable, bound to happen	难免	難	nánmiǎn	*adj.*	丁	14
underestimate	低估		dīgū	*v.*		20
unexpectedly, who knows	谁知	誰	shuízhī	*i.e.*		11
unforeseen event or change	变故	變	biàngù	*n.*		15
unit, ministry, department	部		bù	*n.*	丙	12
unload, remove	卸		xiè	*v.*	丙	12

英文	简体	繁体	拼音	词性	HSK 等级	课数
urge, cause, spur on	促销	銷	cùxiāo	*v.*	丙	18
measure word for poems or songs	首		shǒu	*m.*	乙	19
values	价值观念	價觀	jiàzhí guānniàn	*n.*		16
vegetable grower	菜农	農	càinóng	*n.*		20
village	村		cūn	*n.*	丙	19
violence	暴力		bàolì	*n.*	丙	20
vogue, trend, fashion, fad	时尚	時	shíshàng	*n.*		18
wash clothes, do laundry	洗衣		xǐyī	*v.o.*		12
waste, consume	耗费	費	hàofèi	*n.*	丁	19
weak	弱		ruò	*adj.*	乙	14
webpage	页面	頁	yèmiàn	*n.*		20
well off, rich	富裕		fùyù	*adj.*	丙	17
whether or not	是否		shìfǒu	*adv.*	丙	14
whole wheat	全麦	麥	quánmài	*n.*	乙	18
willing to part with, not begrudge	舍得	捨	shěde	*v.*	丙	13
wish, desire	意愿	願	yìyuàn	*n.*		12
work	干活	幹	gànhuó	*v.o.*	乙	19
wrinkle, furrow (one's brow)	皱	皺	zhòu	*v.*	丙	13
young couple	小两口	兩	xiǎoliǎng kǒu	*n.*		12
zoo	动物园	動園	dòngwù yuán	*n.*	乙	13

Vocabulary Index

Chinese-English

拼音	英文	简体	繁体	词性	HSK 等级	课数
áizhèng	cancer	癌症	癥	*n.*	丙	19
ānquángǎn	sense of security	安全感		*n.*		16
bǎiwàn fùwēng	millionaire	百万富翁	萬	*n.*		17
bàng	good, excellent	棒		*adj.*	丙	13
bāoróng	pardon; forgive; tolerate	包容		*v.*	丁	15
bǎobǎo	baby, "little treasure"	宝宝	寶	*n.*	丙	12
bǎobèi	treasure; endearment (children)	宝贝	寶貝	*n.*	丁	11
bǎomǔ	nanny, housekeeper	保姆		*n.*	丁	12
bǎoxiǎn	sure, safe, insurance	保险	險	*adj./n.*	丙	17
bào	sudden and violent	暴		*adj.*	丙	17
bàolì	violence	暴力		*n.*	丙	20
bēishāng	sad, sorrowful	悲伤	傷	*adj.*	丁	15
bèijǐng	background	背景		*n.*	丙	14
bèizēng	multiplicate, redouble	倍增		*v.*		17
biàngé	transform, reform	变革	變	*n.*	丙	20
biàngù	unforeseen event or change	变故	變	*n.*		15
biàntong	be flexible; adapt	变通	變	*v.*		14
biànxíng jīngāng	transformers (toy, King Kong action figure)	变形金刚	變剛	*n.*		13
biànjí	extend (everywhere)	遍及		*v.p.*		19
biǎotài	make one's position known	表态	態	*v.o.*	乙	11
bìmiǎn	avoid	避免		*v.*	乙	18
bièniu	awkward, uncomfortable	别扭	彆	*adj.*	丁	11
bù	unit, ministry, department	部		*n.*	丙	12
bùhé	not get along well	不和		*adj.*		15
bùjīn	cannot help (doing sth.)	不禁		*adv.*	丙	11
bùliáng	bad, harmful, unhealthy	不良		*attr.*	丁	15
bùtíng	incessantly	不停		*adv.*	丙	13
bùyǐ	endlessly, incessantly	不已		*adv.*		15

拼音	英文	简体	繁体	词性	HSK 等级	课数
bùyòngshuō	needless to say	不用说	說	*i.e.*		11
cáilì	financial resources	财力	財	*n.*	丁	14
càinóng	vegetable grower	菜农	農	*n.*		20
cānyù	partake, participate in	参与	參與	*v.*	丁	17
cānzhuō	dining table	餐桌		*n.*		18
chājù	gap, disparity	差距		*n.*	丁	16
chái	firewood	柴		*n.*	丁	14
chǎnyè	industry	产业	產業	*n.*	丁	20
chángkè	frequent caller	常客		*n.*		18
chāozhī	exceed one's budget	超支		*v.o.*		13
chǎojià	quarrel or argue vehemently	吵架		*v.o.*	丙	15
chǎogǔ	speculate in stocks	炒股		*v.o.*		17
chéngběn	costs	成本		*n.*	丙	17
chénggōng	succeed	成功		*v.*	乙	15
chéngshuāng chéngduì	in a pair, in pairs	成双成对	雙對	*i.e.*		15
chéngyuán	member, members	成员	員	*n.*	丙	15
chéngrèn	admit, acknowledge	承认	認	*v.*	乙	15
chīkǔ	bear hardships, suffer	吃苦		*v.o.*	丙	13
chíxù	sustain, continue	持续	續	*v.*	丁	19
chōngtū	clash, conflict	冲突	衝	*n.*	丙	14
chóng	again; once more	重		*adv.*	乙	12
chóngzǔ	reconstruct, recompose	重组	組	*v.*		15
chóu	prepare, plan	筹	籌	*v.*		17
chòu	stinky, smelly	臭		*adj.*	乙	19
chuānzhuó	dress, apparel	穿着	著	*n.*		18
chuánchéng	inherit, carry on	传承	傳	*v.*		14
chuǎnqì	breathe deeply, pant	喘气	氣	*v.o.*	丙	13
chūshòu	sell	出售		*v.*	丁	17
chūxi	prospects, promise, future	出息		*n.*	丙	13
chūyú	out of, stem from, be due to	出于	於	*v.p.*		12
chún	pure	纯	純	*adj.*	丙	16
cízhí	resign, quit one's job	辞职	辭職	*v.o.*	丁	12
cǐhòu	afterwards	此后	後	*conj.*	丁	18
cùxiāo	urge, cause, spur on	促销	銷	*v.*	丙	18

拼音	英文	简体	繁体	词性	HSK 等级	课数
cūn	village	村		*n.*	丙	19
cún	save, deposit	存		*v.*	乙	16
dǎban	dress up, deck out	打扮		*v.*	乙	18
dàbuliǎo	at the worst	大不了		*adv.*		17
dàfang	generous	大方		*adj.*	丙	13
dàxíng	large scale, big size	大型		*adj.*	乙	13
dàzhòng	general public	大众	眾	*n.*	丙	20
dàijià	price, cost	代价	價	*n.*	丙	19
dàidòng	lead, bring along	带动	帶動	*v.*	丙	18
dānchún	pure, simple	单纯	單純	*adj.*	丙	19
dāndiào	monotonous, dull	单调	單調	*adj.*	乙	18
dānqīn	single parent	单亲	單親	*n.*		15
dāngnián	that year, in those years	当年	當	*n.*	乙	11
dǎozhì	lead to, bring about	导致	導	*v.*	丙	15
dàotuì	go backwards, regress	倒退		*v.*	丁	12
détǐ	appropriate, proper	得体	體	*adj.*		18
déyì	be pleased with oneself	得意		*adj.*	丙	13
déyǐ	can, may	得以		*v.*	丁	18
diànjì	keep thinking of, miss	惦记	記	*v.*	丙	11
diànzǐ	electron, electronic	电子	電	*n. /adj.*	丙	20
dīgū	underestimate	低估		*v.*		20
díquè	indeed, really	的确	確	*adv.*	乙	18
dìtǎn	carpet, rug	地毯		*n.*	丙	14
diē	fall, drop	跌		*v.*	乙	17
dìngzuò	custom make	定做		*v.*		18
dòngtài	trend, development, situation	动态	動態	*n.*	丁	16
dòngwùyuán	zoo	动物园	動園	*n.*	乙	13
dòuzi	pea, bean	豆子		*n.*	丙	18
dòu	tease, play with, tantalize	逗		*v.*	乙	13
dūshì	big city, metropolis	都市		*n.*	丁	18
dúzì	alone, by oneself	独自	獨	*adv.*	丙	15
dù	occasion, time	度		*m.*	乙	12
duān	hold sth. level	端		*v.*	丙	11
duàn	break	断	斷	*v.*	乙	14

拼音	英文	简体	繁体	词性	HSK 等级	课数
duì kàn	look at each other	对看	對	*v.*		11
duōyú	superfluous, extra, unnecessary	多余	餘	*adj.*	丙	16
fāhuī	bring into play, give free rein	发挥	發揮	*v.*	乙	16
fājué	find, detect, discover	发觉	發覺	*v.*	丙	15
fánmáng	busy, bustling	繁忙		*adj.*	丁	12
fánróng	flourishing, prosperous	繁荣	榮	*adj.*	乙	16
fǎn'ér	on the contrary, instead	反而		*adv.*	丙	12
fǎntán	(of price or stock) rebound	反弹	彈	*v.*	丁	17
fǎnyìng	reflect, report	反映		*v.*	乙	18
fǎnzhèng	anyway, anyhow, in any case	反正		*adv.*	乙	13
fǎnhuí	return, come back, go back	返回		*v.*	丁	12
fǎnsī	self-examination, introspection	反思		*v.*	丁	19
fànzuì	commit a crime	犯罪		*v.o.*	丙	20
fànlàn	overflow	泛滥	濫	*v.*	丙	20
fànwéi	scope, range	范围	範圍	*n.*	乙	20
fāngbiànmiàn	instant noodles	方便面		*n.*		18
fángdōng	landlord, landlady	房东	東	*n.*	丁	17
fàngsōng	relax	放松	鬆	*v.*	丙	12
fēi	not, no, non-, un-	非		*adv.*	丙	16
fèichú	abolish, do away with	废除	廢	*v.*	丙	20
fúshì	dress and personal adornment	服饰	飾	*n.*		18
fúzhuāng	clothes, clothing	服装	裝	*n.*	丁	18
fǔyǎng	foster, raise, bring up	抚养	撫養	*v.*	丁	15
fǔbài	corrupt, rotten, decadent	腐败	敗	*adj.*	丁	16
fùchū	pay, expend	付出		*v.*	丁	13
fùmiàn	negative, bad	负面	負	*adj.*		20
fùzhì	duplicate, reproduce, clone	复制	複製	*v.*	丙	14
fùwēng	rich man, man of wealth	富翁		*n.*	丙	17
fùyù	well off, rich	富裕		*adj.*	丙	17
gǎijìn	improve	改进	進	*v.*	乙	20
gāncuì	clear-cut, straightforward	干脆	乾	*adj.*	乙	13
gànhuó	work	干活	幹	*v.o.*	乙	19

拼音	英文	简体	繁体	词性	HSK 等级	课数
Gǎng'àotái	Hong Kong, Macao, and Taiwan	港澳台	臺	*p.n.*		16
gāofā	high-occurring	高发	發	*adj.*		19
gāosù	high-speed	高速		*adj.*	丙	19
gàozhōng	end up	告终	終	*v.p.*		14
gē	dove, pigeon	鸽	鴿	*n.*	丙	13
gē	cut with a knife	割		*v.*	乙	19
gēwǔtīng	song and dance hall	歌舞厅	廳	*n.*		18
gé	separate, be at a distance from, at an interval	隔		*v.*	乙	14
gètǐ	individual, individuality	个体	個體	*n.*	乙	16
gèxìng	individual character, individuality	个性	個	*n.*	丙	18
gēnshang	follow up, catch up	跟上		*v.p.*		13
gēng	custard, a thick soup	羹		*n.*		11
gōnggong	husband's father, father-in-law	公公		*n.*	丁	12
gōngzhǔ	princess	公主		*n.*		14
gōngjī	attack, assault	攻击	擊	*v.*	丙	20
gòuwùzhōngxīn	shopping center, mall	购物中心	購	*n.*		13
gǔ	share of a company	股		*m*	丙	17
gǔpiào	stock, stock certificate	股票		*n.*	丁	16
gǔshì	stock market	股市		*n.*		17
guài	blame	怪		*v.*	丙	11
guānchá	observe carefully, watch	观察	觀	*v.*	乙	17
guānjiàn	key, the most crucial thing	关键	關鍵	*n.*	乙	13
guānyuán	official	官员	員	*n.*	丁	19
guàngjiē	stroll along the street, go (window) shopping	逛街		*v.o.*	丙	18
guīmó	scale, scope, extent	规模	規	*n.*	乙	16
guómín	people of a nation	国民	國	*n.*	丁	16
guómínjīngjì	national economy	国民经济	國經濟	*n.*		16
Guówùyuàn	State Council	国务院	國務	*p.n.*	丙	20
guóyíng	state-run	国营	國營	*attr.*	丙	16
guòfèn	excessive	过分	過	*adj.*	丙	14
hǎiwài	overseas	海外		*n.*	丁	20

拼音	英文	简体	繁体	词性	HSK 等级	课数
Hánguó	Republic of Korea	韩国	韓國	*p.n.*		15
hángqíng	prices of goods on the market	行情		*n.*		17
hàofèi	waste, consume	耗费	費	*n.*	丁	19
hédelái	can get along well with	合得来	來	*i.e.*		11
héfǎ	legal, legitimate	合法		*adj.*	丙	15
héhuǒ	form a partnership	合伙		*v.o.*	丁	17
hélǐ	rational, reasonable	合理		*adj.*	丁	14
hòuguǒ	consequence	后果	後	*n.*	丙	15
Huái Hé	Huai River	淮河		*p.n.*		19
huàn	contract (an illness)	患		*v.*	丙	19
huángguā	cucumber	黄瓜		*n.*	乙	18
huánghūn	dusk, twilight	黄昏		*n.*	丙	11
hūshì	ignore, neglect	忽视	視	*v.*	丙	19
Hùliánwǎng	Internet	互联网	聯網	*p.n.*		20
hūnwàiqíng	extramarital affair	婚外情		*n.*		15
huòqǔ	obtain	获取	獲	*v.*	丁	20
jīyù	opportunity	机遇	機	*n.*	丁	16
jīqǐ	arouse, stir up	激起		*v (c)*	丁	20
jíbìng	disease, sickness	疾病		*n.*	丙	19
jísàn	(of goods) to collect and distribute	集散		*v.*		20
jíshì	fair, market	集市		*n.*	丁	20
jíshǒu	thorny, troublesome	棘手		*adj.*		14
jìyì	remember, memory	记忆	記憶	*v./n.*	乙	19
jìfùmǔ	stepparents	继父母	繼	*n.*	丁	15
jiākuài	accelerate, speed up	加快		*v.p.*		18
jiārù	join	加入		*v.*	丙	15
jiātíngzhǔfù	housewife	家庭主妇	婦	*n.*		12
jiāwù	household duties	家务	務	*n.*	丁	11
jiàqian	price	价钱	價錢	*n.*	丙	13
jiàzhíguānniàn	values	价值观念	價觀	*n.*		16
jiāntóu	shoulder	肩头	頭	*n.*	乙	12
jiǎnhuà	simplify	简化	簡	*v.*	丁	15
jiànjiàn	gradually, by degrees	渐渐	漸	*adv.*	乙	15

拼音	英文	简体	繁体	词性	HSK 等级	课数
jiànshēnfáng	gym	健身房		*n.*		18
jiǎngpǐn	prize, award, trophy	奖品	獎	*n.*	丁	13
jiāoyì	deal, trade, transaction	交易		*n.*	丙	16
jiàomài	peddle goods, hawk one's wares	叫卖	賣	*v.*		20
jiējí	social class	阶级	階級	*n.*	丁	15
jiézòu	rhythm	节奏	節	*n.*	丁	18
jiélùn	conclusion	结论	結論	*n.*	乙	19
jiéwěi	ending	结尾	結	*n.*		14
jiěchú	remove, relieve, get rid of	解除		*v.*	丁	15
jiěfàng	liberate	解放		*v.*	乙	12
jǐnshèn	prudent, careful, cautious	谨慎	謹	*adj.*	丙	17
jìnlì	do all one can, try one's best	尽力	盡	*v.o.*	丙	15
jìnxíngqǔ	march (music)	进行曲	進	*n.*		13
jīngjìshāng	broker, agent, dealer	经纪商	經紀	*n.*	丁	17
jīnglì	go through, experience	经历	經歷	*v.*	乙	15
jīngshāng	engage in trade, be in business	经商	經	*v.o.*	丁	16
jīngrén	astonishing, amazing	惊人	驚	*adj.*	丙	20
jīngyà	surprised, amazed	惊讶	驚訝	*adj.*	丙	17
jīnglì	energy, vigor	精力		*n.*	乙	12
jǐngchá	police	警察		*n.*	乙	20
jiūjìng	actually, exactly, after all	究竟		*adv.*	乙	12
jiǔdiàn	hotel	酒店		*n.*	丙	20
jūliú	detain	拘留		*v.*	丁	20
jú	office, bureau	局		*n.*	丙	19
jǔsàng	discouraged, depressed	沮丧	喪	*adj.*		17
jùlèbù	club	俱乐部	樂	*n.*	乙	15
juéwàng	despairing, hopeless	绝望	絶	*adj.*	丁	17
kǎlā–ok	karaoke	卡拉 OK		*n.*		15
kāixīn	feel happy, rejoice	开心	開	*adj.*	丁	11
kāizhǎn	develop, launch	开展	開	*v.*	乙	18
kāizhāng	open a business	开张	開張	*v.*		16
kān	look after, take care of	看		*v.*	丙	11

拼音	英文	简体	繁体	词性	HSK 等级	课数
kànshang	take a fancy to, take a liking to	看上		*v. c.*		13
kànwàng	call on, pay a visit	看望		*v.*	丁	12
káng	carry on one's shoulders	扛		*v.*	乙	20
kàngyì	protest, demonstrate	抗议	議	*v.*	丙	20
kuàisù	fast	快速		*adj.*	丁	19
kuàngshān	mine	矿山	礦	*n.*	丁	19
kuòsàn	spread	扩散	擴	*v.*	丁	19
làjiāo	hot pepper, chili pepper	辣椒		*n.*	丙	18
lái de kuài	quick in responding	来得快	來	*i.e.*		11
lǎoyézi	old man, old father	老爷子	爺	*n.*		11
lèixíng	type, category	类型	類	*n.*	丙	16
lèng	dumbfounded, stupefied	愣		*adj.*	丙	11
lǐyóu	reason	理由		*n.*	乙	12
lìjīng	experience many times	历经	歷經	*v.*		19
lìlái	always, all through the ages	历来	歷來	*adv.*	丁	12
lìxī	interest	利息		*n.*	丁	17
lìwài	exception	例外		*n.*	丁	18
liánmáng	hastily, hurriedly	连忙	連	*adv.*	乙	11
liě	open one's mouth	咧		*v.*		13
lǐng	receive	领	領	*v.*	乙	13
línghuó	flexible	灵活	靈	*adj.*	乙	16
liúyù	river basin, valley	流域		*n.*	丙	19
shíkè	constantly, always	时刻	時	*adv.*	丙	19
lǒu	hold in one's arms, hug	搂	摟	*v.*	丙	11
lǚyóu	travel, tour	旅游	遊	*v.*	丙	18
lǚyóuyè	tourist industry, tourism	旅游业	遊業	*n.*	丙	18
lún	take turns	轮	輪	*v.*	乙	13
lùntán	forum	论坛	論壇	*n.*		20
luóbo	radish, turnip	萝卜	蘿	*n.*	乙	18
májiàng	mahjong	麻将	將	*n.*		18
mái	cover, bury	埋		*v.*	乙	18
máoyī	sweater	毛衣		*n.*	乙	13
méitóu	eyebrow	眉头	頭	*n.*	丙	13

拼音	英文	简体	繁体	词性	HSK 等级	课数
méijiè	medium	媒介		*n.*	丁	20
mìqiè	close, intimate	密切		*adj.*	乙	19
mínyáo	folk rhyme, folklore, popular verse	民谣	謠	*n.*		16/19
Mínzhèngbù	Ministry of Civil Affairs	民政部		*p.n.*		15
mínzhòng	masses, common people	民众	眾	*n.*	丁	15
mǐn'gǎn	sensitive	敏感		*adj.*	丁	18
mō	touch, feel	摸		*v.*	乙	13
mùdìdì	destination	目的地		*n.*		20
nánguài	no wonder	难怪	難	*adv.*	丙	16
nánmiǎn	unavoidable, bound to happen	难免	難	*adj.*	丁	14
nào	make a noise; give vent	闹	鬧	*v.*	乙	11
néngyuán	energy sources	能源		*n.*	乙	19
nì'ài	spoil (a child)	溺爱	愛	*v.*		14
niúshì	bull market	牛市		*n.*		17
nóngchǎng	farm, ranch	农场	農場	*n.*	丙	19
ōudǎ	beat up	殴打	毆	*v.*	丁	20
ǒurán	accidental, unexpected	偶然		*adj.*	丙	15
páifàng	discharge	排放		*v.*		19
páimíng	rank	排名		*v.o.*		20
péibàn	accompany	陪伴		*v.*		14
pígé	leather	皮革		*n.*	丁	19
piāo	float in the air, flutter	飘	飄	*v.*	乙	18
pínfán	frequently	频繁	頻	*adv.*	丁	19
pǐnpái	brand name	品牌		*n.*		18
pínghéng	balanced	平衡		*adj.*	丙	16
píngtái	platform	平台	臺	*n.*		20
píngmù	(TV or movie) screen	屏幕		*n.*		20
pópo	husband's mother, mother-in-law	婆婆		*n.*	丁	12
pòhuài	destroy, damage	破坏	壞	*v.*	乙	19
pǔchá	census, general investigation	普查		*n.*	丁	19
pǔjí	popularize	普及		*v.*	丙	20
qí	(classical) he, she, it, his, her, its	其		*pron.*	丙	16

拼音	英文	简体	繁体	词性	HSK 等级	课数
qíjì	miracle	奇迹	跡	*n.*	丙	16
qǐdòng	start, initiate, launch	启动	啟動	*v.*		19
qiánfū	ex-husband	前夫		*n.*		15
qiánzài	latent, hidden, potential	潜在	潛	*attr.*	丁	15
qiǎnsòng	send back, repatriate	遣送		*v.*		20
qiángliè	strong, intense	强烈	強	*adj.*	乙	20
qiǎng	force, make an effort, strive	强	強	*v.*	丙	12
qiāoqiāo	gently, softly, stealthily	悄悄		*adv.*	乙	16
qiáo	look, see, watch (colloquial)	瞧		*v.*	乙	11
qiézi	eggplant	茄子		*n.*	丁	18
qīn	kiss	亲	親	*v.*	丙	13
qīngshì	despise, look down on	轻视	輕視	*v.*	丙	16
qīngchè	crystal-clear	清澈		*adj.*		19
qīnglǐ	clean up, clear up, tidy up	清理		*v.*	丁	12
qíngdiào	sentiment	情调	調	*n.*	乙	15
qùshì	die, pass away	去世		*v.o.*	丁	19
quánlì	right, privilege	权利	權	*n.*	丙	15
quánmài	whole wheat	全麦	麥	*n.*	乙	18
quánmiàn	overall, full-scale	全面		*adj.*	乙	17
quánzhí	full-time position	全职	職	*n.*	丙	12
quànshuō	persuade, advise	劝说	勸說	*v.*	乙	15
quēshī	lack, miss	缺失		*v.*		15
qúnzi	skirt	裙子		*n.*	乙	18
rèténgténg	steaming hot, piping hot	热腾腾	熱騰	*adj.*		11
réngé	moral integrity, human dignity	人格		*n.*	丁	12
rénshì	person, personage, public figure	人士		*n.*	丙	15
rénshì	personnel matters	人事		*n.*	丁	12
rènkě	approve of, endorse	认可	認	*v.*	丁	15
rìhòu	in the days to come; future	日后	後	*adv.*		14
róngrù	blend in	融入		*v.*	丁	18
rùshí	fashionable	入时	時	*adj.*		18
ruǎnhuo	soft and warm	软和	軟	*adj.*	乙	13
ruò	weak	弱		*adj.*	乙	14

拼音	英文	简体	繁体	词性	HSK 等级	课数
sèqíng	pornography	色情		*n.*		20
shǎndiàn	lightning	闪电	閃電	*n.*	丙	15
shànyǎng	support, provide for	赡养	贍養	*v.*		14
shāngpǐn	commodity	商品		*n.*	乙	16
shāngrén	businessman, merchant	商人		*n.*	丙	16
shāngtán	discuss, negotiate	商谈	談	*v.*		17
shàngshì	go (appear) on the market	上市		*v.o.*		16
shàngwèi	not yet	尚未		*adv.*	丁	17
shěde	be willing to part with, not begrudge	舍得	捨	*v.*	丙	13
shēngqiān	be promoted	升迁	昇遷	*v.*		19
shēngtiān	go up to heaven, i.e., die	升天	昇	*v.o.*		19
shēngzhí	appreciate, increase in value	升值	昇	*v.o.*		17
shēngyi	business	生意		*n.*	乙	20
shěngxīn	save worry, avoid worry	省心		*v.o.*		11
shīyè	be unemployed, lose one's job	失业	業	*v.o.*	乙	16
shíshàng	vogue, trend, fashion, fad	时尚	時	*n.*		18
shìjiāo	suburb	市郊		*n.*	乙	17
shì	type, style	式		*n.*	丁	15
shìfǒu	whether or not	是否		*adv.*	丙	14
shìfàng	release, set free	释放	釋	*v.*	丁	18
shōugòu	purchase, buy	收购	購	*v.*	丁	16
shōuhuò	results, gains; harvest	收获	穫	*n.*	乙	13
shōuróng	take in, internment	收容		*v.*		20
shōuyì	profit, gain	收益		*n.*	丁	17
shǒuduàn	means, method, approach	手段		*n.*	乙	20
shǒuxù	procedures, formalities	手续	續	*n.*	乙	15
shǒu	measure word for poems or songs	首		*m*	乙	19
shòuhuòyuán	shop assistant	售货员	貨員	*n.*		13
shǔyú	belong to	属于	屬於	*v.*	乙	14
shǔbiāo	(computer) mouse	鼠标	標	*n.*		20
shuāngxìng	double-character surname	双姓	雙	*n.*		14
shuízhī	unexpectedly, who knows…	谁知	誰	*i.e.*		11

拼音	英文	简体	繁体	词性	HSK 等级	课数
shuǐwén	hydrology	水文		*n.*		19
shùnlù	on the way	顺路	順	*adv.*	丙	11
sīwéi	thought, thinking	思维	維	*n.*	丙	20
sǐwáng	death	死亡		*n.*	丙	19
sōusuō	search	搜索		*v.*	丁	20
sùdòng	quick-freeze	速冻	凍	*v.*		18
sūnbèi	grandchildren's generation	孙辈	孫輩	*n.*		14
tàipíng	peaceful	太平		*adj.*	丁	11
tàn	sigh	叹	嘆	*v.*	丁	11
tànqīn	go home to see family	探亲	親	*v.o.*	丁	17
táng	pool, pond	塘		*n.*	丁	19
tāo	dig, scoop out	掏		*v.*	乙	13
téng'ài	be very fond of, love dearly	疼爱	愛	*v.*	乙	14
tǐhuì	realize	体会	體會	*v.*	乙	17
tǐzhì	system of organization	体制	體	*n.*	丁	16
tiān	add, have a baby	添		*v.*	乙	12
tiánmì	sweet, happy, comfortable	甜蜜		*adj.*	丙	12
tiāo	choose, select	挑		*v.*	乙	11
tīnghuà	heed advice; be obedient	听话	聽話	*v.o.*	丁	11
tóngbàn	companion	同伴		*n.*	丙	20
tónghuà	fairy tale	童话	話	*n.*		14
tòumíng	transparent	透明		*adj.*	丙	19
tuán	regiment (in army)	团	團	*n.*	乙	11
tuījìn	promote, push on	推进	進	*v.*	丙	20
wàibiǎo	outward appearance	外表		*n.*	丁	18
wàichū	go out (esp. on business)	外出		*v.p.*	丁	12
wàizài	external	外在		*adj.*		15
wàizǔfù	maternal grandfather	外祖父		*n.*		14
wàizǔmǔ	maternal grandmother	外祖母		*n.*		14
wánjù	toy	玩具		*n.*	丁	13
wǎnjiù	save, rescue	挽救		*v.*	丙	12
wǎncān	dinner; supper	晚餐		*n.*	丁	12
wángzǐ	prince	王子		*n.*		14
wǎnggòu	online shopping	网购	網購	*v./n.*		20

拼音	英文	简体	繁体	词性	HSK 等级	课数
wēixié	threaten	威胁	脅	*v.*	丙	19
wēilì	power, force	威力		*n.*	丁	20
wēixiào	smile	微笑		*v.*	乙	13
wéichí	maintain, keep, preserve	维持	維	*v.*	丙	14
wèicǐ	for this reason	为此	爲	*i.e.*		17
wénmíng	civilization	文明		*n.*	乙	20
wěndìng	stable	稳定	穩	*adj.*	乙	14
wūrǎn	pollute, contaminate, pollution	污染		*v./n.*	乙	16
wū	sound of crying, wind, siren	呜	嗚	*ono.*	丁	11
wúyìyú	no different from, the same as	无异于	無異於	*v.p.*		14
wù	thing, matter, substance	物		*n.*	丁	19
wùzhì	matter, substance, material	物质	質	*n.*	乙	16
xífu	daughter-in-law	媳妇	婦	*n.*	丙	11
xǐyī	wash clothes, do laundry	洗衣		*v.o.*		12
xìshuǐ	play in water	戏水	戲	*v.o.*		19
xiáncài	salted vegetables, pickles	咸菜	鹹	*n.*		13
xiàn	county	县	縣	*n.*	乙	19
xiànmù	admire, envy	羡慕		*v.*	乙	15
xiāngduì	relatively	相对	對	*adv.*	丙	14
xiāngguān	be interrelated	相关	關	*adj.*	丁	19
xiāngjì	one after another	相继	繼	*adv.*	丁	19
xiǎngyǒu	enjoy (rights, privileges, etc.)	享有		*v.*	丁	12
xiàngmù	item, project	项目	項	*n.*	乙	18
xiāolù	sales channels	销路	銷	*n.*	丁	20
xiāoshòu	sell, market	销售	銷	*v.*	丁	16
xiǎoliǎngkǒu	young couple	小两口	兩	*n.*		12
xiàolǜ	efficiency	效率		*n.*	乙	16
xiàoyì	effectiveness, benefit	效益		*n.*	丁	19
xiè	unload, remove	卸		*v.*	丙	12
xīndòng	be interested, be attracted	心动	動	*v.*		17
xīnmù	mind, mind's eye	心目		*n.*	丙	16
xīnxuè	painstaking care or effort	心血		*n.*	丁	13
Xīnjiāpō	Singapore	新加坡		*p.n.*		15
xìngshì	family name	姓氏		*n.*		14

拼音	英文	简体	繁体	词性	HSK 等级	课数
xiónghòu	rich, solid, abundant	雄厚		*adj.*	丁	14
xióngshì	bear market	熊市		*n.*		17
xiūxián	leisure	休闲	閑	*n.*	丙	12
xiūchǐ	shame	羞耻		*n.*	丁	15
xǔkě	allow, permit	许可	許	*v.*	丁	15
xuǎndìng	select, designate	选定	選	*v.*	丁	18
xuǎngòu	choose and buy	选购	選購	*v.*		18
yālì	pressure; burden	压力	壓	*n.*	丙	12
yāzi	duck	鸭子		*n.*	丙	19
Yàzhōu	Asia	亚洲	亞	*p.n.*		15
yán	salt	盐	鹽	*n.*	乙	14
yánjùn	severe	严峻	嚴	*adj.*	丁	19
yánxù	continue, go on, last	延续	續	*v.*	丁	15
yǎngjiā	raise the family	养家	養	*v.o.*		12
yǎoyá	clench one's teeth	咬牙		*v.o.*	乙	13
yèmiàn	webpage	页面	頁	*n.*		20
yī	comply with, yield to	依		*v.*	丁	14
yīlài	depend on; rely on	依赖	賴	*v.*	丁	14
yírìyóu	day tour	一日游	遊	*n.*		18
yíbèizi	all one's life, lifetime	一辈子	輩	*n.*	丙	13
yímín	migrant, immigrant	移民		*n.*	丁	20
yíhuò	be doubtful, uncertain, perplexed	疑惑		*v.*	丁	11
yíxiàng	all along, the whole time, constantly	一向		*adv.*	丙	16
yìfēnwéi'èr	split in two	一分为二	爲	*i.e.*		11
yìpáng	one side, a side	一旁		*n.*	丙	13
yìzhuǎnyǎn	in a second, in a very short time	一转眼	轉	*i.e.*		14
yìyuàn	wish, desire	意愿	願	*n.*		12
yīnsù	factor, element	因素		*n.*	乙	15
yīnyǐng	shadow	阴影	陰	*n.*	丁	15
yǐnfā	trigger	引发	發	*v.*		20
yǐnqíng	engine	引擎		*n.*		20
yǐnshí	diet, food and drink	饮食	飲	*n.*	丁	18

拼音	英文	简体	繁体	词性	HSK 等级	课数
yǐn	addiction	瘾		*n.*		20
yínglì	make a profit	盈利		*v.o.*	丁	17
yōngyǒu	possess, have, own	拥有	擁	*v.*	丁	15
yǒngxiàn	emerge in large numbers	涌现	現	*v.*	丁	16
yōushì	superiority	优势	優勢	*n.*	丙	14
yōulíng	ghost, spirit, phantom	幽灵	靈	*n.*		19
yōuxián	leisurely	悠闲	閑	*adj.*		20
yóujiàn	mail	邮件	郵	*n.*		20
yóu	travel, tour; swim	游	遊	*v.*	丙	18
yóulǎn	tour, go sightseeing	游览	遊覽	*v.*	乙	18
yóuxì	game	游戏	遊戲	*n.*	丙	20
yǒuhài	harmful	有害		*adj.*	丁	20
yúlè	entertainment	娱乐	樂	*n.*	丙	20
yúlùn	public opinion	舆论	輿論	*n.*	丁	20
yǔqí	rather than, better than	与其	與	*conj.*	丙	17
yùmǐ	corn	玉米		*n.*	乙	18
yù	in advance, beforehand	预	預	*adv.*		17
yùdìng	book, reserve	预定	預	*v.*	丁	20
yuánjià	original price	原价	價	*n.*		17
yùndòng	movement	运动	運動	*n.*	甲	12
zāinàn	disaster, catastrophe	灾难	災難	*n.*	丙	15
zàihūn	remarry	再婚		*v.*		15
zàisān	again and again, repeatedly	再三		*adv.*	丙	15
zànshí	temporary	暂时	暫時	*attr.*	乙	12
zànzhù	temporarily reside	暂住	暫	*v.*		20
zànchéng	approve, endorse, agree with	赞成	贊	*v.*	乙	11
zàntóng	approve of, agree with	赞同	贊	*v.*	丁	13
zérèn	responsibility	责任	責	*n.*	乙	12
zhǎohuí	regain, get back	找回		*v.*		12
zhèhuìr	now, at the moment	这会儿	這會兒	*adv.*		13
zhèyàngyīlái	in this way	这样一来	這樣來	*i.e.*	丙	11
zhēnduì	be directed against	针对	針對	*v.*	乙	19
zhīwài	apart from, in addition	之外		*adv.*	丙	18
zhīchū	expenses, expenditure	支出		*n.*	丁	12

拼音	英文	简体	繁体	词性	HSK 等级	课数
zhīshifènzǐ	intellectual	知识分子	識	*n.*	丙	16
zhíxiàn	straight line	直线	綫	*n.*	丁	17
zhíwù	plant	植物		*n.*	乙	20
zhǐzhāng	paper	纸张	紙張	*n.*	丁	19
zhǐbiāo	target, quota	指标	標	*n.*	丙	16
zhǐhuī	command, direct, conduct	指挥	揮	*v.*	乙	11
zhìlǐ	control, manage	治理		*v.*	丁	19
zhì	cause, incur, invite, result in	致		*v.*	丙	19
zhìfù	become rich	致富		*v.o.*	丁	19
zhìlì	intelligence	智力		*n.*	丁	13
zhǒngzi	seed	种子	種	*n.*	乙	20
zhòu	wrinkle, furrow (one's brow)	皱	皺	*v.*	丙	13
zhǔ	lead, manage, take charge of	主		*v.*	丁	12
zhǔliú	mainstream	主流		*n.*	丁	18
zhuā	grab, seize	抓		*v.*	乙	13
zhuǎntóu	turn one's head	转头	轉頭	*v.o.*		13
zhuàn	make money, make a profit	赚	賺	*v.*	丙	12
zhuāngxiū	fix up (a house), renovate	装修	裝	*v.*	丙	17
zhuàng	strong, robust	壮	壯	*adj.*	丙	13
zhuīwèn	question closely	追问	問	*v.*	丁	15
zhuīzhú	pursue, chase	追逐		*v.*		19
zīchǎn	property, estate; capital	资产	資產	*n.*	丙	15
zījīn	fund, capital	资金	資	*n.*	丙	17
zǐ	purple	紫		*adj.*	乙	18
zìláishuǐ	running water, tap water	自来水	來	*n.*	丙	19
zìwǒ	self, oneself, ego	自我		*n.*	乙	12
zìzūn	self-esteem	自尊		*n.*		15
zǒngshù	total, sum total	总数	總數	*n.*	丁	14
zúgòu	enough, ample, sufficient	足够	夠	*adj.*	丙	14
zǔchéng	form; make up; compose	组成	組	*v. c*	丙	14
zuómo	ponder, think over	琢磨		*v.*	丁	11

11 黃昏之戀

"聰聰，走吧，爺爺送你上幼兒園。"

"不去，爺爺，我不去。幼兒園老師要我表演，我不要表演，我不去嘛！"

爺爺一聽，心想糟糕了，上星期六就約好了，星期一把聰聰送進幼兒園，他就到她那裡去。誰知道今天聰聰特別不聽話，說什麼也不肯去幼兒園。他不禁嘆了口氣，唉，想當年，自己能指揮一個團，現在卻連一個五歲的孫子都指揮不了。

於是他只好帶著聰聰一起到她那裡去。她住在北海公園附近，雖然只有一間小小的屋子，但是屋內收拾得乾淨整齊，屋前還種著各種好看的花草。

他推門進去，讓聰聰叫"奶奶"。

"奶奶！"聰聰甜甜地叫了一聲。

她一愣，沒想到他把聰聰帶來了。"哎，"她連忙把聰聰拉過來，拍拍他的頭，讓他坐下，然後端出一碗熱騰騰的雞蛋羹來。這碗雞蛋羹原來是為他做的，既然聰聰來了，就一分為二，讓他和聰聰各吃半碗吧。

他吃了一口雞蛋羹，嘆了口氣："哎，星期天最不好過，兒子媳婦都在家，不好意思出來，可心裡又惦記著你。"

"等哪天把事跟他們說明了，咱們去登記一下，就好了。"她說。

小聰聰疑惑地看看爺爺，又看看"奶奶"，琢磨著他們說的"登記"是什麼意思。他只知道，爺爺奶奶一"登記"，他就有雞蛋羹吃，所以，他希望他們天天都去"登記"，這樣他一定能天天吃到雞蛋羹。

因為遇到一個好奶奶，聰聰一定要玩到吃完晚飯才走。晚飯後，爺孫兩個終於回家了。聰聰邊走邊唱，可高興了。

誰知家裡已經鬧翻了天。

原來，幼兒園老師看見聰聰一天沒來，心裡有點擔心，下班後順路趕到聰聰家，想看看聰聰是不是病了。這樣一來，可就急壞了聰聰的媽媽："都怪你！都怪你！自己不送孩子，一定要那麼早去上班，現在可好，老爺子送孫子去幼兒園，連自己都送丟了！嗚……"

"媽媽、爸爸，" 聰聰猛然推開門，飛跑進來。媽媽一看見寶貝兒子就立刻上去摟住他，又高興又著急地問："寶貝兒，你可回來了！上哪兒去啦？快告訴媽媽。"

"到奶奶家去了，" 聰聰高興地說，"奶奶可好了！給我做雞蛋羹吃，帶我去公園玩兒，還說要給爺爺和我做新衣服呢。"

小倆口先對看了一下，然後一起看著老爺子，心想：哪兒來的這位 "奶奶"？怎麼從來沒聽說過啊？可嘴裡又不好明明白白地問。

"是這樣的，" 老爺子不自然地看了看他們，說："我給聰聰找了個奶奶，我們倆很合得來。你們小倆口商量商量吧，要是沒意見，我就把她接過來一起住；要是有意見，我就搬到她那裡去住。"

兒子一聽就覺得別扭。老爺子這把年紀，還搞起自由戀愛來了，這可讓作兒子的怎麼表態呢？於是他看了看妻子。

倒是兒媳婦來得快，她心想，老爺子可不能走，走了誰看聰聰？來個奶奶也不錯，一定比爺爺還能幹，這樣家務、孩子就都省心了。而且老爺子開心、身體好，家裡也太平啊。於是她就很快表了態："爸，瞧您說的，當初我們結婚，您操了那麼多心；現在您要辦喜事，我們哪能反對呢？我一百個同意！您就挑個好日子吧。""是啊，我們完全贊成！" 兒子也立刻接著說。不用說，小聰聰也把兩隻小手舉得高高的。

12 女性走回廚房：是進步還是倒退？

女性從家庭走向社會，歷來被看作她們在人格上獨立自主、在經濟和社會地位上提高的表現。但有意思的是，近年來，不少能幹而獨立的中國職業女性卻又走回家庭，走進廚房，做起 "全職太太" 來了。這種現象的出現，主要有兩個原因：

一是出於時間和精力上的考慮。過去，傳統的家庭模式是 "男主外，女主內"。男人外出工作，賺錢養家；女人生兒育女，管理家務。可是，在婦女解放運動後走出家庭的婦女們，沒多久就發現，如今雖然享有了工作自由，實現了自我價值，但家務的責任並沒有從肩頭卸下去。這樣一來，職業女性一方面要在外工作，另一方面又要照顧全家人的生活，成了 "自帶工資的保姆"，反而更累了。近年來，職場競爭日益激烈，職業女性的壓力也越來越大。於是，有些女性開始考慮重返傳統家庭模式。

今年二十七歲的小王，原來是一家公司人事部經理，結婚兩年，住在新建的花園公寓，只是離公司太遠，每天上下班要花兩小時，到家後已經精疲力盡，但仍然要強打著精神準備晚餐。星期六、星期天總算不用上班了，但還得買菜、洗衣、清理公寓，去公公婆婆和自己父母家看望老人。小王一星期七天都讓家事排滿了，沒有一天可以放鬆。再加上公司人事複雜、業務繁忙，因此精神上壓力很大，心情也不好，為了一點小事就和丈夫爭執不休。夫妻倆都開始覺得這樣的生活沒什麼意思。為了挽救只有兩年的婚姻，小王決定暫時辭職，回家作“全職太太”。現在，小王的生活不像以前那麼緊張，精神愉快得多，家裡收拾得井井有條，夫妻倆也有時間休息和休閑。錢雖然比以前緊了點，但找回了戀愛時的甜蜜，小兩口還打算在不久的將來再添個小寶寶呢。

另一個原因是經濟方面的考慮。剛過了三十一歲生日的小劉，自從生了個胖兒子，就不再工作了。她的理由是：“現在請個保姆太貴了，又得給她工資，又得給她吃飯，我一個人的工資都不夠，而且好保姆也不容易找，不如自己帶孩子，對孩子的成長更好。”她打算等孩子上學後，再重返工作。而這段時間裡，正好可以學點新知識，為“第二度事業”做些準備。

如今的“全職太太”跟以前的“家庭婦女”有很大的不同。現在的“全職太太”一般都有高等學歷，工作能力強，大多在孩子出生後才辭掉工作，她們的丈夫收入較高，能獨立負擔家庭支出。這種現象究竟是進步，還是倒退呢？有人認為，女性從家庭走進社會是一種進步，而重新回到廚房則是一種倒退。但是也有人認為，應該尊重女性自己的意願，她們有走出家庭的自由，也有返回廚房的自由，這才是真正的婦女解放。

13 貝貝進行曲

貝貝一歲。

那天，小倆口都領了工資。年輕的媽媽下班回來得特別晚，一到家，立刻把寶貝兒子抱起來，親了又親，然後精疲力盡地坐在沙發上。為了給兒子買東西，她跑遍了大半個城市。

這會兒，她一邊喘氣一邊從大包小包裡掏出今天的收穫來，吃的、穿的、玩的、用的……擺滿了半張床。年輕的爸爸看了看，皺皺眉頭：“哇！真捨得買，又花了多少錢？”

“工資去了一半！”她頭也沒抬，逗著貝貝滿床抓玩具。

"哼！到時候沒錢買午餐，又得每天帶飯吃咸菜。"

"哎呀，咱們吃點苦算什麼啊？關鍵是孩子的營養得跟上。只要我兒子長得壯壯的，玩得開開心心的！"她說，"咱們這輩子反正不行了。"

"這倒也是，"年輕的爸爸贊同道，"咱們這輩子不行了，就看他了，就都投資在兒子身上了！"

貝貝三歲。

在購物中心裡。

"請問這件毛衣多少錢？"年輕的媽媽問。

"一百五十元。"售貨員回答。

"咱們貝貝穿著一定很好看！"她問兒子，"嘿，貝貝，喜歡不喜歡？"

"喜歡！"兒子回答得很乾脆。

"買吧？"她摸摸軟和的毛衣，轉頭問丈夫。

"買吧！"他也很大方。

毛衣買好了，他們又來到玩具部。貝貝一眼看上了那個大型的"變形金剛"，一問價錢，三百二。

"哇！太貴了，不能買，今天已經超支了。"爸爸說。

可是貝貝立刻咧開嘴大哭起來："我要，我要買嘛！"

媽媽咬了咬牙，對爸爸說："咳，就算智力投資，給他買吧，我的大衣不買了。"

"可是，天冷了，你……"爸爸看著媽媽，無可奈何地說，"哎！那好吧，就給他買吧。我們這輩子不行了，就看他了。"

貝貝五歲。

在動物園裡，貝貝玩得可高興了。他跑來跑去，小嘴說個不停，好奇地問爸爸媽媽，這種動物叫什麼，那種動物叫什麼？

"貝貝，你知道那是什麼嗎？"輪到媽媽問他了。

"小白鴿。"孩子迅速地回答。

"爸爸來考考你，樹上有五隻白鴿，打死了一隻，還剩幾隻？"

"嗯……，一隻也沒有了，全飛了。"

"喲！咱們貝貝真棒！真聰明，長大一定有出息！"爸爸滿意地說，"來，給你塊巧克力，這是獎品。"貝貝得意地接過巧克力。媽媽在一旁看著聰明的兒子，也不由得微笑起來。

"給媽媽一小塊吧，貝貝，媽媽也有點餓了。"媽媽說。

"不，不給，這是我的，你們不能吃！"

"為什麼不給？這可是我們買的。"爸爸說。

"爸爸媽媽說過，你們吃什麼、穿什麼都沒關系，反正你們這輩子不行了，關鍵是要讓我開開心心的！"貝貝理直氣壯地回答。

"唉！"媽媽轉過臉去，深深地嘆了一口氣，"沒想到，為兒子付出那麼多心血，如今，連一小塊巧克力都嘗不到。"

14 雙獨家庭

獨生子女政策，已經在中國實行差不多 30 年了。一轉眼，生於 70 年代末 80 年代初的第一代獨生子女，如今都到了該結婚成家的年齡。當"小王子"牽著"小公主"的手，走過紅地毯時，他們是否真的像童話故事的結尾所說的那樣，從此永遠過上了幸福快樂的生活呢？

"雙獨家庭"有自己的優勢，比如，相對雄厚的經濟背景，簡單的家庭結構等。與此同時，專家們也指出這種家庭結構中出現的種種問題：

一、家庭穩定性問題：據調查，"雙獨家庭"的穩定性較差，不少婚姻只能維持一兩年。原因是第一代獨生子女，在成長過程中，被父母過分關心和溺愛，所以他們往往非常依賴父母，獨立生活的能力很弱。而且什麼事情都以自我為中心，不懂得怎樣關心別人。結婚後，他們都不太會照顧對方。至於每天必有的家務事，兩個人都不想做，都等著對方做。當浪漫的愛情變成柴米油鹽的現實之後，難免會產生沖突。而習慣以自我為中心的"小王子"和"小公主"互不相讓，所以只要一有沖突，即使是很小的事，也可能以"離婚"告終。

二、隔代教育的問題："雙獨夫婦"沒有帶弟妹的經驗，也不太懂怎麼照顧別人，為了省心，乾脆把孩子的生活教育責任全部推給祖父母或外祖父母，自己則忙事業去了。目前這種隔代教育現象在大城市中越來越普遍，2005 年一項全國調查的結果顯示，上海 0–6 歲的孩子中有 50–60% 屬於隔代教育；廣州佔到總數的一半；北京的比例高達 70%。孩子的年齡越小，跟祖父母生活在一起的比例就越高。祖父母對孫輩常常過分疼愛，事事都依著孩子，處處保護孩子，滿足孩子的不合理要求，這種教育使孩子缺少獨立性，並形成他們以自我爲中心的價值觀。這樣無異於在複制更多的"小皇帝"和"小公主"。

三、贍養老人問題：一對"雙獨夫婦"的家庭結構由 4 個長輩、夫妻 2 人和 1 個小孩組成，被稱爲"421 家庭"。兩個獨生子女小時候獨享了父母的愛，長大後也就只有獨立承擔起對父母的責任。贍養四位老人，負擔會很重。即使有足夠的財力，也沒有時間和精力來陪伴、照顧老人。

四、子女姓氏問題：在中國傳統觀念中，"姓"是非常重要的，因爲家族的傳承主要是通過姓氏。"雙獨夫婦"的孩子姓什麼，已經成爲棘手的家庭問題。以前，孩子一般都是跟父親姓，但是現在獨生女兒的家庭就會覺得他們的家族斷姓了。爲了解決這個問題，廣州等地提出了一個變通的辦法，就是獨生子女的孩子可以用父姓，也可以用母姓，或者由父姓母姓組成的雙姓，比如張王、趙李等。有人認爲，這種雙姓方法發展下去，甚至會改變中國的姓名文化。

"雙獨家庭"是中國剛剛開始大規模出現的婚姻家庭新模式，這種模式必然會對未來社會產生很大的影響。

15 離婚潮

紅今年 42 歲，是上海一家進出口公司的管理人員。她曾經家庭幸福、事業成功，讓許多人羨慕不已。她從沒想到過"離婚"這個詞會跟自己有什麼關系。直到去年有一天，陳紅偶然發現丈夫手機中有一個經常出現的電話號碼，而且這個號碼總是出現在自己出門後的幾分鐘。再三追問之下，丈夫承認了婚外情。經歷了這個突如其來的變故，陳紅離婚了。

剛離婚時，陳紅心裡很難受，尤其是想到自己要獨自撫養 11 歲的女兒，而前夫卻跟另一個女人成雙成對。幾個月之後，她漸漸走出了悲傷。今年情人節時，她參加了離婚者俱樂部的活動，與其他幾十位離婚者一起跳舞、唱卡拉 OK。她還加入了一個有 9.1 萬名成員的離婚者網站，希望再找男朋友。她說："雖然我以前選錯了人，但不等於這一輩子就再沒有機會了。"

離婚，在中國實行改革開放以前，就已經是合法的，但卻不被社會普遍認可。那時人們認爲，離婚給家庭帶來的是災難和羞恥。要求離婚的夫婦，除了要面對來自各方面的責備和壓力以外，還必須先得到工作單位的許可，才能真正解除婚姻關系，而工作單位及親友則常常會盡力勸說，使婚姻關系延續下去。那時候，愛情並不是婚姻關系中的重點；反而常常被認爲是 "資產階級情調"。自 20 世紀 70 年代末以來，隨著社會與經濟的發展，政府對民眾個人生活的控制不斷放鬆，人們的婚姻觀念也因此漸漸改變。社會對離婚和單身人士有了更多的包容和認可。離婚的人越來越多。國家民政部發布的統計報告顯示，2008 年，全國共有 227 萬對夫妻辦理離婚手續，比上一年增加 17 萬對。如今，離婚在中國成了一種普遍的社會現象。中國現在的離婚率已超過日本、韓國、新加坡等離婚率較高的亞洲國家。有人甚至開玩笑說，以前人們見面時互相問的是 "吃了嗎？"，而現在流行的問候語已經成了 "離了嗎？"

據調查，離婚率越來越高的原因有以下幾點：第一，過去人們選擇婚姻伴侶時重視的是對方的經濟條件、家庭社會地位、長相等外在因素；而現在，人們更重視的是感情。結婚後，雙方發覺感情不和時，往往會用離婚來結束婚姻。第二，女性現在的經濟條件和社會地位一般和男性都差不多高，她們不再像上一代女性那樣，擔心離婚的不良後果。她們覺得自己有能力和權利追求幸福的生活。第三，2003 年政府對離婚手續的簡化，導致了一種新的社會婚姻現象 那就是 "閃電式結婚" 和 "閃電式離婚"。報紙曾經報道過年輕人早上結婚，中午吵架，下午離婚的事情。用他們的話說："不求天長地久，只求曾經擁有。"

離婚率增高也帶來了很多不好的後果：比如，在單親家庭裡，父母一方的缺失影響到孩子的成長和對婚姻的看法；在重組家庭裡，存在著孩子與繼父母、或兩家孩子之間的潛在矛盾；在離婚者中，不少人長期走不出孤獨的陰影；另外，再婚者的離婚率也在逐年上升。

有關專家認爲，中國的離婚潮，具有社會進步的意義，體現了女性自我意識和女性社會地位的提高。也說明人們在物質生活水平提高以後，對精神生活的期望值也相應提高。從某種程度上講，這是迅速走向現代化的中國社會必然出現的現象。

16 中國經濟發展動態

　　中國自 1978 年改革開放與發展私有經濟以來，發生了翻天覆地的變化。國民經濟欣欣向榮，人們生活水平不斷提高，中國人的傳統社會價值觀念和就業選擇也悄悄地在改變。

　　改革以前，中國企業基本上都是國營企業，實際上是在政府控制下的 "生產單位"，沒有獨立性，更沒有創造性。它們的生產指標由政府統一規定，產品由政府統一收購、統一銷售，利潤由政府統一分配。對很多人來說，工作只是 "吃大鍋飯"，"幹好幹壞一個樣，幹多幹少一個樣"，所以國營企業的效率非常低。這種情況導致了 70 年代末的經濟體制改革。

　　在改革期間，政府在政策和法律上，明確地認可了非國有經濟市場的地位，並對其採取保護政策。非國有經濟在這段時間實現了突破性的發展，個人經商、大型私人企業和中外合資企業如雨後春筍般涌現出來。中國人被壓抑多年的生產力和創造力終於得到發揮。公司股票上市的規模也不斷擴大，更有了各種類型的交易市場。國家建設日新月異，經濟發展突飛猛進。從 1978 年到 2008 年，中國經濟一直保持著 10% 的年平均增長率。

　　繁榮的商品經濟大大提高了中國人的收入水平和生活水平。從 1978 到 2008 年，中國人均純收入增長了 6 倍。消費市場內容更加豐富、質量全面提高。中國人住房條件明顯改善，私人汽車也正在快速進入百姓家庭。現在人們不僅把多余的錢存在銀行裡，還在股票市場和房地產市場投資。與此同時，人們的社會價值觀念也有了很大的改變。中國人一向 "重文輕商"，知識分子受人尊敬，商人卻被人看不起。而現在，商人的社會地位達到了前所未有的高度，他們的生活水平也遠遠超過知識分子，成為人們羨慕的對象。現在 "經商" 不但不再被人輕視，反而成為新一代人的追求。社會上甚至流傳起 "十億人民九億商，還有一億要開張" 的民謠。

　　經濟發展也改變了人們的擇業觀。上世紀 50 年代到 80 年代期間，中國人最向往的就是能有一個國有單位裡穩定的 "鐵飯碗"。那時，有了 "鐵飯碗" 才有安全感。但是在今天的中國人心目中，"鐵飯碗" 已經漸漸失去了價值。90 年代以來，經濟市場的需要為人們創造了比較靈活的就業市場，也為人們提供了多樣化的工作。所以工作不再只是為了養家糊口，更重要的是為了實現事業上的理想，並過上高質量的生活。因此，興趣、收入及發展前途成了一般人選擇職業的第一考慮，而穩定性就沒有過去那麼重要了。

2009 年，中國國內生產總值 (GDP) 達到世界第三位。（雖然在人均生產總值方面，中國仍然排在 100 名之後，仍屬於發展中國家。）中國在創造經濟奇跡的同時，也產生了經濟發展不平衡，貧富差距增大，政府官員腐敗，環境污染等等問題。要解決這些問題，中國還有很長一段路要走。難怪有人說，中國經濟現在是處在一個"機遇前所未有，挑戰也前所未有"的時代。

17 個人投資：股票與房地產

八十年代初，老萬和弟弟合伙開了一家維修公司，專門維修各單位的舊樓房。兩個人工作上吃苦耐勞，生活上省吃儉用，十年後，在銀行裡有了一筆不小的存款。

九十年代初，市場上開始出現股票交易。老萬的朋友中，有不少人買賣股票賺了錢，老萬和弟弟看了不禁心動，也想投資股票市場。問題是他倆都不懂股票，所以一時不敢參與。後來經過跟朋友的多次商談，又謹慎觀察了一陣股市行情，兩個人終於決心試試看。在投資股票市場之前，他們先做好了心理準備：就當這次是學習經驗，大不了把錢全部輸光。

有了心理準備後，兩人就從銀行提出一部分存款去買股票。開始時，他們選了一隻便宜的股票，買進 300 股。沒想到四個月以後，這隻股票每股比原價漲了 20 元，老萬和弟弟炒股的信心大增，於是他們把銀行裡的存款全部提了出來，投資在股票上。三年後，他們賺了將近 70 萬元。但是他們也體會到，在股票市場中賺錢實在風險太大。股市行情一時暴漲，一時大跌，等你絕望時，它又全面回彈。熊市牛市，變化無常，處理得不好就可能把辛辛苦苦賺來的錢都丟掉。為此，他們雖然日子過得比以前富裕多了，但心情卻更加焦慮和緊張。

九十年代中，老萬的伯父春節期間從香港回上海探親。飯後聊天時，伯父談起香港的房地價，說那真是"寸土如金"，一套普普通通的公寓就要上百萬元。老萬驚訝地說："那擁有一套公寓的人，不就是百萬富翁了嗎？"　"是啊，"伯父說，"如果上海也像香港的話，你們現在的這套住房，沒有百萬，也有幾十萬了。"

伯父的話打動了老萬的心。他想，他和弟弟的工作是維修舊樓房，他們對房屋結構很熟悉，對房屋裝修也很有經驗。何不嘗試買一兩套舊房，裝修後租出去呢？也許這樣做會比股市投資保險得多。於是，伯父一走，老萬和弟弟就將股票賣掉，再向銀行貸款，在市區內買了兩套兩室一廳的舊房，裝修後租給別人，自己做起房東來了。

兩年過去了，人們的生活越來越好，對居住條件的要求也越來越高，房價直線上升。老萬和弟弟的兩套普普通通的房子，一下子價值倍增。老萬和弟弟算了一下，他們那兩套房子，除去裝修和利息成本後，還可以收益近百萬元，而且房價在一段時間內只會漲不會跌。兩人將情況分析過後，覺得與其買房投資，不如建房投資。於是將原有的房子賣掉，然後在市郊買了一大塊地，建了新房出售，兩年後收益兩千多萬元。

這種具有穩定性而利潤又高的商業方式，使許多人像老萬兄弟那樣投資於房地產業。有的人通過籌資甚至貸款買下他們認為會升值的房產；有的人用較少的預付款買下尚未建好的新房，等房價上升後再出售盈利；更有的人趁著房地產熱當起房地產經紀商來了。房地產市場的興起，使許多人考慮到長期投資的可能性。在人均所得越來越高的情況下，投資性買房也會越來越多。

18 都市消費面面觀

中國的消費市場越來越豐富多彩，如今的都市消費有哪些新特點呢？請看下面生活的幾個方面：

一、吃"好"、吃"鮮"、吃"快"

過去，中國人對飲食的要求是能吃飽，現在的要求是要吃好，要有營養。近年來，全麥、玉米、豆子等又變得熱門起來，這反映了老百姓對飲食營養的重視。

追求"鮮"是近年來中國人餐桌上的另一個特色。過去，受季節的影響，中國北方居民往往要靠土豆、蘿蔔和大白菜度過整個冬天；現在呢？每個城市每天都有大量新鮮蔬菜出現在市場上，紅辣椒、紫茄子、黃瓜、青菜……要什麼有什麼。即使冬天也不例外，人們每天都能吃到新鮮的蔬菜。

隨著生活節奏的加快，中國人日常的飲食也變得越來越簡單了。原來居民花很長時間做飯的現象有了很大的改變，速凍餃子、方便面、包子、盒飯……這些中國式快餐已成為許多居民家中餐桌上的"常客"，而且，隨著生活水平的不斷提高，出去吃飯已經很平常了。與此同時，中國孩子們對"洋快餐"也越來越感興趣，兒童們走進"洋"快餐店，既是因為喜歡西式食品，也是因為想得到一份有趣的小禮物。

二、穿出不同

在北京的王府井百貨大樓 當記者問一位正在選購服裝的小姐 "現在什麼服裝最流行" 時，她說："想穿什麼，什麼就是流行"。這就是現在的年輕人對服裝的追求。前些年滿街飄起紅裙子或黃裙子的現象已不見了，取而代之的是既有個性又得體的服裝。一位打扮入時的女士說："如果發現街上有人穿得跟我一樣，第二天我一定會讓自己換一種打扮。為了避免這種情況，我現在常常定做服裝，而不太去商店買衣服了。穿著自己選定的有特色的衣服，感覺特別好。"

的確，這些年來，中國人的外表發生了很大的變化。七十年代初，一位意大利記者在參觀中國首都北京後寫道："北京是一個灰色的城市，人們穿著既單調又統一……" 80 年代初國門打開後，中國人深埋幾十年的愛美之心，開始在服飾上得以釋放。現在，每個人可以根據自己不同的性格、職業、愛好，選擇最適合自己的服裝穿在身上。特別是現在大多數中國年輕一代都會上網，並通過網絡了解歐美同齡人的喜好和興趣，他們對時尚品牌充滿了熱情和敏感，希望融入全球主流。"全球性" 和 "時尚性" 是這些年輕人的追求。

三、 休閑旅游

1994 年 3 月以前，中國人每周只有一個休息日：星期日。此後，有一段時間實行隔周雙休：這一周休息一天，下一周休息兩天。從 1995 年 5 月開始，中國人終於可以每周休息兩天了。實行 "雙休制" 後，人們都感覺到，在工作和家務之外，有了更多屬於自己的自由時間。一個新的熱門話題：休閑，也隨之出現。

據調查：一般城市人外出休閑的選擇是：逛街購物、走親訪友、游覽參觀、去歌舞廳、去健身房和看電影。在家休閑的人主要是看電視、聽音樂和打麻將。商店也利用雙休日這個好機會，開展各種促銷活動，吸引顧客購物消費。

雙休日不僅促進了商業的發展，還帶動了旅游業的迅速發展。如今，周末休閑旅游已經成為熱門的旅游項目。旅游的人們多數參加旅游公司組織的一日游或兩日游，而且常常是一家人親朋好友一塊兒去，既方便又熱鬧。近年來有車族越來越多，自駕游方式已經成為假期旅游一種新時尚，正受到越來越多年輕人的喜愛。

隨著消費市場的發展，中國人的生活水平也在不斷地提高。

19 "癌症村"

　　王子清已記不清村裡死了多少人了。"每死一個人，我的心就像刀割一樣。"從上世紀 90 年代以來，村裡的人就開始紛紛得病。每年村裡因患癌症而死去的少則五六人，多時達 20 多人。由於得癌症的病人多，他們村被當地人稱作 "癌症村"。

　　王子清一家便是這個不幸村庄中的不幸家族。2004 年 6 月，短短一個月內，王子清便失去了 3 位親人：他哥哥、弟弟、叔叔都因癌症而相繼去世。這些年，村裡王姓 130 人中，便有 35 人死於癌症。死者最年長的不到 70 歲，最年輕的只有 30 歲。"人活得都沒有希望了，"王子清說，"村裡的人總擔心，下一個死的會不會是自己。"死亡像一個可怕的幽靈，時刻在威脅著這個村子。

　　王子清家正對著一個大水塘，村裡人吃的用的都是這塘水，村南兩公裡外就是淮河。在王子清的記憶中，從前淮河和水塘裡的水都曾經清澈透明，河塘邊綠樹成蔭，白色的鴨子在河塘內追逐戲水。村裡的人去地裡幹活時，從來不帶水。渴了，隨便從河塘中捧一口水就喝。"可甜了，比現在的自來水都好喝。"王子清說。

　　可是，從 80 年代末開始，淮河邊建起了一些工廠，淮河水開始變壞變臭。據縣水文站提供的一份資料顯示，1990 年、1994 年和 2000 年，淮河水中共查出 90 種污染物，其中致癌物高達 67 種。河水污染了土地和地下水，也污染了空氣。2005 年，國家疾病控制中心曾對淮河流域癌症高發地區進行全面普查，最終結論是：一、淮河流域地區為癌症高發區；二、癌症高發與受污染的淮河水密切相關。以前，曾有 "走千走萬，不如淮河兩岸" 的民謠；而如今，這個自古以來的魚米之鄉，卻變成了 "癌症村" 頻發地區。

　　難怪當地居民中流傳著這樣一首民謠："你們得利，我們得病；你們升遷，我們升天。"這首民謠針對的就是那些建在淮河流域的高污染的紙張、皮革和塑料制造企業。這些企業的工業污水基本上都排放到淮河中，污水一流就是幾十年，遲遲得不到治理。雖然早在 1994 年國家就啟動了治理淮河的工程，歷經二十幾年，投資 600 億，但至今尚未實現 "水體還清" 的目標。

　　上世紀 90 年代，"癌症村" 只在個別地方出現，如今卻擴散到全國 20 個省。在快速致富的過程中，工廠和礦山忽視了環境保護，將有毒的化學品和污水排放到河流湖泊中，使中國各地的水污染達到了觸目驚心的程度。面對那些只重視短期經濟效益和就業機會的企業領導和政府官員時，連國家環保部門也一度感到無能爲力。

中國國家環境保護部副部長潘岳表示，過去幾十年中國經濟的高速發展是以犧牲環境爲代價的。中國創造同等經濟價值的能源耗費量是世界其他地區平均水平的三倍。對環境的嚴重破壞，已經給中國造成了災難性的後果。3 億多農村人口喝不到乾淨的水，三分之一的城市居民呼吸不到清潔空氣。高耗能、高污染、高消費的經濟發展模式使中國成爲了世界耗水第一、污水排放量第一的國家。

近年來頻繁發生的環境污染事件，使人們越來越意識到這種可怕的不斷增長的環境代價。中國社會各界已經開始反思多年來單純追求經濟增長的發展模式。"綠色 GDP"、"可持續發展"的概念已經被越來越多的人所關注和接受。潘岳說，"中國的環境保護形勢依然嚴峻，可以說，環境狀況已經進入了'冬天'，但由於社會各界的廣泛重視，環境保護工作已經進入了'春天'。"

20 互聯網改變中國

中國對大眾開放互聯網服務是從 1995 年開始的。根據中國互聯網網絡信息中心（CNNIC）的統計報告，14 年以後，網民總人數已達到 338 億，排名世界第一。網民增長數量驚人，平均每秒鐘增加兩個網民。對有著 5000 年文明史的中國，14 年是一段很短的時間，但就在這短短的 14 年中，互聯網已進入到中國社會的各方面。網絡正在迅速地改變中國傳統的經濟模式，中國人的日常生活和思維方式，以及中國的文化和政治。

在經濟方面，互聯網推動了新的經營模式和消費模式。搜索引擎已經成爲網民使用互聯網最重要的工具。互聯網逐漸成爲中國最大的市場信息集散和交易平台，它與傳統產業的結合也已經成爲經濟新的推動力。在新的經營模式下，中小企業的商業聯系范圍不斷擴大，大型進出口企業更是依賴互聯網來直接與海外建立生意關系。就連相當落後的農村地區也開始用互聯網來推進業務。不少農民學會了使用互聯網的技術，改進了他們的經營方式。例如，河北省某縣的菜農，以前賣菜大多是肩扛手提。不論酷暑嚴冬，都得早早起床到集市上叫賣。現在他們可以悠閑地坐在蔬菜交易大廳的屏幕前，輕點鼠標，就可以在網上把菜賣個好價錢。據河北省農業廳調查，農民通過網絡學習技術，獲取種子、植物，銷售信息，爲產品找到了更多銷路。這些手段使農民每年的收入大大增加。

人們也通過網絡尋找工作信息。現在一些大學的網站上有專門爲畢業生設計的頁面，不斷更新各單位的招聘信息，瀏覽量相當大。根據一項調查，2004 年人民大學就業的本科畢業生中，通過網絡找到工作的佔 13%；碩士以上畢業生通過網絡求職成功的佔 23%。

中國人的消費方式也由於互聯網的發展，而有了很大的改變。越來越多的人喜歡上了既方便又便宜的網購方式。他們可以搜索各種網上商店，用最理想的價格，購買他們所需要的商品。網站也已成爲人們旅游出門的新媒介。人們不但可以在旅游網站上獲取目的地的信息，也可以購買機票、車票、船票，預定酒店，加入旅行團等，更可以通過旅游網站的論壇，找到興趣相同的旅行同伴，一同去旅游。

對青少年來說，互聯網已經是他們生活中很重要的一部分。根據互聯網網絡信息中心統計報告，當前中國網民的年齡多半在 30 歲以下，這年輕的一代，有半數以上經常在網絡上玩電子游戲、跟朋友聊天、聽音樂、看電影，或在網上交流，用電子郵件交新朋友等。

在政治方面，互聯網爲公眾提供了一個前所未有的開放的輿論平台，使老百姓們有機會參與政治。2003 年 3 月 17 日，大學畢業生孫志剛，從外地到廣州去找工作，但他因爲沒有暫住証而被拘留在移民收容中心，3 月 20 日被警察毆打致死。這個消息在網絡上激起了強烈反應，成千上萬的抗議信，出現在全國各大網站上。互聯網的輿論威力最終促使國務院決定廢除這一實行了多年的收容遣送制度。

互聯網的發展和普及，引發了前所未有的信息革命和產業革命，也引發了深刻的社會變革。但另一方面，網絡攻擊、網絡犯罪、色情暴力信息泛濫、青少年上網成癮等問題，對社會也產生了不可低估的負面影響。

Credits

Woman with dog photo, p. 30: Courtesy of Cecia Li

Parents and child photo, p. 63: © iophoto/iStockphoto

Smokestack photo, p. 247: flickr/rahims, Rahim Sonawalla

Sandstorm photo, p. 272: flickr/Robert Thomson

Tibetan antelope photo, p. 274: flickr/mckaysavage

Cover Design: Joyce Weston

Cover Photographs: Subway © Robert Churchill/iStockphoto; Roof © Hsing-Wen Hsu/iStockphoto

Interior Design: Linda M. Robertson

Editing: Laurel Damashek

Project Management: Laurel Damashek

Production: Victoria E. Kichuk

Manufacturing: JoAnne Sweeney

Proofreading: Eavan Cully, Laurel Damashek, Victoria E. Kichuk

Indexing: Kelly Dagan

Composition: HiSoft

Audio Recording: Jingchan Liu, Pan Luo, Wanhui Qing